Praise for *What Remains?*

'This book is a great work of craft and beauty, truth and humanity, heart and soul. I believe it could be used as a teaching tool and as a comfort. I find Callender's approach to this huge subject deeply loving and moving, but also revolutionary in spirit and courageous.'

SALENA GODDEN, author of *Mrs Death Misses Death*

'Until I read *What Remains?* I had no idea there was a hands-on, old-fashioned alternative to our corporatized Way of Death. Not a fancy hearse but just a car with enough space to transport a body. Not a corpse-size refrigerator, polished wooden coffin and rented pallbearers but a dining room table, cardboard coffin and shallow hole in garden or field, with bugs and birds and animals.... It is what used to happen. And, Callender assures us, that although shocking, perhaps even terrifying and certainly very sad, it is a healing way of death, it is the way death should be. It's about time.'

VICTORIA SWEET, author of *God's Hotel*

'A truly extraordinary book. It is like nothing else I've ever read, or thought I needed. Heartful of the ferocious, transcendent power of love and wonder; it is deeply profound, funny, and wholly and radically moving.'

NICOLA CHESTER, Wainwright-shortlisted author of *On Gallows Down*

'This moving, angry and funny book isn't just about an odd career ushering people off to join the Silent Majority, but a beautiful guide to how to live, grieve and remember well.'

LUKE TURNER, author of *Out of the Woods;* co-founder, The Quietus

'One of the most important books of our age. It had me laughing and crying by turns, sometimes both at the same time, and each page brought a new revelation, a new insight, a new understanding of what it means to be human in this beautiful world, in this strange moment we are passing through. It's a book destined to join the greats of counterculture nonfiction, like *Fear and Loathing in Las Vegas*, *Cosmic Trigger* and *The Electric Kool-Aid Acid Test*.'

C.J. STONE, author of *Fierce Dancing*

'This isn't a grisly book; it is sharp, angry, punchily philosophical and often funny. It basically invents a new type of lifestyle aspiration: deathstyle.'

THE TIMES OF LONDON

'Callender's joyous, thought-provoking book is an account of how his own early encounters with bereavement led to him becoming a new kind of undertaker.'

DAILY MAIL (UK)

'*What Remains?* is a profound and vital book.... As honest, terrifying and truthful as a mirror at midday, it embraces life and death equally and is too compassionate to flinch. Inspiring and unforgettable.'

JOHN HIGGS, author of *William Blake vs the World*

'An exquisitely sensitive, eloquent and courageous guide to its mysteries and terrors, its ordinariness and its humanity.'

MIKE JAY, writer and cultural historian

'If there is one book you should read when death comes knocking or you get the sudden urge to build a crop circle in the middle of the night, then this is that book.'

JIMMY CAUTY, The JAM's, K2 Plant Hire

'It's extraordinary. You'll laugh, you'll cry, your heart will break, your heart will shine, filled with love. You'll be changed. An instant classic.'

ROB HOPKINS, author of *From What Is to What If*

'A fascinating insight into Life's oldest ritual. Dead interesting.'

RÓNÁN HESSION, author of *Leonard and Hungry Paul*

'Rupert Callender takes us to the dark end of the street, but he does so with wit, beauty and no little experience. It's a one-of-a-kind ride, filled with storytelling. This original and gutsy book will do a lot of good in the world.'

MARTIN SHAW, author of *Smoke Hole*

'Vulnerable, raw and moving, this is a book for anyone who strives to die, and live, in an emotionally authentic and honest way. Essential reading. Beautifully written.'

LOUISE WINTER, progressive funeral director, coauthor of *We All Know How This Ends*

WHAT REMAINS?

WHAT REMAINS?

Life, Death and the Human Art of Undertaking

Rupert Callender

Chelsea Green Publishing
White River Junction, Vermont
London, UK

Commissioning Editor: Jonathan Rae
Project Manager: Angela Boyle
Developmental Editor: Muna Reyal
Copy Editor: Susan Pegg
Proofreader: Anne Sheasby
Designer: Melissa Jacobson

Printed in the United States of America.
First printing March 2023.
10 9 8 7 6 5 4 3 2 1   23 24 25 26 27

ISBN 978-1-64502-050-9 (UK hardcover) | ISBN 978-1-91529-412-8 (US hardcover) | ISBN 978-1-64502-051-6 (ebook) | ISBN 978-1-64502-052-3 (audio book)

Library of Congress Cataloging-in-Publication Data is available.

Chelsea Green Publishing
P.O. Box 4529
White River Junction, Vermont USA

Somerset House
London, UK

www.chelseagreen.com

Dedicated to C.J. Stone,
for showing me his
Fierce Dance.

Contents

PROLOGUE

One measures a circle beginning anywhere

It wasn't late late, but it was late enough to be conspicuous. I pulled the car up onto the grass verge, tucked it under the hedge, and turned the engine and the lights off.

The dark rushed in like water.

I breathed out slowly, heart thumping in my ears, and waited, waiting for nothing to happen.

It would have been easier to park in the gateway I had just passed, a hundred yards back along the quiet country lane. Easier but risky. I could be blocked in and credible explanations would, at that point, be very thin on the ground.

Far better to park here and make my way along the edge of the field, ready to run or dive through the hedge at the sight of any approaching headlights.

Logic told me I was being overcautious, that the chances of anyone driving along this rural back lane at 2 a.m. were remote, but things get very atavistic in the dark, even in the gentle English countryside, and the threat was real. There would undoubtedly be anger if I was caught, and very little chance of recourse to the law. Justice would probably be swift and physical.

I stepped out of the car and into the sweet air of a perfectly still summer night. It was mid July, moonless and warm, with clear skies and pinpoint-clear stars everywhere. I looped a plank of wood over my shoulder, the rope that was attached to the plank strapped across my chest, making it look and feel like a quiver of arrows. I put a small bag over my other shoulder, locked the car, hid the keys nearby to avoid any giveaway jangling and started to run quickly up the lane, at my most exposed for this short dash.

I reached the five-bar gate and swiftly clambered over, ducking back behind the hedge at the edge of the field. All good. I consciously exhaled again, deeply. My breathing began to slow.

It is rare that it is truly dark in the countryside, even with no moon, and my eyes had fully adjusted to the night in the ten minutes since I had parked the car. The air was filled with the sweet smell of honeysuckle and cow parsley, sun-warmed earth.

To my right, the soft sodium glow of my home town a mile or so away lit the edges of the dark. Ahead of me, the ten-acre field of ripe wheat stretched and curved away down the hill.

At the bottom lay a farmhouse, the bedroom light still on; always a bedroom light still on – do farmers never sleep? And, of course, in an outhouse kennel, the ever-vigilant farm dog, the night trespasser's mortal enemy.

I tried to cover my psychic footprints, become a natural part of the darkness rather than an anomaly that an intuitive dog could pick up on and become frenzied with outrage. The thought of a loose dog, running, teeth bared, through the darkness, to confront me was the stuff of nightmares.

Prologue

I spent some time crouching in the grass at the edge of the crop, acclimatising to the night. It felt essential to be accepted by what I imagined were the night's inhabitants – as much for symbolic purposes as it did for practical reasons, for, as soon as I got out of the car, I had stepped into ritual space.

Some of the things I would do to appease what I imagined shared the night with me would certainly appear laughable to anyone in fear-banishing daylight. But a dark night is a different country, a metaphysical place where rationality holds no power. The maps and tools you need to navigate and deal with it are subtle and invisible, purely of the imagination.

The roots of the word panic are from the overwhelming fear that overcomes someone who unexpectedly finds themself in the presence of the great god Pan. I didn't literally believe there was a musky, lusty cloven-hoofed deity lurking somewhere on the edge of the woods watching me, but I certainly believed in the utter terror that could overwhelm the senses and send me running blindly through the night.

I took a crumpled water bottle filled with goat's milk out of my bag and poured it slowly onto the cracked earth. All offerings made with good intentions are always welcome and accepted, or so I told myself. I had acknowledged my fear and in doing so gained some control. I started to relax, or rather, tune in.

The field was marked, as most English arable fields are, with parallel lines crossing it vertically and horizontally; a path for the tractor to pass along, spraying, without damaging the wheat or barley.

I started to walk down one and immediately was overwhelmed by the sense of being waist deep in something ghostly. It always felt like the beginning of a dream, when logic is quietly left behind, a stripping away of all reason. Dew was beginning to form on the stalks as I brushed past, wetting my thighs.

I walked the simple up and down, back and forth corridors, which took me into the middle of the field. I stopped when I felt I had reached the right spot, chosen because it was visible from a field a mile away on the corresponding hillside, a field I had made a similar nighttime visit to the summer before.

I stepped slowly and cautiously out into the crop until I was about ten feet in. I took my wooden plank off my shoulder, got down on my knees and lowered it down like a knife between the stalks of wheat. Holding one end stationary, I slowly rotated the plank, flattening the wheat anticlockwise into a circle. The first cut had been made.

When the first circuit was complete, I stood up, taking a short edge of the stomper board to the edge of the flattened wheat. I placed the board flat on the ground, like a petal extending from the centre of a daisy. Holding the loop of attached rope in both hands, I placed my right foot on the wood and began to walk around, pressing the crop down, with each circuit enlarging the circle by the length of the board. After half an hour, I had flattened around thirty foot in diameter.

There was no need for accurate measurements; this was not a complex design that needed precise angles and it was not intended to be seen by anyone or to fool them – though my actions would inadvertently do just that, briefly reactivating the whole great game of belief and pseudoscience that characterised the crop circle phenomenon. This circle was purely for me.

I had got better at it, and had discovered through trial and error techniques to make the edges crisper: walking along the rim one foot placed directly in front of the other, getting down on my hands and knees to flatten stubborn single shafts, shaping the centre into an aesthetically pleasing bowl.

This was probably the fifteenth circle I had made over a three-year period and over an area of about five miles, encircling the town. My intentions were varied and shifted with the years, as had my own experience and attitude to these weirdly powerful yet simple symbols of flattened wheat.

Sometimes it just felt thrilling enough to be abroad on someone else's field without permission, doing something that would be unexplainable and certainly unjustifiable if caught. Right now, I felt less like a burglar or vandal and more like a landscape acupuncturist or a junkie looking for a vein. Somehow I was attempting to encircle the town; why, I knew not. Maybe I was going mad.

Long ago, entering the vast pictograms made by the original circle makers in the early nineties in Wiltshire, I felt like Matthew the Levite, the disciple who followed Jesus and documented his teachings, or Richard Dreyfuss in *Close Encounters* obsessively moulding my mashed potato mountains, searching for meaning and answers to this rising feeling of hopeful transcendence.

But whatever I had once hoped or feared that might be making these indentations – interdimensional beings, Gaia, aliens, a gateway to New Jerusalem, even some kind of military technology – what they had always been, and remain to me to this day, are portals to somewhere else; a way to achieve a different state of consciousness, to gently peel the moment open through a physical ritual, performed alone and in the dark.

I tried to let my mind go blank as I circled outwards, the sound of the crop crunching under my board, a sibilant pulse in the darkness. If I thought of anything, I tried to think of the Greek goddess Demeter, goddess of the harvest, the grieving mother of Persephone who was dragged down into the underworld and whose absence made winter itself.

Making these circles in the crop felt like a renegade act of worship, the creation of a temporary temple for a seriously out-of-fashion deity.

Increasingly, I had come to think of my circles as symbolic tunnels to the underworld, punching through the crust of reality like the gaping sinkholes opening up in the Siberian permafrost. In my imagination, they were pinholes through a burial shroud, inexplicably releasing beams of light. I was cutting through the border fence of the realm of death and I could feel Demeter, in her grief, urging me on. And death shall have no dominion.

I stopped often. Sometimes to scan the field around me, sometimes just to catch my breath. It was easy to animate the distant silhouettes into hostile shapes, let the silence gather and throb in my ears until it became oppressive. But I was alone in a distant field in the middle of the night, the omphalos of my own unfolding universe.

Once I had finished the circle, smoothing it for at least an hour on my hands and knees, I sat back and lit a cigarette, careful to cup the flame so it couldn't be seen. I thought of my grandfather, an officer in the trenches of World War One, and the superstition about lighting many cigarettes from one match; it was the third soldier to light his fag who was most at risk. That was when the sniper, aim found and steadied, would shoot.

A risible comparison; death did not shadow me in these fields, but part of this had to do with my ancestors, and I needed to keep them in mind. In truth, it was death itself that I had come to shrug off within this disc of flattened wheat – or at least to lay down some of its weight.

◆ ◆ ◆

I had been an undertaker for nearly twenty years, after a moment of Damascene, vocational insight that had catapulted me off my stoned indolent sofa existence and into this most unlikely of careers.

The way I practised my trade, first on my own, but soon with a friend who became my partner, was very different from the mainstream funeral establishment, involving a level of deliberate emotional engagement that was considered reckless to our mental health and that of those we helped. Undertakers were meant to guard themselves and their charges against the sadness and emotion like doctors and policeman, not rush towards it like Quakers or protesting Buddhist monks.

I was right that this small, immersive approach, intimate and shorn of all formality and the faux Victoriana traditions that characterised the traditional British funeral, was so much better for the families we were helping. I knew that it was better to cry with them around their unadorned dead than sell them an expensive coffin. I knew that it was better to turn up in a scruffy car and be real, rather than appear in a black suit with a composed persona and a fixed patter. But I also knew we were risking so much of ourselves by opening our hearts and our heads, our very lives, to this unending stream of sadness.

Those early days were filled with zeal and fervour, fuelled by my own many bereavements and a clear understanding of what not to do – always a good starting point for something completely new. But my bluff was called very early, with a sudden, almost immediate immersion into the real nature of death and funerals, suicides, accidents and children – all far from what I imagined, which was an orderly procession of the ill and elderly. It was psychologically and spiritually jarring, but it was also my initiation; I needed to test my mettle.

Back then, the sadness and horror and the out-of-depthness had been things that I had processed and danced out of my system at all-night raves, and I was buoyed up by my belief in what I was doing, which never faltered and never will.

I had started to take the ceremonies too, and had discovered a talent for creating an honest portrait of someone I had never met, for knowing what to say to the living about the dead, about life and death itself. A strange and unexpected mix of ghost writing and sermonising, a high-wire act that could go horribly wrong at any point. The front I had then I don't recognise now, it seems breathtakingly reckless.

And the partnership with my friend Claire had inevitably intensified into love and marriage, so the emotions that were stirred up by our daily confrontations with such deep sorrow were held and contained within our relationship.

We cried as we danced till dawn.

It worked then, keeping the grief flowing through us, healing my own mismanaged childhood grief and allowing us to fully engage with the sadness of each family we encountered.

But that was many years ago. I no longer danced all night long once a month with friends, beatified by ecstasy. And the comfort and security of our marriage had started to crumble, the inevitable result of living and working together alone in a job that has enormous pressures.

Yet the grief and the sadness in our working life continued to grow as our reputation built and we were handed from one family tragedy to another, a secret gift from the most wounded to the newly numb.

As with all jobs that involve trauma, the traditional coping strategies are gallows humour and alcohol. We never went in for the gallows humour, although Claire has a great ability to know when to first crack a joke with a new family, but I had long struggled with self-medicating my own childhood wounds through drink and drugs, and letting off steam could easily slide into compulsion and addiction.

I had a good therapist, but therapy alone wasn't enough to be entirely free from the ringing in the ears that so much death brought. I had started to lean in more to art as a way of reframing myself. Art, and what might be described as ritual magic.

◆ ◆ ◆

As I sat in the darkness in that circle of wheat, I was 47 and dangerously close to a complete burn out.

Compassion fatigue had been and gone, a bleak coping response when the emotions just didn't register for a bit, almost worse than a full emotional breakdown. I was left with the weight of sadness that I held and carried, the existential banality that at times threatened to block out the light and joy of life.

Wilhelm Reich, the maverick psychoanalyst, believed that when a child experienced trauma, they would physically tense up and that this built-up layers of psychic body armour that would be detrimental to their emotional well-being in adult life. I believed my exposure to so much sorrow was doing much the same.

I lay on my back in the centre of the circle, aligning it perfectly up with the centre of the tattooed mandala on my back, which, in turn, aligned with a tattoo over my heart. I closed my eyes and remembered some of the people I had buried or burnt in the previous months.

Some were deaths in what you could call 'the right order': old people, full lives lived with a mix of joy and hardship, their children and grandchildren still alive. Some were sadder: the middle aged, taken too soon by cancer, but still lives lived largely with happiness and achievement.

I held these in my heart and imagined their spirits lifting up into the cosmos of atoms and matter and dark matter, like sparks from a fire rising off me gratefully; I, the last humanity they had randomly encountered in their physical existence, glad to be released, no hard feelings. Then I turned my thoughts to the ones that haunted me.

The child in the car accident, the lonely death of the undiscovered recluse, the tragic fall, the man exactly my age and exactly my cultural tribe who killed himself despite the best efforts of his adoring wife.

The man exactly like me.

All the men exactly like me, dragged under by depression and the lead weight of masculinity, the passive, slow-motion suicides through drink and drugs, and self-disgust and disregard.

I felt into my shoulders. I could feel the small stones that lay under the thin carpet of stalks, but I turned my attention inwards, felt inside to my muscles, the tension, the feeling of plaques of sadness sticking to me like calcified grief.

I tried to melt them, imagining them running together, the individual details of grief and horror becoming indistinct and merging like wax, solidifying into one homogenised colour of loss. I visualised it dripping down my neck and my shoulders, running down my back, pooling in the centre of my tattoo, the drop of my spine.

I held the molten grief there for a moment, searching back for any recent darkness that was evading my patchy memory. I would not be able to return to this circle to do this again once I left it. Then I let it drop, down the portal into the underworld. A long, rippling stalactite of sorrow that stretched and broke and sank into the earth beneath me, and, as it did, I let myself feel the relief of letting it go, shooting an imaginary beam of light up into the night like a searchlight from my heart.

I opened my eyes. Directly above me, around 1,200 miles up, a satellite silently passed over. I sat up, gathered my stuff and walked out of the circle.

I have formed a number of my own superstitions around my own rituals.

One is that as I am leaving a circle I have made, I must not look back. I can see them again from afar in daylight, even re-enter them but, as I am walking away, I must not look back. I had been doing this for quite a while before I realised why.

When Orpheus tried to rescue his wife Eurydice from the underworld, he failed at the last minute because he could not help breaking the one condition of her release – that he not look back at her as they left the underworld.

My circles and the grief they contain may not be looked back on, not then, not in the night they are laid down and shed. I cannot turn and look at them again, in case I weaken my resolve and turn and rush back to them, awkwardly exhorting them to cling to me again, all is forgiven.

My car was where I left it. But my keys?

Don't ever hide anything in a hedge in the dark.

CHAPTER ONE

What does not kill us does some serious damage on the way through

In fairness, it was difficult to tell who was the more screwed up – the funeral industry or me.

Spoiler alert: neither of us are what you would call completely mended, but both of us are changed, or changing, and we have each left a mark on the other. A graze, or a tattoo. Scar tissue perhaps.

Maybe I'm being too unkind to both of us. Maybe I'm being too grandiose. Brace yourself for both of those extremes.

◆ ◆ ◆

This is the story of how my partner Claire and I became the first, and possibly the last, of the punk undertakers by applying the lessons of punk and acid house, and its do-it-yourself ethos, to shake up the stilted funeral industry at the beginning of the twenty-first century.

It is how this most unlikely of vocations propelled me off my sofa as I sat smoking a joint at the tail end of a Monday afternoon, at the tail end of my twenties, and into a life that has opened many unexpected doors of opportunity.

It is the only thing that I have ever done for money, bar a brief period spent being an eel fisherman on an estuary in Cornwall, which was as brutally hard work as it was financially unviable but appeared devastatingly romantic when viewed from the banks of the river.

I have had no training or qualifications other than my own extensive and early experience of bereavement, a graduation from the University of Death as it were.

I crashed in, slipping in through the gaps around the definition of who was or could be an undertaker, flat broke and a little bit mad, driving a tatty old Volvo with no tax or insurance, and using a wide pine board as a stretcher.

The first dead body I touched was of the first man I buried as I dressed and shaved his face with the help of his weeping family, during the first funeral that I ever did.

I have never worked for a funeral director (notice my linguistic differentiation between an undertaker and a funeral director), only with my partner, Claire.

Consequently, we have done and continue to do every aspect of arranging a funeral: looking after the dead (easy but physically exhausting), looking after the living (the real work), cleaning the car, the mortuary, arranging the flowers in the viewing room, doing the paperwork, booking the crematorium, putting the notice in the paper and promoting ourselves, right through to being the person who writes the eulogy and holds the ceremony, traditionally the role of a priest. The only thing we drew the line at was tidying up after the post-funeral party, a lesson learned early when we realised we were the only people sober enough to take down the decorations and wash up.

I have carried and lowered an uncountable number of coffins and shovelled tons of earth onto them. Many times I have been the last person on this earth to see someone's face.

I have held stillborn babies in the palm of my hand.

I have looked into the eyes of dying men who know that the next time we meet they will be dead.

I have watched as children have fired flaming arrows at a pyre upon which sits their father's remains. I have seen bodies that are no longer recognisable as human and bodies that looked so peaceful I have been filled with envy.

All without the permission or regulation of any authority, religious or governmental, other than the families who have engaged my services and trusted me with their dead.

There are some, many in the traditional funeral world, who consider me and my partner as dangerous mavericks, everything that is wrong with the industry, a strong case for the regulation of the market. The industry can be brutal in its need to see off competitors and critics.

There are others who have respect for our transparency and rawness, and credit us with being real agents of change, given us accolades. We have been called 'The greatest undertakers of all time, by a country mile' by an independent funeral guide and I have also received anonymous, negative phone calls for my publicly expressed opinions.

I try not to let either of these extremes break me or go to my head, but my position is that the real problem is that how we deal with death has become an industry.

Although it will often feel like it, this book is not an attack on the funeral industry per se. We are all culpable for the slow, lazy drift away from meaning. The tolerance of outdated ways of thinking due to a resistance to effect change. But it is an attack on the hijacking of our mortality by corporate bodies that pay only lip service to the sorrowed and only engage with the void in order to conjure it up to channel our fear and grief into unnecessary retail purchases.

It is an attack on the belief systems that have failed to accommodate and adapt to our brave new worlds and instead serve up increasingly tepid forms of spiritual comfort.

There are exceptional undertakers and ministers everywhere, but they live in the shadows of faceless multinationals that continue to operate in a deliberately disingenuous way, who dominate the advertising slots of daytime television with emotionally bullying prepayment tactics, guilt-tripping frightened pensioners solely in order to future-proof their businesses.

It is an attack on the complacent entitlement of the industry that refuses to yield to the times because it is still patriarchal in its mindset.

It is an attack on the idea that an expensive flower arrangement and a veneered oak-effect coffin are more important than the content of the funeral itself.

Nothing comes from nothing, and personally I feel part of the long tradition of what can be described as Radical Dissent. My immediate peers are the acid house and punk movements, and my immediate elders are the hippies of the counterculture.

Behind them stand the political and religious nonconformists and irritants. The pacifists of the two world wars, the organic pioneers, the experimental communities of the 1920s and 30s, the social outlaws of the centuries before, who go back at least to that beaten, robed figure standing in front of the fifth procurator of Judea, Pontius Pilate, a representative of the most powerful state on earth at that time, quietly stating the enormous and uncontainable idea that all authority is a form of violence.

I stand for less regulation and more personal responsibility.

I stand for more risk and less caution.

I stand for the electrifying moment of unfettered human to human contact.

I stand for honesty, appropriateness and participation in one of the most real experiences we can go through, our unescapable encounter with death. Our own, and, more significantly, the death of those we love.

The arena I chose in which to live these ideals, or rather was chosen for me by life events, is the reimagining of how we serve the living by dealing with the dead. By ridding ourselves of the well-meaning but outdated traditions that still are the default setting for so many of us, and that are often imposed upon us by the paternalistic mainstream and by our own culpability, through shock, ignorance and deep pain.

I should also make it very clear that I am not alright with death, not alright with it at all. Since death made its dramatic entrance into my life at the age of seven, I have thought of my own death every day. It still scares the shit out of me.

It is what wakes me, Larkin like, at four in the morning, drenched in sweat. It is what whispers in my Caesar-like ears at the moment of my small triumphs. The slave who is really the master, tugging at the links that chain us together.

Working with death for over twenty years has not made me a better person. I do not savour each moment of joy knowing that soon, all too soon, it will all be gone and done. I am not more forgiving of the taxing dullness of life and the feet of clay of those who trudge beside me. I am not part of the death positive movement, although I have the greatest respect for those who are. The only thing worse than death that I can conceive of is immortality.

Freud said that all neuroses are caused by a fear of death. All of them. I think he was trying to soften the blow for us; it's worse than that. But before you throw this book aside with a shiver of anger that you ever mistook this for some kind of self-help book, know this:

What it has given me, and continues to give me, is a dumbstruck awed respect for humanity, for people. Ordinary, everyday people like you and me. Their, okay our, capacity for courage and selflessness, and almost involuntary acts of love when faced with this galloping dust storm of darkness is astonishing. People have, as Patti Smith memorably pointed out, the power.

Everyday people, who muddle and stomp their way clumsily and inattentively through the every days of their lives, have the capacity to overcome their fear and revulsion – for that is what we feel when faced with death and its hideously disfigured offspring: grief. They – sorry, we – rise above it.

We put our own horror and pain aside for the people we love, even if it is just briefly, to try and comfort them, to try and assuage their pain. It is one of the greatest things about humans – our drive towards self-sacrifice.

It really is. It is a privilege to stand beside people as they do this, and in some small way – and believe me it is ridiculously small, however heroic it looks from the outside – help them to facilitate this. It doesn't always happen, and it doesn't happen to everyone, despite either death or bereavement happening to everyone, and it is often the most unlikely of people who step up.

Think about this, your own experience of loss or illness. Maybe you became ill and your best friend disappeared, and that acquaintance you and your friend used to snigger about is suddenly indispensable to you at your most vulnerable, with their unforeseen kindness, in a way which ashamed you. It's often the way.

I have been that person who disappeared, unable to cope with the thought of my friend dying. You probably have too.

I do what I do mainly for strangers, and I do it for selfish reasons: to place another small stone upon the cairn of my own grief. To make up for the mourning I didn't do, through no fault of my own. To try and bribe the ferryman, to get the Reaper to lower his scythe to me. I want death to do it to Julia, not to me. I am also the Ancient Mariner at the gates of the wedding, 'Don't do what I did. Do what I say.'

There will be a fair amount of that. The 'doing what I say' thing. I have never been bothered by the accusations of hypocrisy. If we stuck to that, no one would ever progress in any direction whatsoever, so accuse all you like.

What you won't find here are euphemisms.

'Loved one'.

No no NO.

Euphemisms. They cover the kitchen floor of bereavement like a spilled cat litter tray.

The thing is, not everyone is loved. Some people, many as it happens, are flawed, deeply unpleasant people. Violent abusers, damaged individuals whose actions ripple with tragic consequences down through generation after generation, long after their bones have crumbled in the dust.

It's often not their fault. And they deserve a funeral too, they deserve to be understood, to have the stories of their lives told, to be explained within the context of what happened to them, as close to the truth as anyone can make it.

Once you are dead, I believe you lose all rights to anything except the truth of who you were. The truth. Not an airbrushed, sanitised portrait nor a cruel unfair caricature either. It's a tricky thing to pull off and needs the tacit agreement of all who knew you, and real guts for someone to stand up and say it.

But nobody, nobody, needs the limp bullshit of being described as a 'loved one'.

Euphemisms are at the heart of what I stand against in relation to death and how we deal with it.

'Passed away'.

Say what? It is everywhere within our culture, this mealy-mouthed Victorian term, 'passed away'.

You pass a stool or a parcel, but in this secular age, apparently, we still 'pass away', drift off through some gauzy curtain into the Summerland. Someone better tell Freud.

According to the BBC, even Motorhead's disgracefully behaved lead singer Lemmy 'passed away'. Passed out, yes, plenty of times, but not passed away. It reeks of sanctimonious post-mortem absolution, of infantile priggishness.

Along with the not self-help stuff, there is going to be some graphic descriptions of bodies in extremis. I hope you will stick around for this. Perhaps, like me, you will find these moments of imagined horror a strange and tender privilege instead. Beauty is not just within the eye of the beholder but within the poignancy of the moment.

A dead body is not scary. Seeing one can be deeply moving, incredibly fascinating, perhaps even a little physically repellent, but it is not scary.

More often than not, because you love them, it is reassuringly sad.

At first, you brace yourself for them to open their eyes. That is the conditioning of horror films. That goes, that expectation, and instead is replaced by a deepening sorrow, with the understanding that this is the last thing they are going to do, no matter how much you stare at them.

There it is, the boomerang of pain that is grief:

I'm hurting so much.

What will stop this hurt?

This person coming back.

They will not come back; I hurt so much.

Thud. Thud. Thud. Over and over again.

And, in an essence, that is what we do. Stand holding you as that boomerang hits you over and over again. Teach you some tips to learn how to duck it or, at least, shrug off the bruises.

The only euphemism I have any sympathy for is the most dangerous of all: lost. Loss. This is what we feel, physically. We have lost something.

But, for Christ's sake, don't ever tell a child that they have 'lost' their grandfather; they will spend the rest of their lives checking their pockets for their keys or their wallet. Almost as bad as 'Grandpa has fallen asleep'. That's a lifetime of insomnia and night terrors guaranteed.

Keep it clear and clean, even up to the horizons of your own knowledge.

They have died. I don't know where they have gone, nobody does, but I'm pretty sure it's nowhere bad. I love you. Yes, I'm really sad. It's because I love them and I want them back. I can't change it, but I still love you.

◆ ◆ ◆

Most people who end up working as a funeral director have wanted to do so from an early age. I get contacted by them a lot. They have mixed motives. Most of them are a little introspective, thoughtful, earnest. Some are fascinated by the very notion of mortality, its seriousness, the big questions it asks. Some like the pomp and ceremony of it all. Many have experienced a funeral before and have been changed by it. Some are, I'm not going to lie here, a little morbid.

It had never entered my mind until it landed, a fully fledged, beady-eyed vocation, chirping loudly at me on that Monday afternoon.

I was watching television. I was smoking a joint because, at that time, my only occupation was keeping a full-blown complete nervous breakdown at arm's length and I had decided that self-medicating with hashish was the best way to do it. I also had the means to do it, to cocoon myself, hide in a valley in Cornwall, reading, smoking, trying not to lose it.

I am not endorsing it. I mean, it did work or, at least, I was sane(ish) and alive when my vocation finally found me, but it could have gone several ways.

(There are plenty of other controversial things I will be endorsing, so don't think I'm being cowardly but, for the record, if you are young and existing on the periphery of a perpetual panic attack, smoking dope all day is not going to help.)

I was channel surfing and I briefly rested upon a programme that featured a well-spoken man in his forties being interviewed on a hillside. It was actually a programme about rambling, apt as that was a fair description of what I had been doing for my twenties.

This man was called Nicholas Albery and he changed my life in around five minutes.

He was talking about the different experiences he had around the birth of his son and the death of his father. The former had happened au natural. Just himself and his wife, and an old-school midwife of the sort who had been doing this for millennia, in front of a fire in a rented rural cottage.

No overmedicalisation, no beeping machines, no drugs and, as it turned out, luckily, no problem. A beautiful ecstatic natural birth, a gift of an experience.

The death of his father was at the other end of the spectrum.

A full hospital death, with doctors fighting to save him, even though he was of an appropriate age to die, after a full long life. The sort of death nearly everyone went through then, with death viewed as a professional failure by the medical profession, instead of the natural cessation of life that comes to us all.

The lucky exceptions were those who died in hospices, with doctors who could deal with the cognitive dissonance of breaking the Hippocratic oath, which commanded them to always rail against death and, while not hasten death, allow themselves to ameliorate the suffering, to humanely allow people as much as possible to be without pain, to be with dignity in their final days. A simple yet radical concept.

Nicholas, a boarding school survivor who escaped into the counterculture and who had already dreamed up some wild utopian ideas and put them into practice, was struck by how birth had been liberated by the hippies through the home birth movement, but death remained under the grip of The Man.

He started to investigate and soon discovered that the tight grip that appeared to be held over death by the religious and legal authorities we all assume and defer to was a bit of an illusion. He discovered that in the UK you are not legally obliged to engage the services of a funeral director, that you can as next of kin look after the body of someone who has died.

He clarified that, in fact, as next of kin you ARE the funeral director and that looking after the body of someone who has died is not rocket science. They are, after all, dead. Things can't get much worse than that.

Another man called John Bradfield, shall we say exhumed the fact that you don't have be buried in consecrated ground, that you don't need a priest to oversee things and that with a bit of courage, common sense and adhering to a few basic environmental laws, you can bury someone on your own land. He wrote about all this in his groundbreaking do-it-yourself funeral manual, *Green Burial.*

The Wizard of Oz that was the church and state was actually a shuffling clerk behind a curtain. Death, like everything else in this world, could be approached from a completely different direction.

And so was born The Natural Death Centre, founded by Nicholas Albery, a charity dedicated to informing the public of their rights around funerals and the enormous benefits of doing it yourself or, at the very least, getting seriously involved.

I nearly dropped my joint. I stood up involuntarily. That was it. I was an undertaker.

The thing is, I wasn't an introspective youth who had always dreamed of driving a hearse or putting makeup on a corpse. I was a wounded young man, savagely mauled by bereavement from the age of seven and traumatised by the inadequate response of those around me to help me deal with it.

It wasn't really anyone's fault.

Except perhaps my father's for being so old when he had me, his only child.

And perhaps my mother's for immediately packing me off to boarding school when my father died, but she was traumatised almost into paralysis.

And besides, it was a class thing. I was always going to be packed off to boarding school at the age of seven.

So, yes, it was my parents' fault. Of course, it was, it always is. It's your fault your children are a little fucked up.

But I am getting a little ahead of myself here and, much like that point in *Moby Dick* where Melville stops the action just as Queequeg is about to harpoon a whale from the prow of the ship to give a lengthy and dull lecture of the entire business of whaling from start to finish, I must go back to the moment when the seeds of the Dismal Trade, as the funeral industry was called in Victorian times, were sown in my life. Though hopefully not as dull.

CHAPTER TWO

And faded through the brightening air

Much of what I say about my family history will sound absurdly made up. There are what appear to be too many conveniently looping curlicues of fate, too many cinematically unlikely scenarios.

For instance, my father dropped dead of a heart attack crossing a drawbridge into a granite fortress, built on top of an extinct volcano, underneath a statue of his ancestor, King Robert the Bruce. He actually did.

And I, his only and most unexpected child, was born on the anniversary of the death of his first wife, killed in a car crash as he was driving them to a wedding.

And my mother had been a child bridesmaid at his first wedding, and it was her fellow bridesmaid's wedding that my father and his wife were driving to all those years later. I have the photograph to prove it.

And later my mother married her dead sister's husband. See both *Hamlet* and *Henry VIII* for precedents to this, although it did all turn out a lot better than it did for either of those two.

All of this, and more, is true, and it gives me mild anxiety about the plot twists that await me in my own life – that other people see as unforgivable whimsy, I see as the inevitable loops of family history, so when I find these circumstantial oxbow lakes in the rivers of other people's lives, I am on familiar ground.

My father died on the fifteenth of September 1977 at the age of sixty-three, when I was just seven. It was this that turned me into an undertaker, instead of an actor or a media advisor or plain loser or whatever else I might have been, perhaps a mélange of all three.

I adored my father and had only just started to realise that he was considerably older than all the fathers of my friends when he died. He had fought in World War Two, something which carried considerable cache in Scotland in the 1970s, a country in which nearly everyone from the poorest to the poshest went into the armed forces. Our culture of play as children was still very much based around re-enacting this war, so having a dad who had been there was really something, even if he looked like everyone else's grandfather.

He fought in the worst of it, Burma, against the Japanese, but had emerged remarkably undamaged by this; ebullient, generous, overjoyed to be alive, glad to be given yet another chance at life after the awful tragedy of his first wife's death, with a new young wife, two stepdaughters and a young son.

By the time I was born, he was a highly decorated lieutenant colonel in The Royal Scots and, as a reward for his war effort, had been given a role running the Army Benevolent Fund, which looked after the interests of veterans.

He had an office high up on the basalt cliffs that form part of Edinburgh Castle and his job seemed to consist mainly of chatting to fellow ruddy-cheeked survivors of the war and then retiring to the Regimental bar to enjoy a whisky at lunchtime.

I thought he was God. I would press my face against the glass of the window when he left in the morning and press it again in the afternoon for the first glimpse of his return.

I would stand at the front door with a broom against my shoulder like a rifle, waiting to be drilled by him like a sergeant major, alerted first by the whiff of his pipe tobacco that proceeded him.

But he was ill, or so I had discerned from quietly listening at closed doors to the hushed chat of adults. A lifetime of Scotch and tobacco, cream and sugar, and survivor's bonhomie, well-earned after the horrors of war, had done him no physical favours.

One night, all tear stained, I came down the stairs and shuffled into the sitting room with that round-shouldered gait that sad children have.

My dad was sat in his chair and my mum in hers and, when she asked me what was wrong, I said I would only tell her if she promised not to tell my dad. I whispered my fear that he was going to die and I was assured by my well-meaning but obviously distressed mother that he was okay, that this was not going to happen.

Here begins the first lesson around children, illness, death and bereavement:

Don't lie. Don't do it. Because when it did happen, when he did die, a ball of fury exploded in my heart, which eclipsed any real grieving for many, many years. I was numbly stuck, with my ears ringing from the shockwave of that blast, unable to feel whether I was even injured.

I get the impossible situation she was in, and it wasn't until many years later that I pictured the anguished conversation that probably followed between my parents – the sadness of my father, the pre-emptive fear of my mother. But when it did happen, probably less than a year later, I was filled with the anger of the excluded, of the lied to.

So, if you find yourself faced with this approaching storm cloud, plan what you are going to say long before you are asked. Obviously, you have to be incredibly circumspect to balance the truth and still alleviate as much fear and sadness as you can. But I am not going to tell you what to say – as I said, this is no self-help book.

The day my father died is the last thing I can remember for about the next six months until the day I was dropped off at boarding school, my memory resurfacing then with a vengeance.

He left as usual in the morning, after breakfast. As usual, I pressed my face against the glass until I couldn't see him anymore.

In my memory, I ran outside to see him walk down the street.

In my memory, when he turned the corner I ran down the street to see him crest the hill. I often did. My last sight of him, real or imagined, disappearing over the ridge of the hill.

His walk from our flat to his office in Edinburgh Castle would have been no more than forty minutes, but it does involve a strenuous climb up the granite steps that form much of the terrain of Edinburgh. It was undoubtedly the strain of this exertion that caused his heart attack.

He crossed the wide parade ground known as the Esplanade, where much of the Royal Edinburgh Military Tattoo takes place, and was crossing the drawbridge towards the portcullis, under the statues of William Wallace and Robert the Bruce.

As the guards were saluting him in, he collapsed dead, a picture-perfect death for an old soldier and one I can't help as seeing way beyond cinematic and deep into the territory of the shaman, or, at the very least, the metaphorically overloaded.

There are many faces burnt into my memory. Many of them from people I have buried, most from those I have loved, but one of them is the face of the man who knocked on our door to bring the news that my father was dead.

I opened the door, always first there if I could be, and I remember seeing the ripple of shock that ran across his florid face. He had not been expecting a wee boy to cheerily answer. Years later I worked out that he was somebody from the castle. He was not a policeman, and my father was an important figure there, of course they would have sent someone to break the news to my mother.

A terrible job. My heart goes out to those policemen and women forced to play the role of the angel of death.

I have knocked on doors like that and had them opened by boys like me. The first time it happened it made me feel vertiginous, like a rush of stale air from a long-sealed box, a giddy, forgotten remembrance rushing back, like concussion or coming around from an anaesthetic. I am never there to break the news like he was, that has been done long before I arrive on the doorstep, but we look into each other's eyes and the blank sadness always haunts me.

I was taken away out of the house by my adult sister while he told my mother and, when we returned, I asked my sister for a drink as I was thirsty. She sat me down, gave me a glass of water, and told me that my father had died.

'Yes,' I said. I drank the water and asked for another one. I drank it.

I can still feel the not-feeling of that moment, forty-three years later. Nothing. Even when led to the bedroom of my weeping, hysterical mother.

Nothing, apart from a sense that my status had changed somehow, that I was briefly in a weird position of power. She clung to me, sobbing. My sister put her head around the door and asked if we needed anything. I reeled off a dream list of unimaginable toys, aware that I was in a place of pity that came with odd privileges, a land I wouldn't leave for many years.

My father was gone. Just like that.

I was offered the chance to go to his funeral, but the dice were loaded because I was also offered the chance to go fishing with a friend of the family. I love fishing. So I didn't go.

I have no doubt that the funeral director who performed my father's funeral would have advised my mother that a funeral was too bewildering and distressing for a child, that seeing her upset would hurt me unnecessarily. This was Edinburgh in the 1970s, a dour and often emotionally cold city. Hauntingly beautiful with it, but not much given to sentiment.

My absence at my father's funeral, a huge church do packed with the ludicrously eclectic people my father counted as friends: alcoholic homeless tramps, brigadiers, actors, doctors, artists, the milkman, everyone there apart from me, is the single most important driver behind why I am an undertaker.

I needed to be at my dad's funeral. Would have loved to have heard his friend Reverend Campbell Maclean do his eulogy, had all the teary-eyed old men and women hold me with their shaking liver-spotted hands and tell me tales of his glory.

Of course I would have been upset, and my mother's grief would have hurt and scared me, but I would not have been excluded from the most important thing that had ever happened to me, and that has hurt me a thousand times more.

People still try for the best of intentions to avoid bringing their children or grandchildren to a funeral. I gently ask them whether the child loved that person. I then quietly warn them that unwarranted exclusion from a family's big life events can sometimes lead to them becoming an undertaker. That usually does the trick.

There is a bit in *A Streetcar Named Desire* where Blanche is berating Stella for leaving her at Belle Reve in those death-soaked years, dramatically exclaiming that the Grim Reaper set up residence at their home. It was a bit like that for us. Not four months after my father's death, my two remaining grandparents died and, again, I didn't go to their funerals.

It is clear in retrospect that my mother wasn't coping. To have your husband and both parents die when you are 47, plunging you into a financial black hole with an inchoately angry seven-year-old boy must have been incredibly tough.

But.

I have only dreamed of my father once in my entire life. It was probably about three years after he had died.

I dreamed my mother and I were walking in the street and, suddenly, there he was. In the dream I was dumbstruck. He looked agitated and only had time to explain that he had been on a secret mission and couldn't say more. Then he hurried on.

Deep down in the caves of my subconscious, I clearly didn't really believe he had died, for the simple reason I hadn't seen it with my own eyes.

I hadn't seen his body, or even his coffin, and this disbelief is what lies at the heart of every one of our bereavements, whether we are a child or an adult. The head knows, or at least thinks it knows. It repeats 'the facts' over and over inside like a stutter.

But the heart is a sturdier creature, more suspicious, more loyal, more volatile. It keeps beating No over and over again. NO. NO. NO.

And so that is why now, as an adult undertaker, I lead people into the presence of their dead. Not out of an attempt to cruelly force them to accept the facts, but to allow them to gently see the presence of their absence, the absence of their presence. To see that it is their dead lying there, and that the dead are changed.

Of course, I'm not suggesting that anyone reading this has not seen the body of someone they love and still on some level believes they are alive, but that was my unconscious childhood narrative, buried deep inside my angry core.

I had to learn it the hard way again, by not seeing my mother after she died less than twenty years later. I had to do it, as most of us have to do it, by gawping at a coffin that intellectually I knew her body lay in.

Do as I say, not as I do.

◆ ◆ ◆

All these, I won't call them absences, disappearances, yes, that's what they were, disappearances, created this very real and very true idea that people could and did just vanish. Just walk out of a room and you would never see them again, except in a photograph.

Death became to me as invisible and as omnipresent as the air, and I have thought of my own death every single day of my life since. And, though it terrifies me, it has become my life's work to walk beside people who are experiencing it. I developed a strange compulsion to run towards the darkness, to seek out the thing that scares me the most, but discovering at the age of 29 that I was a circumstantial undertaker was the singular and most important discovery in my life, and this would propel me into such an unexpected direction.

Death, the thing that I still fear the most and that has done so much to shape my psyche for good and bad, has given me the most extraordinary opportunities.

It has opened doors to me that would have remained shut. It has fed and clothed me, brought me a wife and children, given me deep-lasting friendships. It has even given me the opportunity to become more than an undertaker and form an ongoing collaboration with two of my favourite artists to create a pyramid of bricks 23 feet high and containing the cremated remains of over 34,000 people.

Death has shown me unimaginable horror, and the unbreakable core of love and courage that lies at the heart of what it means to be human. It has been an incredible twenty-odd years.

Death is not my friend, neither is it my enemy; it is my destiny, and the knowing of that cannot but make me shake with fear and emotion.

But I would still hit it hard over the head with a shovel if I got the chance, if there was any alternative to it apart from immortality.

Now, before we meet our first dead body, I am afraid that we have to deal with what happened next, my exile to another Scottish castle; Scotland really is filled with castles, but this one was also filled with frightened little boys.

CHAPTER THREE

Banishment into the establishment

The practice of sending young children, in my case at just seven, into the 'care' of other people at a boarding school perplexes most of the rest of the world.

It is brutally archaic, a throwback to when Britain had an empire and needed a tough, practical and emotionally cauterised set of young men to run it. Sequestering them away from the age of seven and subjecting them to a physically brutal regime that prioritised the team over the individual usually did it.

Nowadays, boarding schools are greatly changed; there are mixed-sex schools with incredible facilities and young vocational teachers who give their privileged charges the best possible education they can. Canoeing and counsellors, abseiling down cliffs, with mugs of hot chocolate and marshmallows waiting at the bottom.

I was unlucky enough to be part of the last flush of The Tom Brown's School Days Experience, at best an expensive form of privileged neglect, at worst a gothic replay of *Lord of the Flies*, but without the beach.

Now an almost unrecognisable institution filled, I'm sure, with warmth and opportunity. Then, it was an unimaginably creepy castle stalked by haunted alcoholic veterans of the war.

There was a curious thing where men who had been tortured by the Japanese in prison camps in the Far East were for some ungodly reason immediately welcomed back into the boarding school system as teachers. They prowled the corridors at night, drunk, listening for that most heinous of crimes – whispered conversation after the lights were out – before triumphantly hauling the poor victims before the headmaster, who would often administer a swift brutal beating with a gym shoe that to us was the size of a small car. I personally didn't encounter any paedophilic teachers, but I suffered, as we all did, from the droves of sadistic ones.

It seems of course incredible that I was sent at all. I was a very young, recently bereaved boy, who should have been receiving one-on-one specialist care within the bosom of my family. Instead, I was singled out by one teacher, who literally reacted to my bereavement as if it was actually my fault. This teacher, or 'master' as we were tellingly forced to call them, tried everything he could to break me psychologically, and even today, I still struggle to see what it was in me that he hated so much.

My mother died when I was twenty-five, long before we had had a chance to have 'that conversation'. And were she still alive, I doubt we would have it now. We rarely do confront our parents with their mistakes, it is too fraught a topic. Our hard-won adult relations with them can often not bear such revisiting.

I know that the decision to send me there haunted her considerably; that my sisters, both well into adulthood, argued vehemently with her about it. I think she genuinely thought it was for the best, what my dead father would have wanted and expected, and there was a good chunk of what can only be described as class loyalty.

What I can tell you is that it felt like a betrayal and a punishment for what had happened to me.

It was a place of simmering violence and echoing loneliness. There was always one child in the dormitory weeping all night long. It was just one, because you very quickly learned that these children became the scapegoats, and shoes and hairbrushes were thrown at them with shouts of 'shut up, you little shit', hurled until they dialled down their sorrow to a quiet whimpering.

There is a haunting documentary from the 1970s that follows some of these boys as they go through their first term. What is so shocking is seeing the tautness of their faces as they come back for the holidays. Deep in shock. They left as children and return as a sort of badly engineered pretend adult, desperately trying to carry the responsibility they now believe they have.

It is the severance of innocence that is so brutal and often lasts a lifetime, with what is now described as Boarding School Syndrome – an inability to love or even feel much empathy. It is nowhere more evident than in the coterie of damaged individuals who are currently running the country.

The establishment of Britain has been twisted into its uncaring and distorted shape by this system, and it either produces people who have convinced themselves they were the best days of their lives, or at least accepted the Faustian pact of power that goes with it, or rebel refugees like myself, radicalised and outta there as quickly as possible.

You will be relieved, dear reader, to know that I am not one of those psychopathically damaged ones (although perhaps

I would say that) because I was saved by acid house, whose timing couldn't have been better, but it took me a lot of time and distance to fully see how utterly fucked up this way of educating children is.

It is without a doubt a form of institutional abuse, never mind the unfairness of being able to buy your child a better education – an education, by the way, which is often wasted because the upper middle classes are a remarkably stupid bunch. Privilege and inbreeding doth not make for many geniuses; it just churns out mediocre, overentitled morons by the hundreds.

So, I think you can see where I stand on this, and I am not going to drag you through every Harry Potter moment of it – a franchise, incidentally, that does capture the horror of boarding school remarkably well – but I will talk you through a few pointers and techniques as to how these institutions used to work.

Firstly, be very wary of anyone you meet who went to boarding school, or even school in general, and tells you they were bullied. No shit, Sherlock; it's the actual *modus operandi* of these places.

Everyone is bullied and, unless you were unlucky enough to be particularly socially vulnerable (and there were some children at my school whom I can see clearly now had serious learning issues or conditions like autism), you bullied too. You tried it out for size. It's how the system runs. It's just not possible to control that many children night and day, so you allow little pecking orders to develop.

Individuals are elevated to small positions of power: broom monitor, dormitory head, something like that, with the ultimate promotion being to a prefect – a proxy teacher, a pseudopoliceman. A steady filtration system begins in which the more ruthless or, let's say, more entrenched in the absolute assurance of their family's class position, are identified and rewarded, and the slow, the troubled and the troublesome, the socially doubtful, the communists of the heart are also identified.

There are very few people who emerge from that last gasp of British boarding school cruelty who are indifferent to it. They either buy into it and its rewards in its entirety: a place at the top table of the establishment, a well-paid job in industry or politics (such as the monsters we see currently destroying the country as if it were a game) or they are expelled like a foreign body, gradually and painfully, and live a life on the fringes of privilege, scarred by their septic expulsion, haunted by their damaged childhood.

There is, of course, at first a serious attempt to break the rebels into conformity as, let's be clear, the parents of these pupils are paying a lot of money to these institutions to have someone else raise them. So they are in no hurry to lose you, but they can spot an individual rather than a team member quite quickly, even as you are stuck in the rictus of shock that hits you when your parents, or in my case parent, drive off down the theatrically long drive, leaving you in this nightmare.

The Harry Potter books have given thousands of children a longing to experience boarding school, which I find extraordinary, because the real experience is very like that in tone. Mine actually was a dark, semigothic castle and there were monsters behind every door, portals to horror lay within the switching off of a dormitory light and terror lay down every strip-lit corridor.

The main staircase had deep gouges on one of the landings and, we were told with relish by the older boys on our first day for fuck's sake, that these were the marks left as the owner of the castle, unusually for that time a woman, was dragged out to be burnt alive as a witch.

For decades I assumed the story was simply untrue, a tentacle of fear, coiling around the frightened new boys for dark laughs, but some idle googling one day revealed that the origin story, if embellished with physical traces, was actually true.

The castle and land had passed to a daughter, Euphame MacCalzean in 1558, a spirited and independent woman and the only heir after the death of her father. Jealous relatives who wanted the land framed her for witchcraft (James VI, king of Scotland at that time, was a paranoid and brutal man, much given to frenzied witch burning, and misogyny in general).

She was accused, alongside some servants, of acts of healing witchcraft, in particular of giving pregnant women hagstones, stones with naturally occurring holes, which were said to help women giving birth. This was a sin, as the pain of childbirth was God-given. This defence of physical pain is a very Scottish thing, pure Calvinism, and we will return to its enduring influence later on. But what sealed her death warrant was the accusation that she and others had made 'poppets' of James – small Vodou-like dolls in order to cause his death. This was more than enough and Euphame was burnt to death, alive and without the usual mercy of pre burning strangulation, on the twenty-fifth of June 1591, on the slopes of Edinburgh Castle.

The castle and land were passed to one of the king's favourites, a man obviously. But within twenty years, Euphame had been posthumously pardoned and the act was openly, if tacitly, acknowledged as a plot to take the land and castle away from her, a troublesome woman.

Four hundred years later, this granite monument to the violent power of the establishment was being used to turn young boys such as myself into foot soldiers of the patriarchy.

The truth of what had happened there, so long ago and soaked into the history of the walls, was recounted to us honestly and directly but disguised as garbled myth, a boast of the violent domination men had over women. It was a place of immense dark, psychic power.

But, in expressing my opinion of what I went through, and what I believe the wider experience to have been like, I am firmly and proudly declaring myself a class traitor. There are hundreds of my contemporaries, none of whom I am in touch with for obvious reasons, who will insist they genuinely were the best days of their lives. Arseholes. And there are those who denounce it in various stages of lasting life damage. They, I believe, are the healthy ones.

My time there was not completely without its moments of fun, I admit, but they were far outweighed by the moments of gut-wrenching homesickness and fear, the sudden and shocking understanding that your family have done this to you deliberately, and the cruelty inflicted on you and that you inflict on others. For this hard lesson I am I suppose, quite grateful.

The division of children in general into bullies and bullied is far too arbitrary. There are some children whose already dark home background means they are predisposed to torture and often this inclination is picked up on and shaped by the establishment. But most children, particularly in the largely unsupervised by adults life of a boarding school, a lot of which is conducted under the cover of night, get to try out these costumes of tormenter and tormented.

I was relatively popular, being funny and hard to catch as I was fizzing with ADHD, so I bullied children less gregarious than me. I bullied them for many reasons – being fat, being a bit slow, having disfiguring eczema, being another race

– whatever their obvious weakness was, I exploited it. That was how we all bullied: picking on someone a bit vulnerable. It was normal behaviour. Children can be deeply savage when left to their own devices.

And I, in my turn, was bullied by larger fish, attacked at night by roaming gangs of squads delivering punishment beatings for imagined slights, waiting for it to be my turn, as it was always somebody's turn.

If you are a natural sadist or have psychopathic tendencies, then this kind of thing starts to bring brain-rewarding patterns and, before you know it, you are the CEO of a large company, an extremely successful stockbroker or an MP voting against feeding poor children school meals during the holidays.

But, if you are an ordinary, relatively well-adjusted child, this starts to sit uneasily with your conscience. Do unto others as you would have them do to you comes from the heart of the human soul, not the bible. For me, I was cured of my bullying stage by what almost can be seen today as spontaneous social cognitive behavioural therapy.

I bullied a boy my age solely because he was fat. Routinely and casually, without much thought as to what I was doing. We were probably nine. On the last day of term, a day of such joy and excitement that to compare it with the ending of a jail sentence is not too extreme, I was playing on some grass outside with some friends.

This boy came storming out of a door, hot angry tears streaming down his cheeks. He punched me in the face, hard. Then he turned on his heels and walked away.

I got it. Enough was enough. I never bullied again.

A full life stretch at boarding school is over ten years, from seven until eighteen, split into two sections. The first, from seven until thirteen, is where the real damage is done. The second half, from thirteen to eighteen, can be at times quite fun, although you are of course kicked right back to Go and have to undergo all the arcane rituals to establish your place at the bottom of the social pecking order again. It's all so boring and by this time faintly predictable. This is the bit where, if they have established you as a trouble maker, they do their best to wheedle you into line, talking about the importance of the team and the benefits of settling into the club, which always seemed to be at the expense of the individual.

By this stage, I realised which side I was on, and it was ideological, not merely behavioural. I argued with my fellow classmates, a lot of whom had bought into the extremes of Thatcherism through the osmosis of their parents' belief. I was staggered. Surely now was the time to play the outlaw? And who could accept such brutal and socially divisive politics such as Thatcher's, enacted across the land, without howling in outrage?

We were protected from the outside world by our status of privileged neglect, but we couldn't pretend we were ignorant. Things like The Troubles, as euphemistic a term as you could dream up for a vicious sectarian battle that was being fought in Ireland and Britain, was unavoidable. The 'managed decline' of whole industries and areas of the country, resulting in entire communities being plunged into Victorian levels of poverty, was in every newspaper and on every news programme. How someone could be fourteen and not behave like they were a part of the Weathermen at heart baffled me. It still does.

◆ ◆ ◆

Up until I went to my secondary boarding school, I had led a somewhat schizophrenic existence. During term time I was in an all-male boarding school, taught almost entirely by damaged old men, but during the holidays I was with my widowed mother and her female friends or accompanying her to work, which was as the chief fundraiser for Scotland's first hospice.

My mother was a contradiction. Her politics were left wing to centrist. She was very much a first-wave feminist and her close friends were too. She was active in politics and stood twice in a general election as a candidate for the Liberal Party. All of this clashed with her class loyalty and her somewhat baffling decision to send me off to boarding school but, as Walt Whitman said, 'Do I contradict myself? / Very well then I contradict myself, / (I am large, I contain multitudes.)'

We are all allowed to grow and change, after all, right up until the very last seconds of our life, so I can forgive her contradictions as I hope people can forgive mine. It is one of the most exciting and redeeming features of human beings, this ability to grow even as we die. This idea, that even dying was living is, I think, at the heart of the hospice movement.

They are so entrenched in our culture now that it is hard to think of a time without them, but in the mid 1970s in Scotland, hospices were quite a hard sell. St Columba's Hospice, set in the grounds of a large house on the seafront in the suburbs of Edinburgh, was the first in Scotland and opened in 1977, inspired by an idea by Cicely Saunders to create a place dedicated entirely to palliative care.

The problem was that the deeply held religious beliefs of a lot of people at the time found the idea of ameliorating the pain of the dying as ungodly, that suffering at the end of life was something Christ had gone through in his experience as a human being and this suffering should be part of ours, so throwing a blanket of pain relief around them was fundamentally wrong.

This neatly dovetailed with the Hippocratic oath sworn by doctors when they qualified to always aim to preserve human life at all cost. For many of them, the idea that accepting that this person was dying and there was no more to be done for them apart from to make them peaceful and treat their symptoms of pain and distress in a beautiful place designed to allow them to end their days in peace, clashed with their ideas of almost god-like interventions in hospitals.

As a result, hospices attracted and still attract very special people and, if you are lucky enough to have had a family member die in one, no doubt they have been transformed in your mind from a previous vision of them as charnel houses to places of deep transformative peace, filled with what appear to be angels in human form.

My mother's job was chief fundraiser, which, even back in 1977, meant raising nearly a thousand pounds a day to keep the place running. She toured working men's clubs in the borders of Scotland, Women's Institutes, small rural communities as well as urban ones to persuade people that the idea of a hospice was far from unchristian, but quite the opposite, that it lay at the heart of Christian belief, the idea of mercy. Still, it was a hard sell.

St Columba's Hospice was run, as seemingly are most hospices, by women. The head doctor was a man and so was the groundskeeper, but the rest – all of the medical staff and the administrative staff – were women. In Edinburgh in 1977 this was quite a rarity and, even as a young boy, I could feel the difference. The sisterly camaraderie that flowed through the place felt both strong and light. There was laughter everywhere, and often there were children, sometimes as many as eight or nine, during the school holidays. Childcare was unaffordable to nearly all the mothers there, so they brought us kids in and, up to a certain point, we were given the run of the place. We were not meant to go screaming into the wards or noisily kick a ball inside, and we were encouraged to play outside in the large walled garden, but we pack of kids from all social backgrounds bonded and formed a wild gang.

Of course now, and for good reason, this would be considered completely unacceptable. Health and safety, the peace of the patients, the sheer impracticality of having a gang of kids running around the place, all of it jars with the modern zen-like hospice of today, but it let a much-needed unselfconscious current of life course through the place, which genuinely was appreciated by the patients who watched us zoom our way around the Victorian garden like a feral pack of dogs.

I can remember being brought in to say goodbye to an old lady called Mabel, who was in the last few hours of her life. We had been oblivious to Mabel, but she had watched us out of her window, wheeling and shrieking like a flock of swifts and, to her, we had obviously meant something important. We stood a little awkwardly for a few moments in front of her bed, before saying, 'Can we go now?'

A schizophrenic childhood, half of the time in the bear pit of a boarding school with its entirely male energy, frightened and feral, haunted by fears of my mother being the next to die and ending up an orphan, and the other half spent in the warm embrace of working-class Scots nurses and their children in a place designed specifically for people to die in or hanging out with my mother and her tight set of close strong female friends.

Is it any wonder that Death was such a constant companion to me? My childhood was saturated by it, both negative and positive.

CHAPTER FOUR

Escape into the strobe and the smoke

Assuredly what I didn't need was to immediately inherit a chunk of money equivalent in today's terms to around £700,000 the moment I turned eighteen.

My father had died intestate. Without a shadow of a doubt, he intended to leave his family money to my mother, but Scottish law is a dour, uncharitable beast and so the money was frozen in a trust fund until I was eighteen.

My school had finally expelled me, two weeks before the end of my second to last term, just before the last push for my A levels and probably just after the last tax-free cheque had cleared. (British 'public' schools are defined as charitable institutions and, of course, are not public at all. See if you can pick the individual splinters of irony out of that one.)

I deserved it. If you are going to behave like a teenage Weatherman, don't be surprised if the direction of the wind changes. If there was a complex plot of civil disobedience, a small riot, a clash with the authorities or a plot based around the procurement and consumption of cigarettes and alcohol, I would be at the bottom of it, fingerprints everywhere. So they expelled me and I was out, a newly sprung lifer, blinking in the unfamiliar wide open space of the real world. And who needs A levels when you have a trust fund with stocks and shares in all sorts of horrors?

I have never used my expensive qualifications in any practical way; my schooling gave me a love of literature, a fine antennae tuned to the subtle and pervasive grip of the establishment on British society and a well-modulated BBC voice, which, it seems, vast swathes of the UK still, to their cost, mistake for intelligence. It's served me alright though, as a good part of my professional life is spent speaking.

I was done with education. What has now been diagnosed as ADHD was to the establishment filter clearly just wilfully bad behaviour. To them, I wasn't struggling with a disability, I was trouble and I had broken the class contract.

So I did what any decent class warrior with a guilty clutch of stocks and shares would do; I fled to Cornwall and began a slow-motion nervous breakdown, the sort of which often strikes the newly released institutionalised folk, particularly those a mere decade away from a parental bereavement.

This would occupy the next ten years of my life and find me at twenty-eight with a house but six months into mortgage arrears, all of the money gone, guiltily disposed of through bad business moves, overgenerosity and buying everybody a lot of hash, wine and Indian takeaways. It could have been worse. I could have developed a taste for that panacea of the wounded upper middle classes: heroin or cocaine, and the story would have stopped right there. Luckily, I dodged those particular indulgences.

That time in between leaving school and deliberately shedding all my money was an unsettling mixture of barely concealed panic, wild partying and strange ways to occupy myself and find my vocation.

I looked for it in all sorts of places. I tried to find myself on Bodmin Moor at eighteen by trying my hand at shepherding. It didn't work out, but I was clearly drawn towards the natural world, always had been. I think perhaps I was also deeply repelled by the idea of being drawn into the system, which is still predominantly urban.

Cornwall often attracts the wounded and forlorn, refugees from the wider society, so I was not alone. The bad taste joke of the day, an unacceptable sentiment now, was that the shape of Cornwall resembles a Christmas stocking; the further down you go, the worse your situation. The nuts end up in the toe: Penzance. I wasn't too far gone really, I was around the thigh, firmly trapped in the bride's garter region.

Of course having that sort of money at that age is both ludicrous to the individual and deeply socially immoral. I felt this acutely while simultaneously knowing that it was giving me the space and time to collapse a bit, but feeling terrible for having that space. None of the rest of my family had the wealth I did and my time spent kicking against the pricks at boarding school had given me strong views on the unfairness of inherited wealth, the misery and injustices upon which it was built and the damage that it was doing to the environment – and the world in general and the society that we were all living in.

The dour stereotype that was the Edinburgh lawyer who oversaw my trust fund was able to offer advice, but also unable to stop me from instructing him to sell stocks and shares to fund various crackpot schemes, largely suggested by others. He kept on imploring me to forget I had this money and simply get a job, but frankly I was too in and out of a nervous breakdown to be much use to anyone as an employee of anything and, while liberation from the guilty yoke of a financially comfortable life was not my conscious intention, it was certainly an unconscious driver in my behaviour.

I did some good with it, it didn't all go on hashish and gin. Not that that didn't do some good. There is often a wisdom that goes with self-medication and allowing yourself a break to get your shit together. I gave my mother a sizeable chunk, exactly as my father would have wanted me to, my sisters received some too. I funded a couple of friends' attempts at things like new sailing boat prototypes and I did commission my own first home: a flat-bottomed wooden house boat that sat on a pontoon on a Cornish estuary, a place in which to sit and pretend I was from another century.

It was from this boat that I struck upon my romantic but impossibly macho scheme of becoming a proper riverman, an eel fisherman, licensed to eel as the Beastie Boys nearly said, from the highest tidal reaches of the river I lived on to the tidal breakwater that marked the entrance of the Plymouth Sound.

Out of all the ways I tried to justify my existence and merge with the environment, this was the most ludicrous. I would set fyke nets, as they are called in the business, a sort of extended long version of lobster pots into which, in theory at least, migratory eels would swim.

The idea was to check the nets every low tide, collect the eels and keep them alive in a holding tank. When enough were caught, I could, in theory, summon to me a mythical truck from the Netherlands that would suck up the eels in a vacuum tube, weigh them, and pay me with crisp cash.

The reality was that hauling in heavy mud-soaked nets in the dark, filled with crabs, the odd flat fish, and the even rarer eel, I never caught enough to summon the apocryphal tanker, hawking them instead around local pubs, creating a strange niche market. Clearly I have a talent for identifying and carving out previously unthought-of roles.

I would arrive at these south-east Cornish pubs on my moped, a wet burlap sack of writhing eels between my legs – a source of much amusement and a welcome bit of entertainment in a quiet rural pub – and was quickly dubbed 'Mr Eel', cheery shouts of which would ring out as I entered.

It was as if someone had photoshopped one of the Fabulous Furry Freak Brothers into an eighteenth-century pastoral oil painting of river life. Utterly bizarre, harmless, but risible.

From the outside I was a just another trustafarian; an outwardly confident hippie, taking a good stab at being a rugged outdoors type, if you didn't look for too long or too closely at my still soft hands, dressed like a straggler from one of the crusty late 80s / early 90s festivals I would go to, but inside I was a mess, humming with anxiety and bewilderment.

But destiny waits patiently in the long grass of our youth and the soft singing of our ancestors eventually becomes audible to even the most tone deaf.

Hippies have played a big part in forming who I am. My sisters were hippies, my eldest sister being sixteen when I was born in 1970, and their slightly absent, patchouli and acid-soaked presence saturated my childhood.

My first attempt at inhabiting a post-school persona, was a very late 80s mash-up of hippie and punk, softly morphing through hip hop into a raver – the youth tribe that would come to both save me from the last vestiges of class privilege and give me a social, political and spiritual framework with which to drive forward the rest of my life.

In my houseboat, it was Huckleberry Finn met Wavy Gravy, and the line of transmission stretched back further than Woodstock.

I do believe that ancestral awareness and connection are essential in life to know what your position and direction are. I really do think we go about it all wrong, fetishising the past and misreading the simple basic lives of our predecessors as being morally better than us.

Some of this I think, comes from a belief that we atavistically cling to, even though our logic has long since rejected it. A belief that the dead *know* more than us, that a bigger reveal awaits us, that we get to turn the last page of the cosmic story once we are dead.

I've been around the dead for so long now that I understand the truth to be the opposite.

The dead know less than us, their understanding of the complexity of life stops with their breathing, and, as we pass through history without them, the sadness that they are not with us to marvel, wonder and plain freak out at the increasingly weird and tightening loops of world events makes our separation from them seem even more acute, and their innocence even more enviable.

But it is not my intention to retrospectively slay my ancestors ungratefully (I wouldn't have a chance, being the only male in my line not to have fought in a war ever). I just believe that probably, we, the living, are often the best version of our genetic line, the best model of growth and evolution that is possible, if environmental warping hasn't wreaked its havoc. It is in the nature of forward motion to improve, to learn from the mistakes of the past if we can. After all, they are there for all to see, the mistakes, clearly written on the subway walls of our family lives.

The ancestors that have the biggest effect on us are rarely our flesh and blood.

My social ancestors made themselves known to me at this time, through literature and culture. I discovered the poetry of Bloodaxe Books, the novels of Iain Banks and Ian McEwan, the gonzo political anger of Hunter S. Thompson, the baroque eroticism of Angela Carter, the optimistic song of Walt Whitman, the militant fury of Public Enemy, the fierce integrity of Malcolm X. I started to free myself further from the clumsy social indoctrination of my schooling.

In my eventual decision to become an undertaker, without any of the traditional milestones like apprenticeship or being born into a family business, I feel I was following in the footsteps of these social ancestors, even in my childish rebellion against the awkward and transparently patriarchal boarding school.

I could feel these social ancestors all around me, even as I played at being an outcast. They gathered around me in the oil lamp–lit gloom of my houseboat, most obviously in the form of the hippies I most closely resembled. Their influences felt much stronger and better to me than those of my illustrious Scottish ancestors who, the further one went back with them, became more obviously violently acquisitive warlords, opportunistic people rewarded for tribal brutality with property and status, which they had managed to maintain and historically launder until the facade of social superiority was ensured.

Our cultural ancestors are often still alive. They are the artists, the writers and musicians we love the most. They are our friends and peers, figures from history who resonate. We line up with these non-genetic ancestors, living and dead, like magnetised iron fillings and, in doing so, we can see where we are really headed for, rather than following the somewhat selfish family agenda so much of us are burdened with. It is not a betrayal of flesh to discover your true family, it is a home-coming.

So, in trying to be a hippy, a hippy mark II, I felt I was taking a baton passed from the radical artists and bohemians of the 50s, the poets and novelists, the Beats, who in turn were influenced by the Surrealists and the Pacifists of the First World War. These links in the chain of comradeship go back through the Quakers and the Diggers and the Levellers, through to the Pantisocratic experiments of the 1800s, back down to the early Christian sect.

I identify with a chain of progressive radical thinking that stretches back as far as human society does. These men and women are my ancestors, and some of the most influential still live, and they write and sing. These are the people who form my patchwork quilt of religious gratitude, whom I have appropriated with a combination of chaos magic and Haitian Vodou, a bastardisation of both that would probably anger true adherents of each, to form some sort of rudimentary belief system. A ritual machine through which I can express my gratitude and fear, and focus myself on the heaviness of what I do without losing myself in darkness or becoming calloused to everyday suffering.

But this was all as yet unformed in my head, a barely heard background noise as I sat on my houseboat, chain-smoking spliffs and listening to Irish rebel songs, wondering how in the hell I was going to actualise my destiny and find a vocation while tightly pinched between the twin claws of inherited wealth and inherited trauma.

Several crucial things happened to me at this time of my life.

Culture happened, in the form of meeting other people from very different backgrounds, particularly my future partner Claire, who not only introduced me to new music and literature, swerving me dramatically away from the slightly old-fashioned, almost prewar taste that had been installed in me by my older parents. Claire was also the first person to introduce the idea that perhaps being sent to boarding school at such a young age was an incredibly fucked-up thing to happen.

This idea, which I had been quietly suppressing whenever it arose in my heart, felt true, even as it brought up confusing and contradictory ideas of what it meant to be simultaneously loved and rejected, and it began to give me some historical context for whatever crisis I was silently enduring in my head. These first inklings of self-realisation around my dysfunctional childhood, mixed with my head being torn open culturally, was more of an education than ten years in private school had given me. I started to become my adult self.

Another hugely important thing that happened to me and my peers was acid house culture.

I was eighteen in 1988 when I was spat out by the public school system. My politics were clearly formed by then, left wing with anarcho tendencies, extremely naive and innocent really – typical teenage pious fervour – but the explosion of rave culture gave me my first embodied experiences of these utopian yearnings. I started to go to raves and found that society was indeed complex, rich and multicultured – and way more exciting than the narrow class promontory I had been raised on.

It's a cliche for people of my age to rhapsodise over early acid house culture, but that is because it was life changing for my generation. For a brief period, all the walls of class, ethnicity and gender disintegrated, and the fields and warehouses of Britain were filled with people hugging and dancing.

Football hooligans embraced flamboyant transvestites and woman danced free from the incessant sexual harassment that characterised pre-rave nightclubs. Nobody was drunkenly fighting, nobody cared if your dancing was odd – it didn't matter, this wasn't about looking good, it was about feeling good.

Black, white, nerdy, cool, gay, straight, working class, posh were all swept up in a communal ecstatic drug-fuelled Dionysian ritual that was completely at odds to the prevailing social culture of the country. A generation suddenly scaled the bleak walls of ten years of Conservative authoritarianism and we found ourselves in some sort of an Eden, laughing and hugging each other.

A generation battered by Thatcherism danced on the roofs of our lives, miraculously unbroken by a decade of deliberate social demolition. We bonded with the people that our ruling classes had tried to set us against. We saw through the lie that as individuals we were alone, helpless and doomed. We grinned and danced and threw our hands up in the air.

It must have been a terrifying thing for the dominant social class to see. It had the unmistakable whiff of optimism and solidarity. The sad wreckage of those communal, utopian dreams haunt me as the toad of authoritarianism squats on us all once again.

So this is what I started to do, in between hauling in mud-heavy, largely empty nets and pushing panic attacks down with the help of alcohol and dope. I started going to parties, taking MDMA and gradually recognised and started to transform my trauma through my experiences at raves.

Most of us rely on some drugs to dial down the pressure in the evening or give us the energy at the start of the day, alcohol, sugar and coffee being stitched into the fabric of our society. I still very much believe that we need to rethink our ideas around how we deal with certain drugs, particularly their legal classification, and the way we tolerate their uses.

There is a tremendous amount of hypocrisy around the way we separate drugs through an arbitrary framework with some being demonised and others being available everywhere, and a lot of this globally agreed separation into good drugs and bad drugs owes more to maintaining racist social power structures than it does to benefiting public health issues. The war on drugs has achieved nothing in its fifty years, saved no lives, and has destabilised countries and allowed criminal organisations to become as powerful as nation states.

I have had heroin and alcohol addiction in my own family as a result of terrible trauma and I have buried many young people who have died as a result of drug misadventures, so I am not a naive evangelist. I just know from my own lived experiences that some of the party drugs like MDMA and psychedelics can be immensely healing, while drugs like alcohol or cocaine can cause some of the worst problems in our society.

I am middle aged now and any wild adventures I recount are firmly in my past, but I have a vision of how the power of these substances could be harnessed to create a safety net for all of us.

Alcohol is unarguably one of the most physically and socially harmful drugs, involved in nearly 40 per cent of acts of violence, increasing in proportion around fights near nightclubs and in matters of domestic and sexual abuse.

Alcohol is also one of the most popular and socially acceptable drugs, due to its almost instantaneous ability to dial down stress. It is the traditional drug of choice for all who are involved in professions that involve dealing with trauma: doctors, police, paramedics and, of course, funeral directors, not to mention nearly everyone else who encounters stress in their lives, i.e. all of us – and because it is legal and socially acceptable.

I admit, I have a complicated relationship with substances, as do so many of us, and we should be showing each other immense compassion and understanding around our use of them, not punishing each other and deepening the damage by jailing users. Drug addiction is an illness that is a response to trauma and needs medical help, not punitive incarceration. As a society we need to have honest conversations about the use of drugs, because they are a part of the human experience and will not go away.

For me, aged eighteen, overburdened with guilt and struggling to deal with waves of panic attacks that I now see as the emergence of the grief around my father's death (and that had essentially been forcefully compartmentalised when I entered boarding school), this new drug, MDMA, used in this semi-religious setting was a bit of a life saver.

It plunged me into society, into youth culture and into my body. It took away my fear of other people and allowed me to reflect on what had happened to me. I am eternally grateful and proud that I lived through these times. I sometimes think that without it I would have been unable to safely access my trauma and begin the long slow process of healing.

It is one of the paradoxes of raving that you can be in a crowd of thousands, dancing together as one, and simultaneously be involved in an internal process of extremely insightful and self-forgiving scrutiny.

In my experience, when you take MDMA, it can allow you to revisit events in your past that are deeply painful, while dampening down the fear response in the part of the brain called the amygdala, freeing you from the endless looped memories of PTSD.

There are now well-established clinical trials that have grown into treatment programmes that are incredibly successful for people with treatment-resistant PTSD, undergone in strict medical conditions. I applaud these, but I'm an anarcho-humanist and my experience is that you can tap into these healing moments yourself and surface in a crowd of joyful humans deep in their bodies and their hearts in the middle of a wild, all-night party and grow as much as you can in one night with your friends as you can in any formal therapy session.

I can see a world where these drugs, freed from the random and racist ways they have been presented to society as dangerous, could in fact be the opposite. I feel that MDMA and psychedelics such as psilocybin and LSD could be used to help all those people I mentioned who currently deal with trauma through alcohol, through a blend of ritualised and therapeutical held events, a mixture of a rave and a held support group.

And I can see a world in which these drugs are used in palliative care, not just for the dying, but for the grieving, to help heal the complicated family history that often resurfaces at the end of a life and can cast a sad shadow over a death. I see a world where not just the dying take psilocybin to alleviate their enormous mortal distress, but where whole families sit around the bed of the dying in a hospice and take MDMA together, to properly talk about the untalked about, to heal long-held hurts. I honestly believe we are wasting so many psycho-spiritual substances through our deeply buried, reflexive Puritan prejudices that do not have our best interests at heart.

This timely, self-healing hedonism became one of the first and most powerful tools that I used to begin grappling with my own grief and, later, how I coped with the existential darkness that is inevitable working as a radically connected and involved undertaker.

It also was one of the things that gave me a framework upon which to hang a non-religious ceremony on. A rave is conjured out of very little, simply with the intention to gather and connect and dance all night. This is a powerful social lesson, the striking of a temporary tribal camp in which to enact rituals of pleasure. The healing effects of joy should never be underestimated.

As I came to begin creating ceremonies that stood outside of the established religious power structures, raves were one of the things I leaned on; the sense of togetherness, the lack of hierarchy, the collapsing of the barriers of defence and the light holding of the reins of power.

But there were other drugs I used and alcohol was my dark companion of oblivion, like for so many of us. It switches off those portions of the forebrain that deal with emotions, swiftly and efficiently, and, for most of my life, it has been a strange combination between a confident best friend and a jailer handcuffed to me.

It went hand in hand with dope smoking and, while I can see that these two substances certainly did damage to my growing brain and definitely distanced me emotionally from those around me, they also provided me with an air pocket within which to escape the emerging trauma, buried away since my father's death barely more than a decade before.

But there is only so long you can hide on a mudflat, smoking damn dope and hauling in metaphors in muddy nets like a fevered dream mash-up of Doc Martin and Werner Herzog's *Fitzcarraldo*, so I finally did something sensible with my rapidly diminishing money and bought a collapsed mill so old it was recorded in the *Domesday Book* and a stretch of wild, clean river on the edge of Bodmin Moor.

I breathed my weird version of new life into this ancient place, held wild parties, reopened the silted-up mill stream, attempted to start a small-scale hydro project and, towards the last half of my time there, used it as my workplace when I unexpectedly morphed from a louche trustafarian into a broke, shining-eyed radical undertaker.

Life at the mill was simultaneously bucolic and dull. The summer months were filled with friends camping in the field and swimming in the river. The isolation of the place at the bottom of a remote valley meant I could have long weekend parties without disturbing my distant neighbours, and I certainly did, but the winters were wet and lonely, with not much to do but go to the pub and, just as I was starting to stabilise myself somewhat (if by stabilise I mean become the ring leader of my own private circus rather than just one of the clowns), my mother died.

She was sixty-five, I was twenty-five. An orphan. No matter what age you are when your parents die, you become an orphan. If one or more of your parents are still alive, you will remember these words when the last one dies. Orphaned.

My mother had been ill with Non-Hodgkin lymphoma for several years, her initial diagnosis had come when I was around twenty or twenty-one. I went through the usual sweeping emotional loops that accompany such a diagnosis – immediate shock and catastrophising her imminent death, fear and worry, hope during periods of remission – but ultimately you get used to living with a cancerous family member. It very quickly becomes routine – the pre-emptive grief, the giddy highs of hopeful news – and the highs and the lows cancel each other out to some kind of acceptance.

I was young and preoccupied with my own life, which consisted of mainly keeping my nervous breakdown at arm's length, a full-time job in itself, so her final rapid decline caught me by surprise. I hadn't seen her for a couple of months before I was summoned around Christmastime to see her.

I was deeply shocked the last time we saw each other, too shocked really to take in much of our last conversation. She was in a hospice in Oxford and only lasted a few days but, having worked in one, she made her presence felt, not being able to help pointing out little things that could be changed for the better, mainly for the nurses' benefit. She felt like she was coming home. Not many people get to feel that when they enter a hospice.

She was determined not to ruin Christmas for us all forever so, through sheer force of will, she made herself live until the second of January. The image I had of her then was of a mortally stricken Lancaster bomber, a wounded but cheery David Niven at the joystick, determined to at least clear the village it was imperilling before crashing in the forests beyond.

She held my hand, talking clearly and gently to my shocked face. She told me that although my life was a chaotic mess right now, she knew that one day I would be alright. She told me to go home, that she wasn't going to die that night, but would die tomorrow.

She did and, to my shame, I never returned the next day with my sister and stepfather to be there when she died. The old family dynamic of protective exclusion of me as the youngest kicked into place and I regressed, and colluded in absenting myself from properly participating in one more family death, this time the most important death in my life so far.

Her funeral was something she organised herself, down to the last detail, writing it out after I had left her bedside.

At the top of a definitive list of music and readings, and who was doing them, it said 'Bossy boots still at it'.

There is a school of thought espoused by well-meaning people, and sometimes not-so-well-meaning people with vested financial interests in securing your future funeral, who make a great deal of noise about organising your own funeral, even paying for it up front. Daytime television advertisements are filled with crumbling celebrities of yesteryear promoting various forms of preplanning and prepayment.

I am not one of these people. My mother's control over everything that was to happen, including the entry music, left us with nothing to do in that strange hinterland in between a death and the funeral.

It was well meaning on her part, and part of an understandable desire to continue to control her own narrative right up until the last minute but, if you are asking me now, as an undertaker, whether you should plan your own funeral, I will say no. Leave that up to the people who will be performing it.

It is for them.

It is about you, of course, but death takes your last words with her. (I say Her because, as the poet and novelist Salena Godden has pointed out, of course death is a woman. Only she who can give life can take it.)

Say what you have to say while you live, but let go of the bit right after. Let your family and friends decide what is said about you. They know a side of you that is impossible for you to know yourself, and they need to acknowledge that side and say goodbye to it. It's their work, their grief, their loss, not yours.

My mother's life and death have had a huge impact on my unearthing my vocation, but in different ways. Her work at the hospice and the physical inclusion of myself in that had done much to normalise death for me. The buoyant atmosphere created by the women who ran it, much of which was happiness at achieving some career autonomy, provided a strong counter narrative to the brutal half life I spent in the distorted manhood of boarding school, but it was her death and her overorganised funeral that was to propel me out of my frightened indolence and into an almost Lutheran fervour about becoming what I have always described as a radical undertaker.

My mother was non religious, at least intellectually. She had pretended that she believed in a heaven when my father died as he had been an elder at the Protestant Cramond Kirk throughout his life – the Kirk made famous in both *The Prime of Miss Jean Brodie* and Robert Louis Stevenson's *Kidnapped.*

The minister's well-meaning but clearly nonsensical explanation of where my father had gone was something I tried to desperately believe in but, as an angry and bewildered child, the idea that my father was on a fluffy cloud in the arrivals lounge with Elvis was pretty far out and, while my mother feigned belief to accompany me, she was from the generation that had lived through the Second World War, had read Cyril Connolly's *The Unquiet Grave*, which obliterated any belief in God or an afterlife, and her atheism was part of her political makeup.

But this atheism didn't prevent her from attending the abbey that was the social heart of the village she lived in, and her funeral took place there and was done in the traditional sense. I think the only thing my stepfather had to do was to choose a funeral director and a coffin.

It was a pleasant and sincere enough affair. The beautiful music she had chosen rang around the cloisters, her best friend from childhood wove the complicated and fascinating threads of her life together, grandchildren read poems. This was the first time I had seen the mechanics of a funeral close up – incredible, seeing as my mother was my sixth family member to die.

I was numb. Unreachable really. And this numbness, so common among the newly bereaved, was to envelop me for months to come. Shock is not your best friend, a long, comforting hug of nothing, so don't knock it if it sweeps you up into its consolatory bosom. But don't let it trick you into thinking you don't care. Shock is not something that just happens after a car crash and can be medicated away with strong sugary tea, it is an existential state, a place almost, and it can become comfortingly warm in its coldness.

The short journey from our house to the abbey was in a limousine behind the hearse, a journey of less than two hundred yards, which showed me and my sisters that no shock is deep enough to prevent a bad outbreak of the giggles.

The mock solemnity of the whole affair, walking behind the badly suited, dandruffy old men as they carried my mother was jarring. The faux Victorian pomp out of place and faintly ludicrous.

Who were these strangers looking more upset than me? Did she have a secret life in which these men featured?

When we finally arrived at the village graveyard, I found myself having to jostle to the front edge of the main event, to crane my neck to see them lower my mother into her grave.

As far as the funeral director was concerned, me and my family were spared the heft of the coffin, the awkward physicality of getting my mother from one place to another. Their duty was to deliver her safely to the bottom of her chalky grave; we were free to grieve while others did the work.

I felt excluded and a bit grubby, a feeling which would congeal into guilt.

I hadn't read anything or delivered a eulogy. The grounding physicality of carrying my mother's coffin would have gone a great way to be involved, given me a muscle memory of the day, which would have taken me out of my head and into the moment.

We don't employ professional bearers because of this moment in my life. They are almost always retired old men of the same height, often lugubrious ex-policemen whose job is to shoulder the coffin to and fro. We don't shoulder coffins. It hurts. The reason traditional coffins are shouldered is if you try to lift them by their plastic, mock handles, they would just pull out of the fake hardwood veneer that is stuck on the outside, collapsing scenery, revealing the grim workings backstage, the insincerity of the mock opulence starkly exposed.

For every funeral we have done that has involved any mourners or family at all, we have enlisted their help to do this. It is the last thing that you can do for the person you are burying. Why would you allow this to be done by someone else? It is all part of the emotional infantilising encouraged by the funeral industry, all part of being turned into an audience at one of the most significant moments in your family history, instead of being empowered as a family and a community.

The philosophy that we use as a tagline is simple: honesty, appropriateness and participation. Nearly all of these are absent from the conveyor-belt funeral that had become the default setting for society, and they were all absent from my mother's slick but sterile funeral.

And then it was over, and I was back home in Cornwall, in a fug of dope smoke and numbness.

CHAPTER FIVE

Slowly turning in golden circles

Of course the dope wasn't helping. I can see that now and I would encourage anyone going through grief to only dip into those things that numb you further than you already are and maybe stick with box sets of Scandi noir rather than drink and drugs, but I was in a mess and Netflix was a long way off.

My mother's early death had robbed me of the chance to raise difficult questions with her, such as what had she been thinking in sending me off to boarding school at such a vulnerable young age. But the truth is that had she lived to be a hundred, I probably wouldn't have had the courage to bring this stuff up.

These grand reckonings we like to think we will have with our parents are usually imaginary – they never play out in the real world as we think they will. But even so, I was young and selfish enough to mistake my deep, long-lasting shock, both at her death and from an underlying hidden resentment for my banishment from the safety of my diminished family, for a lack of love for her, a horrible guilty trick to play on myself.

I remained dry eyed for a long time. I cried that night I left her in the hospice, but shock shut me down and there were no real tears at her funeral and no tears for many months, until my grief ambushed me as I danced by myself in my home to some loud music. It broke over me like a wave, frightening my dog who awkwardly left the room as I wailed (always get a female dog, so much better at the big emotional stuff), and I wept for about half an hour. That is a long, long time to really cry.

Grief can be postponed, compartmentalised, shoved in a box at the back of the dusty attic of your heart, but it will always out eventually, when the next death comes along.

My mental shakiness after leaving my boarding school was partly a reaction to its brutality, but I could also see it was my long put-off grief for my father. It took my mother's death to allow me to properly begin grieving for him and, like so many of us, I started the sometimes futile race of catch up, mourning the death behind the death that had just happened.

This is such a common way for us to process our losses. Recognising this is a huge step forward into resynchronising our pain or at least acknowledging that each death we experience contains every death we have ever lived through, Russian dolls of bereavement waiting to be unpacked.

You may never unpack them all perfectly, but understanding that this new pain encloses deeper pain is so much better than being constantly surprised at the vehemence of your grief, the fresh violence of your sadness.

And so I carried on with my strange life, a sort of Great Gatsby in reverse: numbly bereaved and borne forward ceaselessly into the future, throwing bundles of cash into the current to lighten the load.

My mother died in the early part of 1996, not long before big social events like the death of Diana, Princess of Wales, and too late to see the domineering Conservative government fall to Tony Blair and New Labour. It was a time of naive optimism, reflected in the wild hedonic freedom of acid house and in the intersecting world of New Age ideas, which often was woven into the cultural fabric of raving.

Going to raves genuinely helped me so much in these early years of orphanhood. I was flailing around, emotionally and spiritually, and they allowed me to gradually feel into my grief and be safely held by the experience at the same time. I don't think it is too much of an exaggeration to say that raves opened my heart, and perhaps even allowed me to properly love for the first time.

You can call it a chemical delusion or you can call it a social miracle, but I am not alone in being powerfully reshaped for the better by what looks like from the outside a bacchanalian riot, but from the inside feels like an enormous understanding embrace.

My experiences at raves were deeply healing, and the loose, anarchic and spontaneous community that emerged to put them on was showing me both my tribe and what a genuine, shared spiritual experience really felt like. I had been thirsting after these sort of experiences for all of my life, looking to religion to provide them. I could see that what Christ stood for and was saying was a case for radical social reform, and one which I wholeheartedly endorsed, but it seemed to me much more straightforwardly political rather than spiritual. The mystic in me was looking for something more transcendent, a religious ledge to cling on to the mountainside of loss, something that made more sense than the outdated versions of heaven that were still being pushed.

It still baffles me why the big, ruling structures of Christianity, like the Vatican, haven't got together to redefine heaven in modern terms. It feels like an ancient, first-generation website in need of a good designer to rebrand it. But they haven't, and it remains a largely medieval vision.

And so, failing to be comforted by it, the unlikely ledge of belief I found myself clinging to was one of the most popular mysteries of the day. The nocturnal arrival of complex patterns pressed into cereal crops across the sweeping chalk landscape of southern England, particularly around the Neolithic sites around Stonehenge and Avebury – the crop circle phenomenon.

By the time they seized my imagination, the great ontological game was well underway with two sides clearly defined in opposition to each other.

On one side was a group of artists, media graduates and mischief makers who were following the lead of the world's most underappreciated and innovative artist, Doug Bower of Doug and Dave fame, who were claiming, or rather not claiming, but hinting at being the creators of these incredibly beautiful and evolvingly complex patterns in the wheat.

On the other side was a melange of self-proclaimed experts from a wild, rangy field of strangeness, from meteorology to dowsing to mediums channelling alien deities, each with their own pet theory as to what was making them but all united in one basic belief: that no human was making them, they were too precise, too exquisite, too laden with esoteric meaning to come from anything as base as people.

An entire baroque pseudoscience had sprung up around these patterns with machines that owed a debt to the imagination of L. Ron Hubbard – all flickering needles and beeping flashing lights, finding changes in the cell structure of the flattened plants, taking soil samples to send off to labs. They would pompously set up barriers, keep people out with tape while they concluded their measuring and sampling. In retrospect, it was a predictably pigheaded male response to what should have been a simple and obvious answer: it was people at night, quickly mastering an art form that had not existed before.

The patterns were, it had to be said, ever evolving in complexity and beauty, echoing the belief systems of the croppies, anticipating and sculpting the wild theories that grew out of this simple act. The nocturnal flattening of wheat into symbols and the people that were attracted to it were an incredibly English blend of naive eccentrics and thoughtful tricksters, the credulous mixing with the cunning, and, between the wide-eyed believers and their agendas (a lot of whom became extremely wealthy on the backs of the circles) and the people making the circles, something extraordinary grew.

This was the mystery play I fled into, in that first summer of frozen grief. It had a whiff of redemption about it, the feeling that New Jerusalem lay just behind the next hedge or at the end of a flattened corridor of wheat. That someone or something was communicating with us, talking to us in simple symbols that were powerful, activating something dormant in us.

The beauty of them, and the game of chasing them around the Wiltshire Downs, was captivating and very soon I started to have all of the strange experiences that people reported having in them: failing camera batteries that would shut the camera down when in a circle; odd synchronicities; a feeling of familiarity when wandering around them – the stunning beauty and complexity of the formations on the ground was as breathtaking as their image from the air.

Rob Irving, one of the main covert circle makers who dew-soaked and wide-eyed would run out of these fields just before the dawn that could expose him to view and shortly before I entered them, explains in his book, *The Field Guide: the art, history and philosophy of crop circle making*, that people were having an emotional response to a piece of art but, because they didn't realise it was art, they attributed the feelings to another agency, and so it became a paranormal, even metaphysical experience.

It was a completely unique psychological experiment, and unparalleled. The creation of an event, an event that allowed people to layer their own belief system over the top of the flattened wheat, all begun by one imaginative artist trying to mimic a UFO encounter in Australia to fool the public into thinking aliens had landed.

I, luckily, was gently disabused of my ideas that it was anything unexplained to science over the years through a slow and gradual dawning of the truth of the matter. People had put men on the moon. People had created an enormous underground doughnut twenty-seven kilometres long and emptied it of everything in order to fire particles of energy at each other, trying to recreate the first moments of existence.

In light of achievements like this, it didn't seem beyond the realms of possibility that a team of people could flatten a crop into an intricate symbol under the cover of darkness without getting caught.

My gradual realisation of this cut out a lot of fluffy wishful thinking about the world that was to serve me well in the long term. Part of this dawning was as a result of weighing up the two opposing sides and feeling which tribe I felt attracted to. It wasn't that hard really.

The people who believed they were otherworldly, or perhaps worldly but part of some dark military project, became increasingly entrenched and dogmatic as the evidence for human activity overwhelmingly piled up. What had started off appearing as brave intellectual speculation became a defensive orthodoxy, shored up by wilful confirmation bias. Nowadays, this has solidified into something very sinister when it comes to alternative belief systems and conspiracies.

And the people who appeared to be involved in making them were savvy and open minded in a way that the believers weren't. They acknowledged the weirdness that these symbols seemed to attract, the unexplained lights in the sky, the feeling of a playful consciousness interacting, the abyss that came to peer back at them in these dark summery nights.

Stepping over to their side, realising it was people, actually deepened the mystery for me, instead of disabusing me of the realness of magic. It seemed to explain much about things like homeopathy, the placebo effect and the importance of set and setting, for people genuinely were experiencing strange physical and psychological effects, odd synchronicities, spontaneous healing. I understood for the first time how led we are by narrative. I realised that we are really the aliens, that we are the echo of our own curiosity after all.

Many lives were changed irrevocably by crop circles, and not always for the best. People left their families to follow what they thought was the opening up of a portal to some other dimension. Some made a lot of money, guiding New Age tourists around the symbols and interpreting them, and a whole cottage industry sprang up around them: helicopter rides, t-shirts, calendars, glossy coffee table books, posters, conferences. International reputations were created, paranormal celebrities toured the world. Hysterical really.

For me, though, that first summer after my mother's death, they provided a perfect distraction, the 'what if?' factor – a chink of mystery to ameliorate the stark blackness of loss. An interest that consisted of exploring one of the most beautiful and ancient parts of the British landscape during short summer nights and experiencing the astonishing daily rebirth of our world through the routine of dawn.

In one of the glossy hardback books documenting the circles, I saw an aerial photograph of a simple circle that was clearly an ancient symbol of some kind and I decided to have a tattoo done of it. My mother would have had a fit at me having a tattoo, so there was an element of marking my independence from parental authority with it, a scarification of grief, but also the symbol really fascinated me.

It was of two circles linked by a connecting line, and one of the circles had around it a corona, an outside ring, with lines like rays of the sun coming out of it. The book rather pompously called it The Sun Logos, which I suppose was not an unfair description.

I was by this stage largely over any wild ideas I had about their origin, but still was enjoying the metaphysical circus that was played out among these chalk downs. The tattoo marked out the orphan me. It is on my shoulder blade, and gave me huge satisfaction. It still does.

Ten years after I had it done, and long after I had realised the entire thing was a form of underground art, I met and formed a friendship with a writer called Mike Jay. That I should meet him at a funeral and become good friends is not unusual – a good deal of my closest friends have been passed to me by the bony hand of death.

A few months into our relationship, the topic of crop circles came up. Mike said he had been an early experimenter in the field. It was the cleverest way to approach the phenomenon – to see if it was possible to create a crop circle covertly, then see how it was interpreted by the self-declared experts. Mike's had passed with flying colours and formed part of the canon of classic circles. But the weirdness of the phenomenon wasn't done with him yet.

Mike went travelling to Australia and, when he was out there, his sister sent him a t-shirt with a crop circle on it, a random one she had found. She didn't know he had made one, just that he had an interest. Of course, the t-shirt she sent had Mike's very creation on it.

As Mike was telling me this and describing his circle, the hairs on my arm started to stand up. I lifted up my t-shirt and asked him by any chance was this the circle he had made.

Mike is a very clever man and I have only once seen him flummoxed – when I showed him the crop circle he had made a decade and a half ago inked into my shoulder blade.

'You've even got the mistake we made in it, the bit where we went too far!'

Finally I could ask the person who had made it what the symbol stood for.

It was a symbol found carved into rock at an ancient ceremonial site at Chavín in Peru. It depicted a shaman, the emanating lines representing his head ablaze with the mescaline found in the San Pedro cactus that grew on the mountains.

I owe a huge debt to the crop circle game. Doug Bower is one of my ancestors.

Crop circles taught me that it was entirely possible to have a transcendent experience arise from nothing; that a spiritual, semi-religious feeling could be created out of nothing more than awe. At the heart of the crop circle phenomenon is a surprisingly pure centre that isn't about deception or solving a riddle, but instead is about clearing the space to step outside of our daily lives for a moment, the creation of a sacred space from nothing.

One of the photographers who made a fortune photographing them from the air called them 'temporary temples', a brilliant term to describe them.

The circle makers were creating the space for people to have their own religious experience, a simple act of creation that allowed people to superimpose their own belief system on top. They are a spiritual Rorschach test, reflecting back what we want them to.

Hopefully, there is nothing deceptive about the way we create our funeral ceremonies; in fact, we pride ourselves on creating entirely transparent rituals that rely upon nothing more than honesty and connection. Nonetheless, we try to create an atmosphere in which people feel unexpectedly moved by the feeling of the ritual, a sense of profound connection to each other and to the reality of the truth that comes through standing together in a temporary temple, held upright by nothing more than love and each other.

Humanity makes circles; of stone or wheat or flesh, and in the middle of these circles something wonderful can happen, even if it's just our fellow human beings finally coming into focus.

This was who I was as I neared the end of my twenties. A stew of ambiguities and utopian mystical principles hiding a series of deep wounds, class damaged with privileged neglect, stuttering mentally with undiagnosed attention deficit and bleeding internally from unintegrated grief, partying wildly, keeping unfettered panic just under control, flinging my money at a series of unsuitable people and stupid business ideas in an effort to rid myself of the inertia that inherited wealth brings. I was so ready for my life to begin.

CHAPTER SIX

The initiation just waiting around the corner

How do you become an undertaker in the UK?

You just do it.

That might all be about to change as the lumbering corporate beasts of the funeral industry near the end of their 130-year attempt to 'regulate' the profession for their own hidden reasons, but in 1998, if you had a particular mix of fervour, pure naivety and guts, and no clue that what you were about to try and pull off was almost impossible (and had done nothing much but rave and run around wheat fields), then you just did it.

The man I saw on the television for those stoned five minutes, who changed my life so completely, was Nicholas Albery, a remarkably similar public-school-system escapee as me, but older. I've never actually met him in the flesh, though we have talked on the phone, but he is one of the most important people in my life. He is one of my ancestors.

Nicholas was a fully fledged part of the hippie underground, a practical theorist, a dreamer who could turn those dreams into reality. He had been one of the main architects of a remarkable social experiment when he and others, including the radical poet Heathcote Williams, squatted a block of flats in Notting Hill and turned it at first into a self-regulating commune then, influenced by the ideas of R.D. Laing, the maverick anti-psychiatrist, took it a little further, and created a refuge for the emotionally vulnerable – the drug refugees from the 60s that were starting to grow in number. They called this place Frestonia, and it became famous when they tried to secede from the UK and declare themselves a nation state. A lot of this was situationist theatre, but the actual experiment was a beacon in compassionate and tolerant community and existed for many years, providing a safe place for many vulnerable and not so vulnerable people.

Nicholas was a utopian dreamer with the energy and drive of a pamphleteer, a form of disseminating underground ideas that had been popular since the sixteenth century. He produced ideas, all of which were based around empowering and helping ordinary people to jump the train tracks of destiny and live lives filled with meaning, and he largely distributed these ideas via self-published books, densely packed with information, echoing the hippy tomes of the time such as the *Whole Earth Catalog* (an American catalogue and counterculture magazine). Nicholas turned his attention towards the closed-off world of funerals after a dissonant experience between the natural birth of his son and the awful, medicalised death of his father.

Other people had been down this path before. In the US, Jessica Mitford had written a coruscating attack on the funeral world called *The American Way of Death*, later the basis for Evelyn Waugh's comic novel *The Loved One*. Jessica exposed much about the predictably fake nature of death in America, the ludicrous upselling of funeral bling to extremely vulnerable people, the hollow platitudes of the preachers, the straightforward emotionally dishonest and unnecessary process of embalming – a post-mortem continuation of the idea of American exceptionalism that begun in the Civil War as a way of returning bodies to families from across the country and grew into a bizarre art form that could leave a person looking better dead than they were alive, the ultimate cosmetic triumph over the messy truth of death and decay.

And with her disgust at the corporate nature of death, the slick unctuous production line of products and pomp, came a rejection of ceremony and mourning. Jessica can probably be said to be person zero of the 'just bung me in a black bag and put me out with the rubbish' brigade.

Nicholas was coming at it from a different angle.

He saw the consumer excesses, the unnecessary violence and psychological hypocrisy of embalming, the ridiculousness of the aesthetics of the British funeral, still in thrall to the class system and deferring endlessly towards the church. But his experiences in the counterculture were very much of the do-it-yourself mode so, instead of merely criticising the industry, which he certainly did, he uncovered ways for a bereaved family to reclaim the experience, to bypass the so-called professionals and deal with the practicalities themselves, all of which he laid out in clear detail in a series of volumes of a book called *The Natural Death Handbook*.

Within ten years, I would be a trustee of the charity and in charge of editing and rewriting the fifth volume of the handbook.

He was not alone in researching ways to reclaim the experience of death. John Bradfield, of *Green Burial* fame, had researched whether it was necessary to be buried in a churchyard or cemetery, and discovered it wasn't. This ripped open the world of funerals, and particularly burials. As long as a few common-sense laws around water contamination were adhered to, anybody could be buried on private land.

Nicholas also unpicked the legalities around using a funeral director, with the same countercultural zeal that the hippies had dismantled so many previously seemingly intractable social constructs, arriving at the conclusion that the family were, in fact, the funeral directors, and that given enough information, they could legally and practically do it all themselves.

In the UK, you are still, just, not required to use a funeral director by law. It still is entirely possible to do the whole thing yourself, including making the coffin and looking after the body at home and even burying them on your own land. The industry itself was aware of this on a subconscious level, and so had made a number of moves to prove themselves indispensable, mainly by overstating the complexities of a post-mortem body and by inferring that people were not actually up to doing all of this themselves.

They were largely right. Few people have the guts to do it all themselves, but some do, and the first three editions of *The Natural Death Handbook* provided all of the practical ways to do this, but most still wanted the help of someone who was used to what could happen.

My Damascene moment was quite profound. I saw my future laid out before me in a flash. I would become an undertaker, a new type – one who didn't exclude the family or lead them down predictable paths of tradition that ended up with the dusty vicar of a religion the family didn't really believe in.

I am a social anarchist, I believe as Patti Smith says, that people really do have the power, and anarchy doesn't mean no rules, it means no rulers. Having somebody who has been licensed by the state directly control what happens between you and your dead is a ruler in my book. A low-level one in terms of the might of the state, but possibly more meaningfully impactful than nearly any other form of authority you might encounter.

So, it was clear that there was a niche for someone to set up as an antiundertaker, or perhaps more accurately, an old-style undertaker, the name they called themselves before they morphed into the more paternalist capital F funeral capital D director.

I would be the gatekeeper who opened the gates, a Wizard of Oz stepping out proudly from behind the curtain; I would accompany, not steer them, and together we would do the practicalities of what needs to happen, the ritual and practical transfer of a body from the world of the living to a place of transformation, the grave or the fire and, in doing so, I would slowly mourn for and rebury my own dead – all of my family's funerals that I had been excluded from, that had turned me and not my dead into a ghost, long lingering at these unattended events.

I rang Nicholas the next day to order a copy of the latest volume of *The Natural Death Handbook* and began telling everyone of my grand plans.

The news was treated with an amused dismissal by nearly everyone. It seemed so unlikely that I, who had done so little in the way of paid work, should make a success of this bold plan, a plan that involved not only gatecrashing a centuries-old industry that went hand in glove with the religious status quo, but meant creating a new niche within it, a niche that would appeal enough to people that they would agree to use my services, despite my lack of experience.

This amused dismissal was well deserved. I didn't fully understand then that the funeral world was such a bastion of conservatism, complete with dominating multinationals who called the shots and beset with hundreds of small competing independent funeral directors, all of whom were scrabbling to survive under the belly of these industry beasts.

If I had, I don't think I would have had the courage to just go for it. I didn't realise it was an almost impossible business to set up in, that it took years to earn a reputation and that reputation could be lost in a second. I didn't fully realise what a working-class family-inherited trade it was or how bitchy and competitive it could be.

I knew none of this. I just knew that the current model had let me down time and time again and that the funerals I had attended and the funerals I had missed were stuck in a post-war framework that was failing a lot of people.

I babbled about this to anyone who would listen, much as I had babbled about crop circles a few years earlier. I read every book that came my way about grief and funerals, rituals of letting go, about death, death, death.

Everything I read was pushing me forward, making me more certain that this was indeed my vocation. That I could be an agent of change because I was the result of what happened when funerals were done badly.

Being an undertaker at its most basic means looking after the body. I realised my next step was to arrange to actually see a dead body, just to make sure I didn't faint. Our culture and our news feed are pornographically saturated with images of death and the dead, both real and invented, but so few of us ever have the chance to actually see a real dead body, until we are faced with our own dead.

There was a woman in Minehead, a Quaker in her seventies called Barbara Butler, one of the original industry upsetters who ran a business called Green Undertakings. She is another ancestor of mine, and someone I owe a huge debt of thanks to. She led me into a light and airy room in her premises and there in his coffin was my first corpse.

Twenty-one years later, I have seen countless dead bodies, numbering in the thousands, but I can still see in sharp detail this old man, dressed in his tweed jacket with his cap in his hands.

He had a moustache and the unruly tendrils of an old man's eyebrows, and he wore the peaceful face that is often death's gift – all the tension and animation gone from the skin, a slackness that clearly shows not just the absence of life, but also tells of an absence of pain and worry.

Here, for the first time, I balanced between the contradictions. I wasn't sure whether there was a presence of an absence or an absence of a presence, but I could feel the tip of the fulcrum of existence and the implications as they hung in the air.

St Paul, that most problematic of converts to Christianity, once said, 'Behold, I show you a mystery. We shall not all sleep, but we shall all be changed.' And in this cryptic phrase lies a truth about the dead.

We are so alike, yet so different. The dead show us a future self that is unimaginable, yet there is in front of us an incontrovertible fact. One day, we too will be changed into this unmoving weight of flesh, the spark that animated us darkened, the biology of life freed from its humanness, matter once more. My first encounters with the dead made my ears ring with loud silence, held my gaze.

The good news for me was that I didn't faint. I felt a mixture of fascination and compassion and awe. After a while, this fascination with the dead fades, they become logistical things to be lifted, washed, dressed, placed in coffins, lowered into graves. The living becomes the thing you keep the eyes of the heart on; they are the ones who can be hurt and healed by this experience, they are the priority, the focus of the work.

Yet when the living are brought into the presence of their dead, a transformation occurs. The dead indeed do not sleep, and are changed, and change again, as the soft wave of sadness and love breaks over the people who loved them. Love returns their personalities, the story of their lives hangs in the air like the faint scent of flowers and time seems to stand still, outplayed by the enormity of the moment.

But all of these experiences lay in front of me.

At the age of twenty-nine, I was certain of what I needed to do, but I was also flat broke, my trust fund successfully liberated and dispersed to the wind, the last of it going to the most predictably crooked business partner I could find among my acquaintances. He had skipped the country leaving me owing the bank sixty thousand pounds and six months in arrears on my mortgage. I wasn't just starting from zero, I was starting from considerably less than zero.

My brief visit to see the body of the old man was literally all I did in terms of practical training. The next body I would see, and indeed the first body I would actually touch, would be the body of the first person I buried.

All my information came from books and my gut instinct. *The Natural Death Handbook* gave me a list of things that I needed to start: somewhere to use as a mortuary, something to carry a body from wherever they were to that mortuary and a vehicle to do it in. That was pretty much the funeral director 'start from scratch' kit.

I had the space at the mill to do this and I converted a tiny one-room barn into a makeshift chapel of rest and bought a refrigerated unit, around which I built an insulated space to safely contain a body.

Logic told me I needed to buy a stretcher, but they are remarkably expensive bits of kit and my lack of money and fervour to take things back to basics and make it as natural as possible meant instead I used a thin oak board with some handles carved into it.

This was to prove ludicrously impractical and, as soon as my partner, Claire, joined with her keen critical eye for the clownish, we bought a real stretcher. But for the first few funerals I did, I lifted the bodies of my clients onto this Flintstones' version of a stretcher and secured them with some straps that were originally seatbelts.

Everything was dictated by my dire lack of funds, so the car I bought was a tatty old Volvo estate, the car of choice for broke funeral directors and antique dealers due to its capacious boot. It was dark blue, slightly scratched with what looked suspiciously like a bullet hole in the windscreen. The hydraulics on the boot had gone, which meant that in order to stop it slamming down as I was loading a body in, it had to be propped open with a piece of wood. The car remained untaxed and without an MOT for most of the time I used it and I never got the windscreen or the hydraulics fixed.

This type of car, tipped slightly towards outside the law, was fairly common in Cornwall at that time, but not as a hearse. It is a testament to the power of my earnest sincerity that the families who used me in those early days chose to overlook this battered vehicle.

I managed to make the propping up of the boot with a piece of four-by-two into some kind of solemn ritual, trying to give it some gravitas, as if undertakers had been symbolically jamming open the gates to the underworld ever thus.

My gauche transparency worked. The families who picked me did so because they did not want the slick, unctuous machine that was the old-school funeral director model, but even so, now I look back two decades, I am filled with gratitude that these families trusted me enough with the bodies of their dead.

Everything Claire and I learned about how to do this work with excellence and attention was through the generosity of the families who invited us to share the intimacy of their grief, and we learned something from each and every funeral, and took it with us on to the next family. Still do.

But I had to start somewhere, I had to make myself known. So I did a press release and had an article about my plans written in the largest regional newspaper, with a photograph of me accompanying it, dressed in a dark suit, leaning against a tree, with *The Oxford Book of Death* tucked under my arm, a strange comic hybrid of Walt Whitman and Gomez Addams.

After this came a slot on the early morning show of BBC Radio Cornwall, a short interview at 6.30 in the morning, which is actually peak listening time for the mainly elderly listeners that make up the demographic of local BBC radio. Ten minutes after it had aired, at 6.50 a.m., my phone rang and I had my first funeral.

I was stunned. This was it. I was an undertaker.

The first person I buried was an ex-postman called Barry. He fitted the profile of what I was expecting; a late middle-aged man who refused to take seriously the idea that white bread, bacon and cigarettes were bad for the heart. A classic death, almost from an earlier age, the way all men including my own father used to die; one unequivocal heart attack.

As it turned out, this funeral was to be one of the most complicated I have ever done, involving as it did a church service, followed by a burial in the garden of a couple who were good friends. It was the friends who contacted me and were doing most of the arrangements.

I immediately felt utterly out of my depth, but was incredibly supported by the staff in the hospital mortuary, who were generous beyond the call of duty, talking me through it and allowing me to turn up on the day of the funeral to dress him and put him in the cardboard coffin I had brought.

I hadn't even managed to buy my bullet-ridden Volvo estate by then, so I had to enlist the help of my local pub landlord who had an estate car big enough. He was, it has to be said, a little freaked out by all of this, but he drove the car like a seasoned hearse driver.

Despite the complications, the three things that had to fit together in sequence – dressing his body with the help of his sobbing family, including me shaving him and putting him in his coffin; getting him to the church for the service; then getting him back to their home and lowering him down into his deep grave in the corner of their rural back garden – these things went okay.

Timing is everything with a funeral and getting stuck in an accident between A and B can cause the whole delicate framework to collapse so, until a coffin is successfully resting at the bottom of a grave or on the catafalque of the crematorium, you just can't relax.

The only thing that went wrong was in the church.

His postman colleagues had turned out mob-handed. The pews were filled with men in red jackets wearing shorts, postbags slung to one side like some peaceful militia of correspondence. Barry's friend was delivering the eulogy and she stood up after the vicar had done his welcoming prayers and we had sung a hymn.

I was hovering at the back, my mind racing with logistics such as how to get the volunteer bearers to turn around as we carried Barry out. A coffin is always carried feetfirst, largely because to carry a coffin headfirst feels like you are carrying them backward or upside down. A coffin always faces the altar feet first because, if you are doing a church funeral, sticking with tradition is the path of least resistance. It is in these practical details that my mind fixates on.

Getting family and friends to carry the coffin is an incredibly important part of the philosophy of practical inclusiveness that is at the heart of what we do, but it means that for each funeral we are having to give instructions to people who are often deep in shock, almost to the point of having an out-of-body experience. Not using the intrusive old men who at least know what to do is both a blessing for the family and an extra worry for us.

But it wasn't the carrying out of Barry that would be the most memorable point of my first funeral, or lowering him into his grave as the heavens opened, it was his eulogy.

His friend opened it with, 'Barry didn't believe in all this crap.'

I was stunned, though not as stunned as the vicar, whose face visibly changed like a cuttlefish. Turned out neither Barry nor any of his family or friends had a religious bone in their bodies.

The eulogy spent a good while picking apart what his friend saw as the delusions of Christianity, causing the vicar to deliver a strong counterattack on ungodliness in general.

I was baffled. Sure, a church was a big space, big enough to accommodate all of his colleagues, but I thought I'd made it clear that we could do it anywhere – that was one of the strong points of my position.

I have done funerals on beaches, cliff tops, in pubs, village halls, private homes, woods at twilight, hilltops at dawn. Churches are fine, but I was aiming for no compromises, no default retrogression to the old power structures unless they were appropriate. And delivering a Richard Dawkins' style anti-religion diatribe from a pulpit was definitely a wild card I hadn't reckoned on being dealt.

Despite this and the logistical stresses of getting six postmen to rotate anticlockwise with Barry's cardboard coffin on the spot like the arms of a clock, Barry's funeral happened. In the end, one way or another, they always do.

His coffin eventually rested in his grave, and I felt like I had run a marathon and invented the lightbulb while doing it. The high lasted for days.

Another funeral followed quite quickly, a little old lady in her late eighties made small and wizened through a brief one-sided fight with pancreatic cancer. And then another old lady, also in her late eighties, who was buried in a new natural burial site down near Land's End.

Her family asked me if I would take the ceremony and, though it hadn't properly occurred to me that this was what I would soon be doing for almost every funeral I did, I quickly accepted. After all, I had something to say about all of this business of life and death.

Her funeral was a small and deeply moving affair. It was June, and a bee swarm briefly invaded the orchard she was being buried in, a buzzing congregation of life, enfolding and protecting the Queen as she decided where to settle. It provided just the right amount of drama and gave us a feeling that even nature itself was participating in and approving of what we were doing.

I talked a little bit about her life with the information I had gleaned from her family, but also about this new way of doing things, this endeavour to do things differently that we were all jointly doing here, the environmental and the social benefits that come with shrugging off outdated traditions.

I talked about how we were sacralising the landscape, blessing it with the bodies of those we love. She was the second person to be buried there, and the first woman, something I felt important to point out. It was a significant moment for both the family and the fledgling burial ground in which she was being laid down in. Her brother was an opera singer and sung a short mournful aria, his old man's voice quivering with emotion and age.

It seems I had quite naturally stepped into the role usually occupied by the priest, and I found myself to be weirdly at home there. I did have something to say, about death and life, ritual and remembrance. A preacher lies hidden just under my surface. It felt a huge responsibility to be entrusted with not just the logistics of someone's death, but also with what would be said over their body as they departed this physical plane but, somehow, I managed to strike the right tone.

I continue to take nearly all of the ceremonies we do, unless a family comes with a minister or a celebrant they have in mind. It makes the process much less cluttered for the family, who have only to deal with Claire and myself from the first phone call to the last shovelful of earth.

It is a weird and unexpected talent I have developed, part ghost writing, part sermonising, part channelling, if I believed in that. I am a natural mimic, but have stretched this ability to allow me to mimic and inhabit people I have never met, and to know things about them that the family haven't told me.

I don't mean that in a remotely paranormal way, although the people I have only met when dead are strangely alive in my memory. It comes from listening to what the family are saying and, more importantly, not saying – the gaps in between the words. It also means trying to get away from the still-overwhelming social pressure to speak only about the dead person's good points – as if they can hear.

To properly honour someone, they – we – should be seen in our entirety.

If you want the last word, get it in before you die because after that the telling of your story falls from other lips. If I am your undertaker, mine are the lips it falls from.

Only once you are dead can the full arc of your life be clearly seen, and telling that story out loud and truthfully to the people who shared it is a powerful social act that both binds us together and places us within our culture. Even without the moral structures of religion, we have so much to learn about ourselves from the death of others. To not seize these moments and use them to illuminate our own lives is a wasted opportunity.

It is always really obvious what needs to be said at a funeral, just as it is obvious what needs to be done. It is having the courage to say it and do it that elevates a funeral from the humdrum ordinariness of what we have become accustomed to, to the heart-thumping familiarity of an authentic moment, of a shared human experience.

A funeral is an incredible opportunity to say something important. If you can catch and hold people's attention, they are open and receptive to big concepts. Death obliterates the trivial, puts all of the banality of our unthinking daily routine in the shade for a moment. If you can command and hold that space, you can say something enormous yet deeply simple, that nobody can disagree with, about what it means to live our lives.

Being a funeral autodidact means I have a way of working with a ceremony that differs from most celebrants who have been trained by an organisation. If possible, I don't show the family what I am going to say before I say it because I feel that too much back and forth with the script robs it of its ceremonial impact.

My ultimate aim is to show the family that they have shown me an aspect of their relationship with the dead person that they haven't realised they have revealed. That the strength of their connection is so strong that it is visible beyond death to someone who has never met them before – through their grief, their affection and the love that is revealed as they fall silent.

The risks are getting the biographical details wrong, but if you step free from the type of eulogy that is more of a timeline of their life, a CV of their achievements, and into how their life feels in retrospect to a stranger, and how their life meshed with the lives of the mourners, then people listen intently. It is thrilling and liberating to hear the truth about someone's faults and foibles as well as their capacity for love, not just the more attractive aspects of their personality.

But the honing of this priestly part of me was to come slowly and was inspired by witnessing some extraordinary ordinary people do this most skilled of balancing act, and in particular, one person.

My first three funerals were very much as I expected them to be. People dying of what I presumed were the normal things: cancer, heart attack, extreme old age. This is how I thought it was going to continue, a steady unfolding of what I believed to be the 'natural order' of death, a slow procession of the sad but suitable. I thought that generally that was how this life of ours worked. You lived, you grew old, you died. Or the lottery of sickness drew your number a little earlier than was fair and you grappled with it, and lost, and died.

I knew on one level that more than just old people or sick people died, but I didn't know how many young people died – of accidents and bad luck; what Thomas Lynch, the American funeral director, poet and author of the brilliant *The Undertaking*, describes as 'the everyday lapses of caution that do us in'.

I didn't know how many people kill themselves. I didn't realise that the next twenty years of my life would be so taken up with helping their families, their poor maimed husbands and wives, mothers and fathers, who would never again feel the buoyant lightness of life we, the unwounded, take for granted.

Suicide is not just 'one thing'. There are many reasons and circumstances in which people take their own lives. Even though the phrase itself, with its old legal status of a crime being committed, and the religious condemnation that accompanies it has changed, there is still an enormous social stigma that goes with it, a shame that accompanies the horror.

It is not always tragic, sometimes it is a liberation, but it is the loneliest of bereavements. The idea that this person chose to do this, even though that idea of 'choice' is blurred, haunts those who continue to live in its shadow and yet it does not have one unifying factor, other than the fact that it is a death born from self-determination to die.

Some suicides are completely understandable; the last grizzly stages of a cruel disease, the pain that can overwhelm us as a cancer advances, or the refusal to be shut down, muscle by muscle and sense by sense at the remorseless march of something like motor neurone disease or Huntington's disease. In a world where assisted dying was legal, these deaths would be a very different experience for all.

There are some that seem like an entirely logical step. A beloved spouse has died after decades of a shared life. What remains is a flat existence, the trials of old age endured alone. Sometimes these people take a passive approach, suicide by neglect, sometimes they methodically plan what is, in their hearts and heads, a reunion of sorts.

Then there are the people blindsided by fate and circumstance. People who have, either deliberately or through no fault of their own, found themselves at the heart of a terrible thing – a car accident in which someone died or after committing an awful crime that haunts them – multiple lives forever destroyed by a terrible event. And bad things happen randomly to good people for no reason, as well as the bad things we do ourselves, and the consequences of either can be impossible to live with.

Then there are the young people, the teenagers, overcome by a moment of shame or exposure that to an adult would be excruciating but not unbearable. The children who do this do so in a storm of pain that is not fully thought through, who don't realise the finality of it all. The twenty-somethings wrestling with themselves and finding they are pinned to the floor by their own perceived character flaws, suffocated by their own chokehold.

And then there are those for whom life has been drained of its colour, who fight a darkness with their hands tied behind their back – those who find the world to be a vistaless grey soup or, at least, their vision of the world to be blinded by ocular floaters of horror. The unreachables, who gradually slide down a slippery slope of sadness, deaf to the help and the pleadings of those who love them, who turn away from life with a terrible slow-motion inevitability.

They are mostly men, though not always, men my age and younger. The rate of suicide in the UK is climbing steadily, and it remains the most common cause of death in men under 50, but there is a worrying upsurge in the number of young women taking their lives. This world is increasingly hard to live in.

But I had no idea of this, three funerals in to my unexpected vocation, no idea of how death really was. I had no idea of the magnitude of emotional suffering that I would be exposed to or that the idea of immersive undertaking that I was trying to pioneer would result in more and more of these funerals coming my way as we were handed on from wounded family to wounded family. I was protected by my encasing bubble of naivety, my meniscus of belief, which was just as well because I was plunged into the boiling oil of grief.

And so my fourth funeral was a suicide, a violent, inexplicable and devastating one, and I was as far out of my depth as it is possible to be in this life, with my battered old car and my head full of idealistic notions of participation and transparency, my lack of previous experience in anything but escapism and survival and postponed grief. It was the last funeral I would do on my own.

Nobody, including myself, would have blamed me if I had turned away from the business of undertaking at this point, but this job has a way of very quickly and strongly calling your bluff and this funeral turned out to be my initiation. The lessons I learned, about how to be in the face of such horror, about the dignity and power of those who are engulfed in it and, most importantly, about how to structure and hold a ceremony for such a funeral, are among the most significant things I have ever been taught in my life.

The person who taught me, the ordinary person who found themselves at the epicentre of this maelstrom of grief, is also a living ancestor of mine and I am indebted beyond words to them and their generosity in allowing me to accompany them for the two weeks that it took to organise and direct the funeral.

The phone call came like the three calls before. I had started to recognise the controlled flatness in the voices of the freshly bereaved, the steeling of courage that is needed to ring the number of an undertaker.

It is a hugely significant moment in their timeline of loss, something that is done in the ear-popping high altitude of deep shock. People often audibly choke when I answer. Those first moments of connection are often me patiently and gently waiting for them to speak.

This woman spoke with that flatness of speech, but was in control of herself. She asked if I did the funerals with the cardboard coffins, if I was the man she had heard about, who had just started up. We talked for a bit before she mentioned her husband was in the care of the coroner.

I had no experience so far of a coroner. I knew they were involved when the death was far from straightforward, unresolved of cause, suspicious. She also mentioned the police.

Her husband had killed himself. He was not, apparently, in any of the categories I have listed above. This death had come sliding out of the blackness, like a spinning car, completely unexpected and unequivocally violent. No cry for help, no mistake, no warning, no answers.

We met and talked. My inexperience was obvious. I didn't hide it, and I couldn't keep the shock from my face. She was deeper in shock, but completely free from any hysteria. She had a calmness and control that was incredible to see, but is more familiar to me now. Not disconnected, but with the deep focus that comes from a need to hold it together.

The relationship between an undertaker and a client is like that between a therapist and their client in the sense that that is all there is – the entirety of it hangs or should hang on the personal dynamic. She didn't choose me because of my funeral-directing hardware: the smooth premises, the discrete matching livery of the non-existent employees, the formality of my appearance.

I arrived in the comedy car that was also my hearse, wearing what I always wear, my ordinary clothes. I was thirty, probably looked younger. We talked. She told me what she knew. We looked at each other and drank tea. I tried not to flinch or look as scared and overwhelmed as I felt. She asked me if I was up to helping her, if I would do this for, or rather with her. I said I would.

I stubbornly call myself an undertaker. Twenty years later it has become fashionable again – the stripped-backed honesty of the name gives it a raw authenticity, unlike the slightly pompous term funeral director, with all its implication of authority and control, of etiquette and gatekeeping – but back then there was a radical honesty about calling oneself an undertaker.

People usually assume the origin of the word comes from the act of burial, that one takes the body under the ground, but what it actually means is to make a pledge. You promise to undertake to deal with the dead for the sake of the living. You agree to help them with both the practicalities of fetching and looking after the body, and helping them get that body to a safe place of bodily change, to the fire or the earth. To be with the living until this part of the process is done and the long lonely business of grieving can begin.

And this pledge, this undertaking, involves agreement and trust on both sides. It is not something that we have ever formalised with a contract; it is such a powerful thing to be asked to do, such a huge amount of trust is placed, that the idea of anything making it more binding is ridiculous.

We agreed to do it together.

Everything I experienced during this funeral was wildly out of anything I had ever experienced in my life. Visiting the police station to collect his belongings, the ordinary handheld clutter of a life suddenly transmuted into something different, the dumb witness of everyday matter to those last moments changes these objects into relics of an almost supernatural intensity, into evidence of a tragedy.

I went to the large hospital to collect his body from their mortuary. I am not going to describe him, this, my first body in extremis, though I will describe other bodies. I won't describe him for his privacy and mine. There is something deeply intimate about meeting the body of someone you didn't know in life.

In a strange sense it is the corpse's last relationship, a secret one, and the undertaker hangs in the liminal space created by their death and the pain of those who love them; the last link between what they once were and what they have become; a human bridge for the bereaved, one they eventually have to cross alone, walking away from the dead back into the world of the living.

It is one of the reasons for the working model that Claire and I created, of just two people for it all. No disconnection, no one whose job it is to collect the body and never see them again, to hand the family on to another person who makes the arrangements, and then another who directs on the day, and another who takes the ceremony. An endless stream of strangers you have to retell the story to.

We form a proper relationship, we make a pledge to their families to accompany them through this first wave of grief, a short-term, intense relationship, one in which you can become very intimate very quickly, and it is in this relationship that our work is done.

It is a huge risk to us in doing it, this level of engagement. There is not as much of a theoretical, academic framework to the trade of undertaking as you might think. The history is documented, but there is not a huge amount written about the psychological impact of this work. The orthodox, lived experience of many undertakers, and indeed many people whose job involves interacting with trauma, is that you need to maintain some kind of emotional barrier between yourself and the horror, that to enter too far into their world would be putting yourself and, possibly them, at risk of drowning in despair.

It is why people often say that an undertaker they know is one of the funniest people they have ever met. What they usually mean by that is the undertaker has a gallows humour with which they present themselves to the world, always ready with a quip, often jokingly measuring acquaintances at the bar with a tape measure. It is a protective, forced bonhomie, a way of keeping the sorrow out. That and alcohol to numb the horror.

Right from the start, right from this funeral, my first exposure to the furnace blast of white-hot grief, I knew that this distance was not for me, and not for the people I was helping. The numbness that I experienced through my own bereavement had not served me at all, it had merely postponed the pain until it would not be denied any longer. The only way through grief was to work through it and the only way to properly help these families was to accompany them through as much of the emotional turmoil as possible.

And so I cried as I dressed this stranger, cried for whatever black vision had swept over him causing him to do this to himself. I cried for his family, and I cried for myself, because if I was going to let this stuff in, I would let it out too.

But I never cried with his widow. That would be a presumptive owning of a grief that wasn't mine, a participatory step too far at this point of my career. I would cry with families later but, in this, my first serious funeral, she needed me to lean on and we had promised each other we would do this together.

I took my courage from her steady presence, stayed calm in the face of her ice-cool anger, laughed with her in those pockets of normality that you briefly escape into in the middle of an ongoing trauma.

There were so many levels to my initiation. There was the courage I needed to find to dress this man and place him in his coffin, all the while grappling with the reality of what his death meant to his family. There was the learning to lean into the sadness of it all, to form a relationship with his wife, who was light years away from me in this new world, yet side by side with me in the moment.

And there was how it was when we gathered for his funeral.

His funeral was simple, but incredibly profound. This man was deeply loved, a pillar of his community, and this community turned out in strength to his funeral. It took place in a village hall and I had never before in my life been in such a crowd of people so deeply in shock. It felt like we were in one of those centrifugal spinning fairground rides, in which the floor drops away and you are pinned to the wall above an abyss. Everyone was rooted to the spot with grief.

He was in a simple, cardboard coffin and his wife took the ceremony before we carried him to the nearby churchyard, or rather the congregation walked slowly behind my tattered Volvo.

My mind was partly taken up with the practicalities. I checked the grave endlessly to make sure it was the right size and I worried about who was going to carry the coffin and how I would instruct them in both this and the lowering into the grave, so I was not really prepared for the impact that the ceremony would have on me, and everyone who saw it.

It was not a complicated funeral. The best are stripped right back – no viola-playing grandchildren, as Claire puts it. It was almost entirely his wife doing the talking, though I think his oldest friend and best man at their wedding also spoke.

There was one piece of music, a Pink Floyd track, the one that starts with lots of alarm clocks going off, but really, it was his wife, standing with a quiet dignity, a hand resting at all times on her husband's simple white cardboard coffin that was at the heart of this. The way she was at that funeral, the things she said, changed my life.

She maintained a perfect balance between the sudden awfulness of the manner of his death; the need to look out for each other because despair can grow, hidden and silently, between even the closest of people; how it was to suddenly find yourself alone in the world when you had been part of a loving partnership for so long, and the happiness and achievement of the rest of his life and their relationship – his strong parenting and the simple fulfilment and companionship they had shared together as a family.

It was an incredibly skilled and bold thing to do, to take this opportunity to teach us all a serious lesson about depression and stress and grief, while refusing to allow the manner of his death to completely overshadow his life.

She held these opposite ideas in both hands, his life and his death, the horror and the happiness, and took us all back and forth between them.

It was moving and powerful and, like all good funerals, was as much about all of us. It showed me how to write a eulogy and hold a ceremony. How to address the truth of the matter, of someone's life and true character as well as their death, but not allow either of these things to completely dominate.

She showed me how to grab people's attention, something the church did well in the past, albeit with threats of eternal punishment, and how to hold on to it. What was said over the dead had to have the feel of authenticity around it, but be tempered with compassion and forgiveness of the stress points around the human heart, the fragility of our existence, the ways we can all too easily get lost in the fog of sadness.

His friends carried his coffin. We lowered him down into the soil of the ancient village churchyard and, as his coffin rested on the bottom of his grave, I knew that I was now an undertaker. That I was right to pursue this unlikely idea, and that I had indeed found my vocation.

I had no one then to debrief with, but there was a wild party in a friend's barn and so I went and danced all night in the darkness, and let my tears run down my face, changed forever by the intensity of my initiation.

I could do this.

CHAPTER SEVEN

The wild-eyed riders of the storm

So, much to everyone's astonishment, most of all mine, my unlikely transformation from idle trustafarian to alternative green undertaker had happened in the time it takes to close a coffin lid.

Funerals would at first be few and far between, but the philosophy and approach which had landed in my head and my heart almost immediately remain unchanged to this day.

It all felt very obvious. The funeral industry was beset by poor practice, hampered by venture capitalists on one side and many small family-based undertakers on the other, who were all still shackled to a religious tradition and a faux Victorian style that was increasingly out of step with most people's culture and beliefs.

I would do it as differently as I possibly could, drop the formality, the etiquette and the social control that went with it and try to reshape the experience of how we deal with our dead into something that would be more like how it was a hundred or more years ago, before the corpse was made unwelcome from its own funeral. All of it suffused with the lessons I had learned about connection and authenticity from acid house, about transcendence and emotion from crop circles, and trauma and absence from my early bereavements.

I had the philosophy and the fervour, but I had all the nous of the former boarding-school boy I was. My only experience of handling money was how to shed it. There had to be a serious supportive framework around these radical ideas and that is where Claire came in. Without her involvement, both organisational and creatively, and how she instinctively interacted with families, this fledgling idea would have crashed and burned within a year, ignited by my scatterbrained incompetence.

It is hard to write about Claire at the moment, partly because our partnership of twenty-one years has, at this time of writing, finally finished, and our marriage finished a couple of years before, but also because Claire is someone who fiercely guards her privacy and does not like her story being told.

But I am going to have to tell some of it because, at this point, it is our story.

I met Claire when I was trying to be a boat gypsy trying to be an eel fisherman. She and her then partner had sailed up the estuary I lived on and tied their boat onto the pontoon. Immediately I could see they were not like the conservative types who usually sailed. Claire had a couple of chunky peroxide blonde dreadlocks perched on the top of her head and dressed like the comic book character Tank Girl.

They were a few years older than me and were escaping the music industry in London. Her boyfriend, David, had been a musician in a punk duo famous and notorious throughout Eastern Europe. Claire had been working for Mute Records, a unique label in that it was run on entirely egalitarian lines, where costs and the profits were split between the artist and the label. There were no contracts binding them together, everything hung on a handshake and trust and, once on the label, the artist was entirely free from any commercial pressure on what they recorded. Mute's success was based on this trust and transparency of the artist/label relationship and legendary founder Daniel Miller's eye for talent. The commercial success of such acts as Depeche Mode and Erasure bankrolled some of the more controversial and avant-garde acts like Einstürzende Neubauten and Diamanda Galás, and Nick Cave's The Birthday Party.

Culturally and socially, we were worlds apart. Claire had a cool urban vibe, which made her very conspicuous in the sleepy Cornish boatyard that we had both washed up in. She was seven years older than me, a punk and post-punk by tribe, and we quickly became friends.

In case you hadn't realised yet, being incarcerated in a boarding school from seven to eighteen meant that you had little cultural exposure that wasn't at least a hundred years old. Claire introduced me to books and music that were way beyond my experience at that point, and I am very grateful for this cultural download that led me away from the bland mainstream. I probably would have got there myself, but Claire provided me with an education that ripped open my mind a lot sooner than I expected.

We met and became friends ten years before we started working together. She and her partner sailed off to Spain and missed the bonfire of my finances years and, by the time they returned, Claire had two small children and her boat adventure days were over – as were mine. I was broke, but already babbling about my newly discovered vocation.

Claire watched me do my early funerals and, after my initiatory fourth funeral, she expressed an interest in working with me to build it up. She suggested she joined as a partner, and I accepted, having worked out that you really did need two people to do this job, physically and emotionally, and I couldn't keep calling on random local friends to come and help me lift a dead old lady onto a plank and slide them into my knackered Volvo forever – I needed a partner. Now, at this point, Claire had little or no experience of death and bereavement, but she could see that this was an area of life ripe for a new approach.

Punk had not only swept through music like a furious emetic, it had moved through all areas of society. Its DIY ethos, the famous instructions in the punk fanzine *Sideburns* showing three basic guitar chords and an exhortation to NOW FORM A BAND, regardless of musical background or expectation, was revolutionary, and that attitude had swept through all parts of society and work since punk had flared up and died back.

Claire could immediately see that what I was suggesting was essentially a punk attitude, and she got it. So four funerals in, I had a partner, someone with exactly the same attitude that I had – that we could take these lessons of punk and rave, and bring them to the musty world of funerals.

It's not that we wanted to do funerals for punks and ravers (when we started, they were all very much alive), we just knew that everybody could benefit from the creative freedom that these youth movements brought. If we had produced a fanzine, the front cover would have said, 'Here's a dead body, here's a coffin, now go create a funeral.'

I suppose in those days I felt a lot of anger towards the funeral industry. I still do. Its own identification as an industry for a start. I know it is. I know that the sheer volume of deaths and the need to respond to this has created a system that turns over enough money to accurately describe itself as an industry, but it isn't really, or shouldn't be.

It was a largely male institution, heavily Masonic and was tied into a pattern of behaviour that had evolved out of the way that death had been almost industrialised following the two world wars. It had become a conveyor-belt process in which almost everybody was cremated and almost everybody defaulted to a religious framework. There was very little wiggle room for creativity or involvement by the family. That was until The Natural Death Centre got involved.

Funeral directing is a competitive world, everywhere in the world. Certainly, in the last thirty years, due to life expectancy extending and the population explosion that marked the end of the Second World War and created the swollen baby boomer generation, there have been a similar explosion in the number of funeral directors setting up in order to catch this market.

There is a graph that has been promising an inevitable wave of death when this generation dies, and it is these stock market-like future predictions that has attracted big business in. And how each funeral company gets its custom varies hugely.

The best rely on reputation. They grow slowly, and are passed from family to family over the years as trusted and recommended people who can genuinely help with the tumult of grief. Others, the larger national and even international chains, rely on advertising and the securing of prepaid funeral plans or their old reputation as friends of the working class, organisations like the Co-op, which grew out of a collective socialist culture, a place where food and amenities could be purchased cheaply and with a reliable dignity.

Venture capitalists have not been slow to see the money potential hiding in plain sight in this ageing population eventually going, almost simultaneously. They invest in funeral companies, which have become corporations, which have shareholders, and that is where the balance of power shifts for the worse.

One of the most pernicious things to have grown with such intensity in the past twenty years is the securing of future deaths through the aggressive marketing of prepaid funeral plans. I loathe them. They embody the worst of the industry; they are tacky, misleading, a modern version of the medieval sale of indulgences and, to get to the truth of them, are really just a way of securing a lead over the competition. Advertised on daytime television with a well-known celebrity usually as the face of it, they talk about rising costs, the peace of mind that goes with paying for it all in advance – a peace of mind they imply is really for your children who are freed from the terrible burden of cost, and with it, freedom from grief, or at least freedom from the money worry.

I get it. Funerals are unexpectedly expensive, especially if you blindly buy them off the shelf, as so many of us do. Shopping around takes guts and can be exhausting, but compared to a lot of big purchases, a wedding for instance, whose final destination is far from certain, a funeral can and should be a fully satisfying thing with an assured outcome. It's just that with these funeral plans, so much of the money goes on the wrong thing.

And no amount of financial relief can take away those inevitable feelings of loss. No one reads the small print about the solid, unrelenting patience of grief, the need to go through it, not around it, which no amount of preplanning or prepaying can spare you.

Class is the hidden factor behind the showy pomp of so many of these funerals, the weaponisation of class and guilt to convince ordinary people that they need to put on a big public spectacle to prove their loss. Sixty or more years ago, the only chance that an ordinary person might get to travel in a car of the gentry would be as a corpse in a hearse. How desperately sad, and what an echo of the promises of Christianity, that this bartered some kind of comfort and relief in the next life, as long as you knuckled down to the hardships and privations of this one.

It is such a big mission. What to replace this crumbling edifice of collapsing belief and fossilising tradition with? What to raise up in the dust of these cultural and spiritual ruins? It is such a huge conversation that we need to have, and it is a conversation that can make the armpits prickle with uncomfortableness, because we are talking about death, the finality of it all, and the mind does indeed blank at the glare.

There is also undoubtedly a deep current of cultural disgust that society feels about the job, which I don't want to add to. There definitely are strong atavistic feelings that people have towards those who choose to do this work. We are either viewed with the suspicion that we are ghoulishly attracted towards the dead or, at the very least, are tainted by our physical involvement with them. Or we are lazy conmen preying upon people at their most vulnerable to sell them expensive, shitty coffins. Of course, some of that goes on and the hypercapitalisation of the industry into huge international corporations has not helped, but there really are easier ways to earn money, easier on the head and the heart.

I feel that we should reserve this kind of moral disgust for jobs like futures traders in the stock exchange, work that is genuinely at odds against the greatest benefit for all, but people are more basic and helpless in their visceral response. Undertakers are a persistent reminder that all of us are going to die – we have a whiff of the untouchables about us, a touch of the old role of sin eaters. But this work, even done half-heartedly, makes the ears ring with existential tinnitus. This work makes the heart ache with sadness and foreboding.

Nonetheless, in 1999, the UK funeral industry was its own worst enemy, still stuck in a model that was outdated and patronising, and that was not working for the vast majority of people. It was deeply resistant to change but, like that stupid vent in the Death Star, it had a weak point. It was and remains (if just for a few months more) unregulated as to who can become an undertaker because, unlike in most of the US, you do not need to be a licensed, official funeral director to deal with a body – and rightly so. The stark fact of death marks the limit of our horizon as a species, practically and spiritually. Nobody is an expert, nobody knows for certain what occurs, and the right way of doing this is, like everything, mere fashion.

I can hear the murmur of unease that arises at the thought that someone like me could just have an idea and suddenly declare themselves an undertaker. Where are the safeguards? Surely some kind of medical training is needed, what about the dignity of the body?

My argument has always been that a hundred and fifty years of 'professionalism' is no guarantee of respect. The point where the problem arises is when there is a disconnect between how you say you are going to be with the body and with the bereaved, and how you actually are. Because if you think about it, the dead in this situation are the least vulnerable of all of the players in this drama. They cannot be hurt further – they are literally beyond offence.

Of course, a family is entrusting you with them, the cypher of their love, and that trust is enormous because this once-animated body is all they physically have left of the person they loved. The body needs to be kept in as much of a stable and dignified condition as is possible until they are taken to the lip of the grave or the furnace, but this is not complicated. It involves washing them and dressing and keeping them refrigerated.

The position of *The Natural Death Handbook*, and the position that I adopted, is that an empowered family can step out of this uneven relationship of funeral director and client, can refuse to accept the pressure to give up the body entirely to a professional, can refuse to accept the limited options that are offered to 'personalise' a funeral beyond the cookie-cutter format of a regular funeral that largely suits the funeral director in its predictability. And, all of this can be done in partnership with a good undertaker, alternative or as straight as a die.

Even today, well over twenty years after this quiet revolution in funerals, the largest players in the business in the UK still offer very little in the way of real change. They publish endless meaningless polls in the national press about how funerals are changing to a 'celebration of life', a phrase which makes my blood boil.

They fixate on things like wacky coffins or funeral directors dressing up in fancy dress for young people, all of which is just surface change, cosmetic things that make for a good visual image on the day and a great PR shot for lazy journalists, but do nothing to help shift the glacier of grief, which can slowly grind the spirit of the bereaved down to dust.

They allow people to do things like carry the coffin (as long as it's not one of those crappy chipboard coffins with plastic handles that rip out if you try to lift it by them) and they have introduced a lot more secular celebrants (even if too many of these are well meaning but dull people given to whimsy and bad poetry), but they are still driven by logistics: a fixed timeframe for the funeral that suits them first, the selling of their particular chipboard coffins, the transformation of the dead into these hyperreal embalmed uncanny versions of what we are.

They are often reluctant to allow relatively spontaneous visits to see the dead because, in an urban branch of a big company, the body is often not at the premises the family visit, but held in a vast centralised, Amazon-like warehouse of corpses, all on shelves, in identikit numbered chipboard coffins.

They become the barrier in between the dead and their living, often from the best of intentions but with the worst of results.

And yet there are good people still at work in this world. Not everyone is for sale and this extends to people working within the body of these multinationals, who often leave to set up on their own, doing the exact opposite of the working model they have been shoehorned into. And, of course, there are family firms whose ambition has led them to ape the corporate beasts, who try to follow that model of acquisition of small one-man bands with a good reputation, to ride on this good-will and absorb it into their own ambitious empire.

I tell you, it is like the Wild West out there.

Instead, Claire and I would form a tight, two-person unit that would fulfil all of the roles that a funeral director and a priest would do, but which primarily lay in dropping all of the formality and the bad theatre, and would pay more attention to the living than the dead.

We started by getting rid of the undertaker's uniform, the pinstriped trousers, the suit and tie, and, more importantly, the mock lugubriousness, which has been lampooned since

Charles Dickens, the face that seems to say that this is their death too, that the pain is shared equally.

How we look when we first meet a family is everything. A formal outfit screams of an authority to be deferred to, someone who is going to tell you what to do next, school you in the etiquette of bereavement, which, in the UK, means not making too much of a public display of grief, not scaring others with the rawness of your loss.

There is a shared culpability in this, a false comfort that comes with allowing yourself to be told what to do next. So we dress normally, which in Claire's case is with a great deal of style and flair, jeans and extremely funky trainers, and this makes an immediate impression.

We see people's faces relax a little, realising that we are not some kind of mortal bailiffs, come to demand their tears and their money in exchange for the love they have for their freshly dead. And we don't look like we are more upset than they are. The bereaved don't need this, this guilty feeling that we are going through it too, and that they need to treat us with as much care as we are treating them. They need to feel that this situation is normal. Devastating, disorientating, but not so unusual that it has destabilised even the undertakers.

My experiences in the party world means that I am familiar with what it is like to be around people who are tripping, and that is what early grief is like. It is deeply hallucinatory. It doesn't matter how long the death has been anticipated and expected, nothing can prepare you for the time immediately following the death of someone you love. Everything is tinged with unreality. You feel outraged that the sun rises so thoughtlessly into the sky, that birds continue to sing with joy, strangers laugh with each other, buses, trains, television adverts roll on, schedules uninterrupted, while for you, the world has changed completely.

So we approach a room full of the newly bereaved as if we had walked into a room full of people tripping on acid. They need to be handled gently. Someone will be strong and practical, someone will be shell-shocked, someone might be mildly hysterical with the dark humour of the situation.

They need people to come in slowly and delicately, to assess the situation, to feel who needs the cup of strong tea, who needs to be given a wide berth for the moment because of their seething anger, who needs to be joked to, to feel the relief of a bark of seemingly inappropriate laughter.

That moment, the moment when you say something that is funny, when you invite and allow humour in is an extraordinarily crucial part of starting the relationship. It is not about making light of the situation, it is a way of dropping down to meet the family on their emotional level, which is so much more genuine than by attempting to mirror their misery.

When she started to work with me, unlike myself, who had a Wildean litany of careless family deaths under my belt, Claire had had very little personal experience of bereavement other than a couple of grandparents. Yet straightaway she got it, showing an uncanny ability to know whom to make a joke with, and what that joke should be about.

There is a lot of humour around death and, yes, some of it is dark, but a lot of it is incredulity at the sheer absurdity of it, the throbbing dissonance between what you have been anticipating for so long and the fact that it has happened, that everything has changed – and nothing has changed.

One of the ways that the traditional model does badly is that it leaves no room for this authentic behaviour. When faced with a deeply serious undertaker, a family react as we all do to figures of authority; they play the part that they think is expected of them.

Once you have laughed with a family or showed them that it is okay for them to laugh, you are giving them permission to briefly step out of that numbness, a banishing ritual which relieves the pressure. It shows a family that they can go through this experience as they really are, not who they think they have to pretend to be, with all the entangled limbs of their family dynamic intact, all of their own different responses honoured, all of their different needs met.

None of this is rocket science. And not all of it is the fault of the church or the institutional way that funerals have become entwined with it; it's all of our faults, the way we have allowed ourselves to be led away from the presence of our dead, the way we have allowed our rituals of farewell to become meaningless – an echo of a faded belief system, someone else's gestures and beliefs. It lies in our collusion that things like an expensive coffin, or thousands of pounds worth of flowers, or a line of Mercedes limousines to take us to the doors of the crematorium can cover for feelings of guilt about the way we reacted during their illness, or during their lives in general. It lies in the compromises we make with ourselves to tell little white lies about the way they really were.

None of this honours them, and it doesn't serve us in our grief either.

You get one shot at a funeral, one chance to tell the story of a life in a way that is truthful and honouring at the same time. That puts to rest any lingering ghosts and allows our grief to unfold in a way which is deeply painful, but not crippled and bonsaied by the shape of things unsaid.

All of this ideology was formed almost instantly, the moment my vocation revealed itself to me. It remains pretty much unchanged, although I have softened my view on certain things. I am even friends now with some of the people who run the crematoriums, certainly those good men and women who are at that edge, the chapel attendants upon whom the experience of the family in their grief hangs. This is what elevates a crematorium from a socially mechanical experience filled with a sense of being part of some indifferent machine of disposal to a shared moment of human sympathy: the quality of the person interacting with them at this crucial moment. Like Blanche Dubois, we are all, in a sense, reliant on the kindness of strangers. Good undertaking is done through endless small acts of thoughtfulness, of anticipating how the family is feeling about whatever is happening right then, and acting on it.

It is, or should be, a way of life that takes you every day to the edge of a huge existential cliff, that asks of you again and again huge questions about what is important in your life, where you are going and where you came from.

As an undertaker and a celebrant I have no more idea of the answers to the big questions than a barista or a train driver, but I am privileged to be in a position where these questions come up, where the bullshit and facade of so much of our consumerist, late-capitalist lives falls away for a moment and we can see what really matters.

And, of course, what really matters is nothing to do with an afterlife or lack of one, those meaty existential questions we can't help but grapple with. What matters is love, or the lack of it, in a life. Love, or the lack of it, is what forms the body of a life that sets the trajectory, that allows us to take the opportunities that life gives us or shoves us off down steep-sided chutes of consequence that rob us of any real agency, that slides us down into a world of pain avoidance, regret and patterns of disfunction that can rattle down through generations.

My own noisy entrance into the world of undertaking was brash and opinionated, covered by a lot of press and, if I was a nearby undertaker, I would have reacted exactly as the old lumbering prog rock dinosaurs did to punk, with resentment and hostility, but this was not the case.

One of my nearest 'competitors' was a small independent going by the Hardyesque name of Garfield Gubbin. Garfield operates from a premises adjoining his house, a good sign of someone with integrity, in a part of North Cornwall that is rolling dairy farming country.

We couldn't have been more different in appearance and style. That community is largely Christian, Methodist to be precise – Cornwall is where John Wesley's stripped back, earthy and austere preaching had a huge impact. Most of Garfield's funerals are part of this low-key Christian culture and he was the go-to funeral director for the farming community that lay all around him, so he really had nothing to fear from me, but his warmth and generosity towards my spiky, arrogant arrival was extraordinary. He came by to introduce himself and offer any assistance I needed in a practical way – the hire of a hearse, space to store bodies, anything.

It slightly wrong-footed me as my anger towards the industry had not prepared me for the integrity of many working within it. And it was not just individual funeral directors who were welcoming and patient. There were mortuary technicians working within the large hospitals that I rocked up to, looking like a lost relative, who showed me great patience.

People like Tim, the amateur opera singer and leading light of the Spiritualist Church who, for some reason liked my naive fervour, and did everything to gently initiate me into the strange world of working with the dead.

There were the people who did the administration at the local crematoriums who patiently helped me get the hang of the crucial paperwork, a nightmarish system of checks and double checks and doctor's visits and cross-references, whose accurate completion was quite rightly essential to the irreversible act of cremation.

These people, though few and far between admittedly, professionals with decades of experience, showed me a warmth and an encouragement that confirmed to me I was into something important. That this shabby, earnest and emotionally involved way with its spaces for things to go slightly wrong had an authentic power that held its own against the more formulaic, slick and predictable funerals that the mainstream churned out. When these people started to say that they would want me to do their funerals, I felt an emotion that was beyond words. It seemed I had a future as an undertaker. At last someone else could mind the eels.

So, with the thanks out of the way, not that this will be the last of them, it feels right to spell out in detail my objections to the mainstream funeral world, and that can be summed up in one word: patriarchy.

There is a particularly male energy that has formed the modern traditional funeral, which is consolidated in the relationship between the funeral director and the clergy (and, if I was straying into the Eisenhower military-industrial complex area of speechifying, I would say the financial sector too) and it relies upon the mistaken belief that a family needs protecting from much of the process. That they are unable to cope with the realities of what has happened and need steering down particular avenues.

If each death is approached with a fresh and open mind, then sometimes, yes this might be true. But too often this steering is done for the convenience of the funeral director, who has fallen into the lazy pattern of pushing a cremation, with a retired minister to take the service, known to all in the business as Crem Cowboys, part of the old-school 'insert name here' and waffle on for a bit. Three bits of music, one for carrying in, one during the service, and one at the end, the Lord's Prayer and wham bang thank you ma'am, out in twenty minutes.

These funerals are incredibly easy to organise. They need little deep involvement from the funeral director who might, in the larger organisations, not even meet the family until the day or have any real idea of who they are cremating until they see the list of names for the day. The minister too needs little deep contact with the family. A few badly told anecdotes at best, mixed with a little guff about their place in heaven and how much happier they are now.

The family just jumped through a series of preordained hoops, a shiny but badly made coffin, an order of service with a cross on the front or images of a dove ascending, a floral display to mask the unpleasantness of the coffin and the obligatory four retired blokes to carry the coffin to the catafalque, who, job done, left the chapel to smoke fags around the back.

Most families who go through these funerals are just grateful if the vicar gets the name of the dead person right or they don't get the giggles. These default funerals were depressingly common when I started, far from finished now, and people accepted them with a grim stoicism. I suppose the reasoning was that nobody actually likes a funeral – it is the physical disposal of someone they generally like, so the awfulness of the actual event was just part of it.

Of course not all of them were like this, but a shocking number were. The pompous self-assurance of the often middle- to upper-class minister, whose relationship with the largely working-class undertaker was shot through with the class deference that mirrors the relationship between an officer and the ordinary enlisted soldier in the army (and, sadly, so much of our interactions as professional men) seemed to be more about them and their place in this world rather than the family. At best all the family could hope for was some basic kindness towards them, something they would be pathetically grateful for.

If a funeral didn't go disastrously wrong, then a family would use the same funeral director for the next family death, and the same formula, regardless of their actual beliefs. People just accepted this whole shit show, their expectations around funerals were, and remain, pathetically low.

Their dead were spirited away to be dressed in strange pink paper gowns with frilly necks, making them look like very camp choirboys. I have no idea where these bizarre disposable gowns came from, or who thought it would be appropriate to dress an elderly heterosexual man who had fought in the war as if they were a baby. They look no more appropriate on women. They are literally things you wouldn't want to be seen dead in, yet when you went in to see your dead, there they were, dressed as if Liberace were being played by Charlie Chaplin, covered in strange rouge makeup. Talk about walking into the uncanny valley.

That is, only if the funeral director felt that the body was viewable, and that almost always meant embalmed.

CHAPTER EIGHT

The unthinkable

Embalming was, and remains, a red line for us. It was the first thing that outraged me on an environmental, social and psychological level.

It was done as a matter of course when I started, often without seeking permission, and certainly only with some very vague description of what it actually entailed. It is euphemistically called Hygienic Treatment in the trade and is what the funeral industry uses to describes the ultra-violent and completely unnecessary art of embalming.

Hygienic Treatment.

Hygiene. Like somebody has made sure you have a clean bum instead of draining your blood, puncturing your organs with an enormous, syringed vacuum cleaner and replacing that blood with a pink-dyed carcinogenic chemical that if done well makes you look like you have just had the best holiday of your life.

Hyperreal. High definition. High weirdness.

No wonder so many people's experience with the bodies of the people they love is such a cognitively jarring experience. They look alive.

Well, not on my watch.

If you have had someone you loved go through this and hadn't fully grasped it: I'm sorry. Me too. Don't blame me, blame a culture that thinks that we cannot handle the truth of who we were and who we are right now.

For smaller undertakers, it negated the need for a refrigeration unit and meant bodies could be stored for as long as the funeral director needed but, for many it was, and for some remains, the only way they will allow the family to see their dead. They believe an unembalmed body to be too dead for the delicate bereaved. Too close to the reality of what has actually happened.

◆ ◆ ◆

As most people know, embalming as an art has a long, fascinating history and, done properly, is indeed an art. Forms of preservation, particularly mummification, were practised by all sorts of ancient cultures: the Aztecs, the Toltecs, the Mayans and the Tibetans to mention a few, but it was the Egyptians who perfected it as part of their complex belief system around the continuation in some form of the physical body into the next world. So many cultures since the beginning of time have found different methods from preventing the complete deterioration of the body, but Western embalming came out of the medical enlightenment whose epicentre was Scotland in the seventeenth and eighteenth centuries.

An English physician called William Harvey was the first person to properly map the system of blood circulation throughout the body by injecting dye, but it was a Scottish surgeon and his brother, William and John Hunter, who were to perfect the technique of arterial and cavity preservation in the mid eighteenth century and start offering it to the public.

There was much to be grateful for about this new advanced method of preserving a body longer than nature intended. It took away the risk of smell, apart from the chemical sterility that clung to the body. It meant people could transport their dead by railway to be buried elsewhere, something that was surprisingly popular with the Victorians, who had their very own Necropolis railway line.

It also meant that soldiers in the American Civil War could be returned home to be buried and that funerals in general didn't have to be organised with such haste. There had been preservation techniques before involving packing the body in ice and straw, but in 1867, a German chemist discovered a chemical called formaldehyde and everything changed.

Now, we have always been vehemently opposed to embalming for many reasons. Modern mortuary refrigeration has made it largely irrelevant and the process itself is hugely violent and intrusive. Trigger warning: this is what happens.

An incision is made in the neck and the inner thigh, which allows the blood to drain out of the body. This goes down the drain. Once as much of the blood as possible has left the body, it is replaced with a mixture of various chemicals, mainly a varying concentrate of formaldehyde, whose strength is based on how long the body needs to be preserved for, and a dye is added to give the body a healthy pink glow, then the chemicals are massaged to the extremities.

Then a cut is made in the abdomen and a long-spiked tube like a giant syringe is inserted. This is attached to a vacuum machine and the spike, known as a trocar, is moved around vigorously, stabbing soft organs and sucking all the blood and guts stuff out.

It makes that exact sound you have in your head right now.

It's then used to fill the abdomen with preserving chemicals and the body is sealed up. A skilled embalmer will put a tiny bit more fluid in than came out, resulting in the smoothing out of your wrinkles, a post-mortem facelift as it were.

This is a simplified version of what happens and, don't get me wrong, there is a lot of skill involved, but for me there is so much that is just plain abhorrent.

The violence of the procedure is difficult not to see as a weird form of ritualised desecration. If you were watching someone you loved undergoing it, you would physically stop it happening. The chemicals involved are horrendous, both for the environment and for the embalming practitioner. Formaldehyde is incredibly carcinogenic and I certainly know of embalmers who have died of unusual and aggressive cancers. Some have a very gung-ho approach to them. One embalmer told me they never got any colds or bronchial infections because of inhaling formaldehyde fumes. Apparently a good whiff burns off all of your bronchial hairs. I suffer from the usual evolutionary baffling male-ageing problem of excessive hair growing out of the nose and ears, but to scorch them off with formaldehyde feels like dealing with dandelions on your lawn with petrol.

But these objections – the environmental concerns for the practitioner, the ground the body is going into or the air it is being sent up in as smoke and gas – are not my real concerns.

The real issues are what it does to the bereaved psychologically and this is encapsulated, as so much often is, in one of the earliest examples of the modern practice. In 1775, a dentist called Martin Van Butchell had his wife embalmed and ostentatiously displayed in the window of his home. She was filled with the new combination of preserving fluids and dyes; her eyes, which after death naturally sink back into the head and the eyelids dip inward as the vitreous fluid drains back, were replaced with glass eyes, and she was dressed in a beautiful lace dress. Her body was then set in a plaster of Paris mould and sealed in a glass coffin, seemingly in perpetuity.

Clearly there was something very wrong about Mr Van Butchell's mourning. A generous assessment of his psychological state might say he was suffering from complicated grief, a common-enough emotional state for people to be in. I have encountered in many people, mainly parents of young children who are deeply reluctant to let go of the body, a sort of Sleeping Beauty syndrome, but Mr Van Butchell's post-mortem enforced exhibitionism of his presumably non-consenting wife seems weird.

The public felt uneasy at this display and a rumour started, possibly put around by Mr Van Butchell himself, claiming that due to a clause in his marriage certificate, he could only maintain control of his wife's estate if she remained unburied. Whatever his motives, I imagine the distaste of the public was not at seeing a dead body – in the eighteenth century a person would encounter lots of dead bodies from an early age – but from the cognitive dissonance at seeing someone dead look so alive.

And this is where we radically differ from the mainstream position on this. When I started it was a hunch, an instinct, an ideological position, but after twenty-one years of showing people their unembalmed dead, we know it as a truth.

It is deeply disconcerting to see someone you know is dead looking so alive – and sometimes wearing discernibly comic makeup. The well-meaning aim of a good embalmer is to make the dead look alive, but what a terrible head- and heart-fuck that is.

When you come into the presence of someone who is dead, you are torn. Your head knows they are dead. Or at least keeps telling you that – a looping form of early PTSD. But the heart is more loyal and sceptical. It refuses to believe and when you first encounter them, lying in the still of some chapel of rest, all you want them to do is to open their eyes and sit up and say 'Gotcha! Had you going, didn't I?' And if they look like they have just stepped of the plane from a fabulous holiday in Magaluf that feeling is magnified.

The mainstream thinks that you, the bereaved, the client, would rather see your father glowing with rude health than in the state they actually are in. They don't think you can cope with the sunken cheeks, the grey colour, the strange way they are there and not there, the absence of a presence. They don't think you can handle seeing them naturally dead.

So, so wrong.

The American poet and undertaker Thomas Lynch, who is very different in the way he directs funerals but also very much a living ancestor of mine, talks about how to deal with people's reluctance to see the body; 'I want to remember him as he was' is a familiar refrain. Thomas says, 'Ah, but remembering them as they were starts with accepting how they are now.' This is so true.

We carry this knowledge, the truth about our mortality and our physical decay, deep inside us. It is encoded in our DNA, part of what makes us human, the awful sadness that Philip Larkin describes as standing plain as a wardrobe. And so seeing somebody as they really are is a heavy but often vital part of the long process of acceptance.

'So it's true. That really is them. There hasn't been some awful but brilliant mix up and they really are dead. However much I want them to, the last thing they are going to do is sit up.'

This is at the heart of how we work; brokering this reunion between the dead and the living. Supporting the living by being straight about the dead, allowing them to come back to see them again and again as the body subtly changes. Give them the space and opportunity to talk to them, to express love and regret and, yes, anger too.

Some of the most profound, moving and challenging moments of my life have been in the presence of the dead and the living who love them.

The bone-wracking sobs of a mother searching the body of their child who has taken their own life for every last wound.

The tender intimacy of daughters filling the arthritic, bent arms of their ancient mother with wild flowers.

The time-stopping experience of watching a wife caress the face of her husband one last time as she takes a hammer to nail his coffin shut herself.

Following a crocodile of five year olds as they file into a summerhouse to see the body of their school friend, watching them pass quickly through curiosity, sadness and then normalcy and boredom, the whole thing just another novel experience in the busy day of a small child where everything is new.

Bringing cups of tea to a woman meditating on the slow decay of her beloved husband over a period of weeks.

Helping a mother to wash the battered body of her daughter, snatched from life by a car crash.

Standing by while a wife alternates between rage and adoration at the body of her husband who has hung himself.

This is the work, standing with families in that unimaginable horror of what has happened, helping them with tea and normal interactions when they surface into a brief bubble of normality, knowing there is nothing to say but witness and support and hold.

This was the starting point of our work, bringing home the body to the stone cottage we used as a chapel and a mortuary, lighting the blazing fireplace, which was the centre of the mill in the kitchen, and giving back access to these families.

Slowing everything down, forming a relationship, asking simple questions like 'what happened?', and not immediately producing a list of questions with tick boxes – church or natural burial ground, brochures of coffins – a bombardment of options to rush through.

All of this would follow, but slowly, gently.

'What happened?' is a really good springboard into the family dynamic. It starts with the story of the person's death and widens out into a broader picture of their life.

The information I obtain to paint my portrait of the person is gleaned slowly and obliquely. One family remarked at the end of the whole thing that I hadn't asked one direct question about the person's life. I had allowed them to tell me with long, meandering stories about almost irrelevant things.

It is the things left unsaid, the stories that peter out, the silence that suddenly falls that reveals the true nature of a person. It takes complete concentration because these things are not uncovered and revealed twice, and they may be revelations to the person saying them, a moment of clarity that comes as they are telling a story they have told so many times in which a sudden realisation sweeps over them as to what was really going on there. They may not even realise what they have said.

Witnessing these moments of realisation, the reframing of an old narrative, an understanding into what that person was going through is an incredible privilege. The emotion that overcomes someone when they understand the love behind an act, or the selfishness and neglect that can equally lie behind an act, is so powerful to witness.

These long, seemingly inconsequential conversations with the family; in their home, in our premises, even wandering around the various natural burial sites to choose from, are where the slivers of truth about a life are shared.

It is exhausting to do because your focus needs to be completely but unobtrusively focused on what they are saying – and also what they are not saying. Silence has such loud eloquence and truths are not pronounced clearly, but hang in the air unspoken between us all.

This approach, slow funerals I suppose you could call them, came naturally to us, helped by the fact that in the early days our funerals were far and few. The central staring point, the guest of honour, the Kaaba stone around which we would all slowly revolve, was the body, the unmoving material solidness of what is a very cerebral event, a physical event and a metaphysical event at the same time.

They were, at first, a form of deep fascination for me.

I remember collecting with a friend my second body – the pancreatic old lady, light as a bleached stick held in the overhanging branches of a flooded river. We carried her into my large kitchen on my impractically rustic wooden stretcher and laid it on the kitchen table.

There she was, here but long gone, a long life reduced to a small yellow body, thrumming with hints and implications about what life meant by being so clearly absent. I couldn't take my eyes off her.

Of course, this fascination has naturally abated as over a thousand of these people have passed through our care, but it can still catch me unaware, the seeming agency of a body that clearly had none, the shock of seeing a dead friend's face.

The difference between the living and the dead is so huge and so ineffable. Yet there is something deeply complete about the whole experience, a truth about our short and cosmically tiny existences that has little to do with ideas of a soul or an afterlife, but which hint at a wider context to our lives that subtly colours the sky of bereavement like the northern lights; focus too much on them and they disappear.

So we started with the body. We took ownership of them from whatever authority had them, usually a hospital mortuary, brought them back to the valley and the ancient mill house I lived in, and started to gently hand back the ownership of the experience to the bereaved.

Not always I hasten to add; not every family we deal with are dragged forcibly and reluctantly in to be faced with the body of someone they have loved.

Or hated. Let's not forget them. Remember not everyone is loved, but they largely still have families who need to organise the funeral. No default 'loved ones passing over' with us. Only people who have died.

The need for this encounter varies greatly due to the circumstance of a death. Some people die at a great age, peacefully in their beds surrounded and nursed through their final illness by the people who love them, often their children for whom they performed similar offices during their childhood. They sit beside the body for hours after death, allowing that incredible mix of sadness, relief, awe and dissolved tension to wash over them.

Anyone who has held vigil like this, after what is described as 'a good death' is lucky and much less likely to need to come back again and again to see that they really have gone – and are changing by the day.

But these 'good deaths' are rare. Family members can sit around a hospital bed for days until exhaustion sends them home to snatch an hour or two's sleep. They may be an hour away, speeding down a motorway, summoned by the nurses because of the sudden worsening of the patient's condition. They may have only got up to go to the toilet and that is the time the dying person seems to choose to slip away. Most dying people do so in a brief moment of privacy. Perhaps the love keeps them hanging on out of a sense of guilt and sorrow.

The death might not be, probably wasn't, peaceful, at least to an observer. Dying isn't something that happens to you, it is something you do, and it is arduous. Sitting beside someone as they draw what seems an interminable number of last breaths, the phlegm rattling in their throat as the swallow mechanism shuts down is a more distressing experience to witness than it is to experience.

They may not be ill or old. They might have walked out of the door that morning, waving a cheery goodbye or grunting a monosyllabic farewell, unaware that this will be the last interaction they have with the people they love on this earth.

They may have killed themselves or been killed by a drunk driver or a violent predator or, more likely, their partner. They may have just not woken up or lain on the sofa for days until the smell drives the neighbours to call the police.

These are the times when it is important to see the body. This is the work.

Even now at the time of writing, the tail end of this awful and frightening pandemic, it is a truth that a dead body is remarkably uninfectious. It is the living, with our seething armies of billions of bacteria and our messy wide dispersal of them through breathing and touching and just bloody living, which are the real culprits.

A dead body in far-gone decay can be a gory thing, difficult to stomach and needs to be dealt with in a way that both allows the dead dignity and protects the living from smelling the unmistakable smell of death, but there is little risk of much cross-contamination.

Not that the old-school mainstream funeral directors with their insistence on performing their violent 'hygienic treatment' would suggest this. For them, the body is a source of literal and perhaps even moral contamination, certainly a psychological bridge too far, and so they take a quasi-medical ownership of their own, the transformation of the dead into chemical-filled waxy simulacra.

For us, we make sure a body is clean and dignified, and lightly disinfected, but the access we allow to people is pretty much unrestricted, even if the body is in a state of advanced decay.

We are entirely straight with a person about how their dead look. If they are too far gone, we will offer our personal opinion about the benefits and drawbacks of seeing them, but we would never forbid them to see them.

I remember receiving a phone call from a woman whose mother had died at home and gone undiscovered for a number of weeks. Her body was indeed so far gone in decay that she was certainly a grim sight, well past what you would think of as a corpse. The daughter got in touch with us because her well-meaning but extremely old-school funeral director was refusing to allow her to see her mother.

We talked at length with her, outlining the details of how she undoubtedly looked and smelled. Our conversations with the undertaker confirmed this; she was in a dreadful and advanced state of decay. And yet the daughter still had an overpowering atavistic need to see her mother.

We negotiated between them and he agreed to allow her to come to his premises to see her. The experience was traumatic but healing for her; it was not as bad as she had imagined.

Not as bad as she had imagined. Sometimes this is what we need to see. An awful thing has happened, but we need to know for ourselves how awful.

Transparency without crass gratuitousness. A refusal to obfuscate or gatekeep. Ever-shifting lines of judgement about what is going to help people and what is going to fuck with their heads for the next thirty years, but always the truth of the matter shared with them in some way.

An encounter with death is the most out-of-control event we go through and wrestling back a little bit of control, even if that is making an informed decision based on a description of what their dead are like right now, is a victory, a secure, narrow stepping stone over the rushing black waters of existential wildness.

So, the dead were our guide into the world of undertaking, which is, of course, more about the care of the living. A funeral dictates how our grief is lived. Done badly and a hangnail of pain is torn that will catch on the everyday emotional matter of our lives and never heals. Done well, it can allow you to move through the lifelong consequences of a loss in a normal and healthy way.

Remember, nobody feels nothing, unless they feel nothing. And even then, grief, that opportunistic and hugely creative parasite, will swiftly jump in and start a malignant residency. We love people or we hate them, and they die and that hurts a staggering amount either way. There is no way around it. It can be postponed but, like malaria, it can hide in your system until the next death and up it flares again, stronger and more feverish.

◆ ◆ ◆

There is only one thing you really need to thrive in this world of funerals and that is a bottomless interest in the lives of ordinary people and, like me, Claire had it in buckets. That and a strong back.

Her early encounters with the dead were moments of apprehension filtered through the conditioning of cultural fear that soon gave way to awe and compassion. Her no-nonsense way of cutting through the shit and saying it as it is was something she brought to our early interactions with the bereaved that left me slack-jawed.

Say the wrong thing to someone deep in the initial rawness of grief and the fragile relationship is shattered. Somehow, Claire knew instinctively what to say, when to lighten the mood and make a joke, and when to be utterly straight.

My fourth funeral, the violent suicide and subsequent masterclass in how to speak truth to horror, how to change people's lives through the power of honesty and bravery was my full initiation into this world I had discovered, and Claire's was not far behind.

We did a few more funerals together, each interesting, unique and relatively straightforward, and they went well. We worked well together and our friendship of ten years meant there were few surprises about any faults and foibles we had.

But Claire's girls were still extremely young and, while our funerals were few and far between, she felt that it was a little too soon to commit to a full-time job, so she was just about to tell me that she was out, much as she loved it, and would be back when they were older, when her bluff was called, and her own initiation presented itself.

A child died. A girl in the same nursery class as Claire's youngest daughter. Her name was Tallulah. She had been ill for nearly all of her life with a serious condition that was incredibly hard to diagnose but everyone, including her parents, had become used to living in the war zone of illness, the way you become institutionalised to dread, which forms a background hum to the everyday domestic business of raising kids. She had a sister who was a few years older than her and who had had to live with this shadow, like the rest of her family.

The request to help her family came to Claire and was unrefusable.

One of the scariest things about doing this work is when the deaths are just too close for comfort. Later on, when we married, when we did the funeral for someone in a couple like us, we could sense a high-pitched, inaudible bat squeak of fear, a shiver of recognition of us and our own fragility, but that was nothing compared to the courage it took for Claire to agree to this funeral, with two girls of her own almost exactly that age.

Tallulah had died in a specialist hospital from what was meant to be a routine exploratory procedure. Her parents were immediately cut off from the rest of life by this event.

When an extraordinary grief suddenly comes smashing out of nowhere on a humdrum Tuesday afternoon, when the teenager who cheerily walks out of the back door leaving the usual thoughtless detritus behind only to never return, your life is transformed in an instant. It is like a thick, transparent Perspex wall has suddenly descended, cutting you off from the rest of life, neatly dividing your past from your present.

You can hear and see everyone on the outside, muffled but visible with pinpoint detail, but you are in a different place, frozen in an horrific present and you would give anything to be back on the other side of that impossible divide.

All of what seemed like such difficult problems and issues at the time – work issues, an emotionally fallow patch in your marriage, money worries – are revealed to be the bliss of everyday life before the detonation of grief.

People's lives can change in a flash and without warning, and the past is revealed to be a paradise, with its shallow concerns and complicated needy friendships, all trivial bollocks compared to the deep pain of a loss like this which taints every joy for decades, if not forever.

So, I try to remind myself, when my baseless moods set in, that actually I am, before this possible moment, living in the rosy past that a future bereaved me would consider a literal heaven. The terrible, terrible thing has not happened yet, and may never. I am living before the fall.

Because of my job and the profundity of it, people expect me to live every day as though it were my last, to savour every moment, to tell my kids and friends I love them every day, but it doesn't work like that. I still moan about trivial things, allow the grumpiness of middle age to squat toad-like on the perfectly pleasant path of my day. Claire would still berate the children for leaving wet towels on the bathroom floor, we would bicker and snipe like any couple, be overcome by the drudgery of everyday life.

There is an episode of *The Simpsons* where Homer thinks he has eaten the toxic liver of the fugu fish, a dangerous delicacy in Japanese food that needs expert preparation that done well gives a mild tingling to the fingertips like a nettle sting but prepared badly means death. That is the thrill.

Homer believes he has twenty-four hours to live and tries to cram as much into his last day as possible. It is worth watching alone for Homer going through all of Elisabeth Kübler-Ross's five stages of grief at a terminal diagnosis: denial, anger, bargaining, depression and acceptance, in around five seconds. But the bit that sticks with me is that, after the twenty-four hours is up and he is still alive, he stands up triumphantly to proclaim, 'From this day forward, I vow to live life to its fullest!' Cut to him the next day sitting on the sofa, watching TV and throwing potato chips into his mouth.

Working with trauma is like that. You cannot maintain that level of existential alertness without burning out, but every so often I consciously think of this. I am living before an awful event that may never happen, but if it did, this life I lead now with my gripes and fears would be an Eden I had been expelled from.

Tallulah's funeral was our first child and it really was a different level of grief and loss. Her parents were bewildered by this event, the atmosphere of their lives suddenly thickened with a heavier gravity, their movements slowed down as if they were thigh deep in some viscous liquid.

Every action decided around the body of this little girl was a complete thing in itself. We were out of our depths, Claire for the first time.

We brought the child back home from the hospital and, as my premises were an hour away in Cornwall, her parents felt that was too far away from them, so we looked around some of the local undertakers' premises to see whether she could stay with them while the funeral was organised.

They were typical of the small-town undertakers' parlours of the time: bleak, weird, practical, but with all of the unheimlichness that these places can have. They were generous to allow us to look around, but her father rejected them all. I don't blame him. Backstage at a funeral parlour is often a deeply strange place. But the child's body had to rest somewhere.

Everything we were doing at this point was based on theory. I had read as many books about funerals and bodies and grief as I could and most of that information had come from the third edition of *The Natural Death Handbook*.

I knew in theory that we could keep her body at home and by using those plastic freezable blocks, the type you use to keep a bag full of picnic stuff chilled, a body could be kept as cool as a mortuary fridge. It would require attention and routine, but no more than the needs of the girl while she was alive, whose condition had required twenty-four-hour vigilance.

In the US, there is a different system used by people having what could fall under the umbrella term 'a home funeral' and that involves dry ice, a solid form of CO_2. There, buying pellets of dry ice was easy and cheap, but in the UK, it was not generally available for use by anybody other than licensed and trained handlers, so we had to go with the much more low-tech solution of the frozen ice blocks. They were incredibly cheap and could be refrozen and used over and over again.

When someone dies, immediately following their death there is a brief surge in temperature as individual cells keep doing their thing until the message of death reaches them from the brain, but the body's exhaust system of sweating and farting has stopped releasing the heat from this feverish last burst of activity.

This is brief, before the body goes into algor mortis proper, which is the gradual acclimatisation of the body to the ambient room temperature. The average living body temperature is 37° Celsius, but can be raised by disease and drugs. Life is surprisingly hot, and it is not until we feel how cold we are when it is gone that we realise quite how hot.

Getting the body temperature to be lower than room temperature is essential to stop body decomposition and it is really the torso that this needs to happen to. Instant refrigeration in a mortuary fridge is the easiest solution but, as in this case, sometimes that wasn't possible or desirable for the family.

At first, as the ice blocks are packed around the body, the heat exchange is fast and the blocks begin to thaw within a few hours, so the freezer always has at least eight blocks refreezing in it. But, as the body begins to cool down, those packs stay cold for longer and so, with regular changing, it is possible to keep a body at home for as long as was needed.

The family had a small summer house at the end of their terraced garden, just a single simple wooden room, and we suggested this was where she could rest until it came time to bury her.

With so much of this work, there are moments of suggesting things which, at first, might seem outlandish and utterly unacceptable to a family, and sometimes they are just that. It is delicate work, putting forward ideas and allowing them to filter through or be roundly rejected. It all goes with the gentle back and forth exchange of power between ourselves and the bereaved.

Everything we are doing is an attempt to make them take back the ownership of the death, without feeling that they are lumbered with all of the practicalities. We hold them through these decisions, reassuring them there is no right or wrong, only what feels that way.

Her father had a strong reaction against the idea at first, he felt it a little macabre and possibly would affect his other daughter too much. But he and his partner quickly came around to the idea, and so we began preparations, all of the while holding the body of the girl down in my chapel in Cornwall.

Her family decorated the bare pine walls of the summer garden house with drapes as well as drawings that Tallulah had done. They made a soft bed with pillows and we cleared the freezer part of their fridge and filled it with around twenty or so of these small cheap plastic blocks.

The idea was that her body, mainly her torso, would be surrounded by these freezer packs, probably no more than six at a time. These would need replacing and refreezing every six hours or so, slowing down to every twelve hours as her body cooled down.

The practicalities of doing this came very naturally to both parents. It felt like a continuation of the caring they had done for Tallulah during her whole short life, a natural thing, and one they quickly embraced with love.

When you have been caring for someone who is ill or nearing death, be it a child or an ancient parent with Alzheimer's, you get used to doing the earthy practicalities that go with such a stage of life. Those feelings of natural responsibility, the desire to do these things yourself and not to hand them over to strangers remains very strong.

To watch them prepare her body for the night, to repack her bird-like torso with ice packs, to dry any moisture from the condensation that formed, to hear them murmuring comforting things exactly as if they were putting her to bed, was an incredible privilege and a vindication of everything *The Natural Death Handbook* had said. It just took a certain amount of courage to allow all of this to happen.

It was an extraordinary time, the week or so in which her body lay in state. Tallulah's father in particular warmed to the task of attending her body and, at one point, I thought we had made a mistake when he talked about keeping her body like this forever, a Sleeping Beauty that he would assiduously attend, fending off the decay.

But he knew this was not possible and, as the slow, subtle changes occurred to the body of this beautiful child, the slight discolouration of her skin, her transformation into what looked like a dead child from a renaissance painting, he gradually accepted that it was getting time to lay her down to rest.

I will never forget that week. Her schoolmates all coming to see her body, the worry and discomfort of all of their parents contrasting so completely with the insouciance of the kids, their absolute normality around her body.

They came in a steady stream to say goodbye to their friend. The sound of laughter and chatter rang around her body all day and, as the evening descended and they left, the noises of play were replaced by the quiet sad murmurs of the adults who came to sit with her in the candle light, cry over this sadness, be with her parents in their unbearable loss.

Once you remove as many of the obstacles as you can, physical and psychological, that prevent people from actually being in the presence of their dead, something extraordinary happens. It becomes normal. Or, if not normal, then a natural part of life. The people immediately around it lose their disempowered helplessness and become an active part of it. It is a deeply familiar social thing, this being with our dead before we let them go, an experience we have only lost touch with in the last one hundred years or so.

And so the time came to bury Tallulah, and the slow, brave release of the body that every family goes through, and by now is such a familiar thing to me, took place.

Tallulah's funeral was in the local church, whose minister was open hearted enough to allow nearly any gathering to happen there that benefited the community, Christian or not.

It was a ceremony filled with the chatter of children, the singing of familiar nursery songs and, at the end, everyone filed past her open coffin to sprinkle rose petals on her body. By the time Tallulah's mother shut her bamboo coffin for the last time, she was already buried under a drift of red petals. We carried her out, singing and crying, to the graveyard.

Claire's fate as an undertaker was sealed. There was no going back from this.

CHAPTER NINE

Car parks, waiting rooms, chimneys and smoke

Quite early on, somebody asked me who, in my work, I was really burying, and that question stopped me in my tracks.

I was, of course, atoning for my own mismanaged grief, my literal absence from the funerals of people I deeply loved when I was a small boy – my father, my grandmother and grandfather, and my aunt, all dead within a cruelly short time, all funerals that I did not attend, as well as my emotional absence from the funeral of my mother. The numbness that set in like concrete to protect me from the wave of unresolved grief that I had pushed down through my need to survive boarding school, the pain that I could not outrun.

Every time I helped a family, I faced a little bit more of my own sadness, I placed another small rock on the cairn of remembrance.

And I also rather provocatively took the opportunity to throw small rocks at the edifice that had been placed in between all of us and our authentic loss – the granite walls of distorted masculinity that had so many unclimbable edges that shored up the patriarchy.

Some of these I had been hurling rocks at all my life. The intrinsically unfair way I had been segregated educationally, unfair to society and unfair to me, with its tight gold chains of privileged neglect, but also the way the grip of masculine authoritarianism had tightened over us all and had settled into late-stage capitalism: Moloch.

Acid house had showed me a more egalitarian vision of how things could be and I refused to see these experiences as just youthful hedonism that was something to be grown out of. It had showed me that honest cooperation working towards a common good was actually the norm, not the exception. That individual connection not competition was easier than the state would lead us to believe, and this cooperation was perhaps all we really had to hold our fragile society together.

This was how we both started this work – no apprenticeship, no gradual learning of the way each part of the jigsaw fitted together, no sheltering under the wing of a more experienced funeral director, starting off washing cars, then carrying and lowering coffins, perhaps answering the phone or collecting bodies at night, no chance to say, 'Help, what do I do?' From the very first funeral, every buck for every mistake stopped with us.

Our position was that everything needed to change about funerals. No one was howling from the rooftops about the merciless outrage of death, this cliff we all drop off to who knows where. No one was saying anything honest about the person who had died in a respectful way that actually helped the living. No one was dealing with the appalling unnecessary environmental aspects of a funeral. It was all so clear that everything had to change.

The fervour of youth, the power of idealism that sees no obstacles, that makes things happen through sheer will and the knowledge that what you are doing is right and will work.

So, we loudly proclaimed our differences, made a virtue out of our inexperience, scoffed at professionalism as the benchmark for being an undertaker, replacing it with a radical authenticity and a willingness to approach each funeral as though it were the first.

We would be who we were and, if people didn't like us or what we stood for, that was fine, the marketplace more than catered for the opposite of us. But it was obvious from the start that a lot of people found our lack of pomp refreshing and, even if they didn't know it, were hungry for participation and their own genuine creative input, particularly those who had sat through those offensively evasive identikit funerals where nothing real was said or felt.

It helped that we were handed on from family to family, particularly those ones who had lost someone out of the natural sequence, a child or a young person. Helpful but extreme, to be confronted again and again by the unavoidable and unfair tragedies of life, the truth of death – that it was not just the old and tired who died, but the young.

One truth that became very self-evident to us was that getting a child successfully through the risk-taking years is pure luck. It has nothing to do with parenting or social status though, of course, sometimes elements of these were factors; nonetheless it is a lottery.

Children and young people die through so many ways, silly little mistakes that an adult would avoid: getting into a car with a driver impaired through drink, an experimental drug misadventure, an on-rush of shame that causes them to take their own lives, a phenomenon amplified by the unrelenting magnifying never-turned-off recording lens of social media.

These are the deaths that are everywhere, and always will be. They are not a reflection of a broken society, although without a doubt, many lives would be saved if our politicians had the courage to implement a drug policy that actually was about keeping people safe, rather than playing to an audience who feels that these substances and experiences need to be eradicated. Life is inherently risky and no one is owed safe passage or a happy ending. Once we had shown ourselves to be willing to really accompany these families through this extreme darkness, we became the go-to undertakers for the most wounded families.

But the paradox was that these families, each completely different in their own way, all had something in common: deep wells of courage and compassion, a strength that you would think belongs only to the exceptional, but actually lies within most of us and, above all, is reachable.

Being around people like this is one of the pay-offs to the endless weight of grief we work with. Discovering that people are fundamentally good and brave, that they can survive the most awful things and still live a meaningful life filled with small acts of kindness.

These weren't the only funerals we did. We buried plenty of people who had lived long lives, full of happiness and fulfilment, and families found us through many ways. We very quickly decided we weren't going to go down the traditional route of a series of formal weekly newspaper ads proclaiming in florid script our '24-hour personal service' or our 'dedicated chapel of repose'. We understood that interviews with journalists were the best way of getting our message across, appearances on local radio stations talking about our philosophy and, more often than not, what we were opposed to.

Soon we were being featured in all sorts of publications and had taken to posing like a moody post-punk synth duo, accentuating our differences. Claire, it has to be said, pulled this off better than me, but I grew into myself as my mum might have said.

I'm sure this put some people off, and this was almost intentional. We didn't want to exclude any strata of society from using us either because of cost or belief system, but we didn't want to find ourselves helping a family who felt that fundamentally we stood in opposition to their way of life. Sometimes, one of our funerals can take well over two weeks and that is a long time to have someone in your head that you don't get on with. Only just yesterday a woman rang me up, refusing to give her name and with the number withheld, to complain that a photo I had used in a newspaper article, a parody that she clearly didn't get of the classic 1930 American painting by Grant Wood called 'American Gothic', in which Claire and I replace the two grumpy-looking figures and I hold a shovel instead of a pitchfork, made us look miserable and she wouldn't be using us. I replied that I wouldn't want to work with anyone who felt an anonymous critique of a photograph was the way to express an opinion and she should look a little deeper than her reflexive prejudice. No one had died, I hasten to add, she just didn't like the cut of my jib and I don't blame her.

We are not for everyone. Sometimes you come face to face with someone who is an implacable foe, and there is something of a liberation in that. Often, you are being clearly seen for who you are and you can clearly see them in return. They are right and so are you. At least it is free from sickly insincerity. There have been times when my outspokenness has undoubtedly showed myself to those who disapproved of me and they have not always come at me so directly, but this trouble was many moons away. We were just at the beginning of our maverick career.

But the earliest indication that we were doing something different and doing it well came with the way established death-care professionals treated us. Really cutting-edge bereavement councillors started to recommend us. Mortuary technicians, whose working day was spent dissecting bodies for post-mortems and releasing those bodies to a steady stream of funeral directors, started to say they would like us to do their funerals.

Independent family-run undertakers who had every right to bristle at our arrogant attacks on embalming and modern cremation quietly told us to keep going, and they were there for us for anything we needed. People who worked in hospices, radical chaplains, senior nurses, GPs, all got it.

Their encouragement spurred us on, gave us the confidence to put much of this theory into practice. These were people who had interacted with the funeral industry and the church for years. They knew that things needed shaking up.

I could feel a clear link between what we were doing, putting these counterculture values into practice through the philosophy of The Natural Death Centre and a long line of ancestral rebels, going back through various dissenting traditions. Once you know that you are on a well-trampled path, even if you are taking it into new territory, it gives you some courage.

I felt the quiet determination of people like the Quakers, the Levellers and the Diggers behind us, both the original English Diggers in the 1600s, whose defiant practice of digging up the so-called common ground to plant and grow food was the forerunner of anarchism, and the San Francisco Diggers, an art activist theatre group who acted as informal moral leaders and surrogate parents to the huge explosion of young hippies that flocked to Haight-Ashbury in the 1960s. Both groups were set against the establishment and both groups believed that radical participation in your own life was the way to make change happen. But we were up against such a solid and established empire of tradition and control. How could two people make a scratch of difference to this Death Star machine?

One of the first big things we came up against was the inflexibility of the system around cremation. I don't just mean the legal checks, all of which I agree with completely and are self-evidently good. I mean the way the system presented itself to the public, which was very much on their terms.

It was, and in many places remains, a fortress of uncooperation.

In the UK, nearly 75 per cent of people are cremated. It is the default position. In the US, it is creeping up to nearly 50 per cent. The two countries have different philosophical positions on it, with the US, considering it to be more environmentally friendly than burial, which it is so not, unless you are considering the extremely weird American habit of burying somebody in a hermetically sealed casket within a concrete-lined vault. It also used to be considered somewhat futuristic, a Californian thing, modern.

In the UK, people don't so much as want cremation, they just don't want to be buried. People have strong views on it – there is either fear of the worms or fear of the fire. Very few people anywhere in the world are ambivalent about it.

The evolution of cremation in the UK into its position as the primary form of body disposal came about partly through the industrialisation of death through the horror of two world wars in quick succession, but also through society falling dutifully into a pattern where the funeral service would take place at a church with a vicar presiding, then would follow on to the crematorium with perhaps just the family attending. There would be a brief addendum to the church service, the committal, and the coffin would be consigned to the fire. This model worked well in the early part of the twentieth century, but remains defiantly old-fashioned and unfit for purpose today.

By the way, despite persistent rumours, the staff at crematoriums do not remove bodies to reuse the coffins. They are not undertakers, and are no more used to dealing with a corpse than a chef.

And the profit margins on coffins are such that there is no need for that to happen anyway.

The coffins are 'shot' into the fiery furnace and burnt at between 800 and 1,000° Celsius for around an hour and a half to three hours, the timing dependent on the body and its fat content. Nearly everything apart from the bones are incinerated into the sky. The ashes are allowed to cool, then raked out and crumbled in the crassly named cremulator to grind them down to the consistency of cement – and with the same look.

It is an environmental nightmare. It uses the same technology as when it was first industrialised in the late 1800s. It takes roughly the same amount of energy to cremate a body as it does to supply a living person with all of their energy needs for three months and, despite technical modernisation to the chimney flue, they still disgorge a significant amount of greenhouse gases and soot particulates, plastic coffin detritus and all the shit like formaldehyde and glues that go into their construction up into the air. It even puts up to a ton and a half of mercury gas into the atmosphere, or used to until expensive mercury abatement filters were put in place. These filters do nothing to stop the emission of CO_2, and a staggering amount is released into the global atmosphere as a result of this.

Yet, as radical undertakers starting up, we were not in a position to refuse to do cremations. That would have made a difficult starting position impossible and, frankly, would be a little pious to boot, and so we do do them and always have done, and make them as environmentally sound as possible by using a simple willow coffin.

But the thing we came up against, which grated the most, wasn't the way that it was so terrible for the environment, it was the way it was so terrible for the family.

It was, and largely remains, a conveyor-belt process in buildings, which are aesthetically horrendous, the worst of post-war municipal architecture, brutalist concrete structures, and are often staffed by men who are little more than glorified nightclub bouncers or car park attendants. They are more concerned with the flow of funerals in and out than they are with the quality of the ritual taking place within.

Unlike society, which has largely moved on from the certainties of Christian belief that were so dominant such a short time ago, these places remain set up for the tail end of a Christian ceremony, unchanged in design and allowing extremely short time slots for each funeral.

Most of the crematoriums we still use on a regular basis allow thirty minutes or, at best, forty-five minutes. This includes time to get a family in and, more difficult, time to get a family out. That often leaves around twenty to twenty-five minutes for the ceremony, barely enough time to settle everyone down before it is over.

They open for public cremations from nine till five and don't open on a weekend. My heart sinks when a family insists on doing the entire ceremony at a crematorium: the plastic flowers, the line of mourners still sobbing from the previous funeral before shuffling out of sight, the puff of smoke emerging from the chimney as the coffin is burnt off, the narrowing down of an important social and spiritual thing into a mechanical process, the feeling that we are all just shuffling through the gift shop of life before dropping off a conveyor belt into a skip.

The irony is that the story to legalise and mainstream cremation in the UK is one of a fiery public elemental event, an angry mob, a case in the High Court and a theological debate about the resurrection, all driven by radical Welsh eccentric, the magnificent Dr William Price.

Dr Price is the closest thing that the cremation industry has to a patron saint. His story is extraordinary and I feel more kinship with the good doctor than I do with any modern crematorium. He is another of my ancestors.

Dr William Price was born in Wales in 1800 and lived a long, righteous and eccentric life. He held strong beliefs about many things.

He was a Chartist, an early form of revolutionary socialism, and believed in radical change in a number of areas of society, including the liberation of Wales to govern itself. He was implacably opposed to marriage and believed in 'free love', something which was to be very much part of the story of cremation.

He was a practising doctor, a GP who refused to treat people if they smoked, but nonetheless who ran a National Health-style practice long before it was imagined. He was a vegetarian, almost unheard of in those days, and he had a penchant for naked hill walking, wearing nothing but a fox skin headdress and holding a staff topped with a brass crescent moon.

Naturist rambling was not the only thing he had a penchant for and he fathered a child when he was 83 with a young farmer's daughter called Gwenllian, who was aged just 23. In a typical act of public provocation, Dr Price named his son Iesu Grist, Welsh for Jesus Christ. William held the conventional church in as much contempt as he did his fellow doctors, whom he thought quacks pedalling ineffective cures, and the government, whom he thought enslavers of man. Perhaps Dr Price could be summed up by the song that Groucho Marx sings in *Horse Feathers*: 'Whatever it is, I'm against it!'

I think that his defiant stand against the religious and social status quo was a genuinely revolutionary act and that his identification with a mythic Wales, complete with an invented druidical heritage, holds a gnostic truth and was part of the struggle to prise the choking fingers of capitalism from the throat of the common man. You can see why I like Dr Price.

Sadly Gwenllian and William's son died at just five months old, and it was here that Dr Price's hitherto indulged eccentricities ran into the contradictory granite wall of the implacable Welsh conventionality.

Dr Price arose early on a Sunday and took the body of Jesus Christ up onto a hill, where he tried to cremate him with paraffin, due to his belief that burial was detrimental to the body of the earth.

The flames were spotted by worshippers in a nearby chapel and they poured out of it enraged, like a disturbed wasps' nest. This time Dr Price had gone too far, and the mob nearly lynched him, ancient though he was.

The fire was put out before the child was immolated and checks were made by local doctors to ensure he had not been murdered. To this day, the checks that are made around the preparations for a cremation echo this first examination and the laws around outraging public decency are the result of his angry mob and their reaction to seeing the partly burnt body of the boy.

And so the stage was set for an extraordinary court case that captured the imagination of the country and covered the front pages of the nation's broadsheet newspapers.

It was essentially a battle between Dr Price and the Church, but the country held its breath. Crematoriums were already being constructed, but their legality was uncertain, largely due to the hesitant disapproval of the Church on the grounds of what would happen come the last trump of judgement, when Christ (the original one, not the poor lad who crumpled at such a tender age, possibly under the weight of expectation of his name) would raise up the bodies of the dead to be judged on their lives.

Dr Price argued convincingly that if Christ could raise a mouldering body or indeed a crumbling skeleton interred years before, then surely he could reassemble a pile of bone ash into a recognisable character to face the music. There was no real theological answer to that and Richard Dawkins himself couldn't have put it better. The case collapsed and Dr Price triumphantly cremated the eponymous Jesus Christ on the spot he had previously attempted it with his own Druidic rituals.

When Dr Price finally died nine years later, his last words being, 'Bring me a glass of Champagne,' which he promptly downed and died, ground zero for champagne socialists, he was burnt on a funeral pyre on top of the hill he had cremated his son on, in front of a crowd of twenty thousand onlookers. They had to get in more police to manage the onlookers, who drank the town's pubs dry, snatching bits of sheered-off steel from Dr Price's enormous metal sarcophagus as souvenirs.

It had everything. Drama, the mountain top, the hushed crowd watching the spectacle, flames rising up into the morning sky, the emotional resolution of the whole thing, which transcends any belief in an afterlife. In a wonderful piece of natural theatre, the tons of coal that had been used to ensure his complete immolation, compounded by the oven-like properties of his enormous iron coffin that glowed white hot, meant that his skeleton had all but disappeared, an extraordinary act of reverse transubstantiation, an almost-occult vanishing trick.

What an extraordinary contrast with the pale imitation it so quickly became, reclaimed by the Protestant Christian church and defanged into a dismal procession of cars and people around a one-way system, no time for reflection, no chance to warm yourself around the pyre.

Time and time again authority takes our spiritual needs and commodifies them. Over and over, our more atavistic sides are pruned down for the sake of control and money. This is how an existential experience solidified into an industry, and where corporations began to move in and take over from local councils, shrouding the process in euphemisms and corporate logos, gauzy layers of obfuscation, charging huge amounts of money for what is a simple and relatively cheap process.

It's not generally the fault of the people who work there. My local crematorium has a lovely chapel attendant called Dee, coincidentally also an old punk. Nothing is too much bother or too out there for her, and sometimes that is all you need; a warm friendly face reassuring you that it is okay to move the chairs into a circle or that actually you have more time than you think. Someone who can think on their feet and make a judgement about what to allow to happen that will help the mourners. But still far too many crematoriums are run with a rather brusque attitude, funnelling people in and out like an airport, treating every unusual request as if you had asked to stage an orgy, instead of allowing the family to quietly encircle the coffin.

I started a campaign when I joined The Natural Death Centre in 2009 to re-legalise outdoor funeral pyres, which had an ambiguous legal status, the last officially sanctioned funeral pyres taking place during World War Two, teaming up with a Hindu man called Davender Ghai of the Anglo Asian Friendship Society.

His desire to be burnt on a funeral pyre was from the standpoint of his religious beliefs, but it was not universally supported by his fellow Hindus in this country, who felt that the compromises of the crematorium were just part and parcel of integrated living in the UK and that he was portraying their beliefs in an unnecessarily old-fashioned way.

My own motivation was my desire for a fiery immolation on top of a hill, a funeral that would be simple and yet magnificent in its spectacle, an all-night affair taking place, in my imagination, on a warm midsummer eve, the time of my birthday. I know, ego the size of a planet with the fragility of an empty eggshell, but I also wanted to try and reach out to ethnic minorities around death, to try and stop the natural death movement from being a just white middle-class concern.

At the time of our campaign, we seemed to have worked out a way which was environmentally sound. We would use hazel, an indigenous tree that is easily coppiced and burns at an extremely high temperature. The growing of the hazel would provide an environmentally friendly cottage industry and our reckoning was that not that many people would go for it to make it a real worry.

Sadly the last twenty years of accelerated climate change make it look unlikely, but I was responding to a genuine response from people I met, who, as soon as they found out I was an undertaker, would immediately say, 'Oh, I want one of them Viking funerals.'

The public's enthusiasm for a 'Viking' funeral mainly came from the film *The Vikings* with Tony Curtis, in which flaming arrows were fired at a longship. A strong image indeed, but probably fanciful. The Vikings did burn people on longships, but largely on the shore. This practice was usually reserved for high-status individuals and would also involve the butchering of a few slaves to accompany them to the afterlife.

Recent archeological digs have revealed that it is as much an indigenous British way of dealing with your dead as it is Norse. Stonehenge appears to have been a vast place of burning bodies for the Beaker people, as they are known, interring their bone ash within the complex. The bodies were burnt a mile away and then the remains processed and buried within Stonehenge itself. Like most of our knowledge about the Beaker people, the details on this are hazy.

As for the campaign, well it never gained much serious traction, although several bodies were burnt on funeral pyres to test the reaction of both the public and the police. The upshot was that it would be down to the director of public prosecutions to decide whether to press charges and, as long as the required paperwork for a cremation ensuring the death was ascertained and without any questions around it, then it would probably be okay.

I have burnt one person on a pyre, the body of a tiny preterm baby.

It was entirely legal because the child was below the legal age of existence as a person, the miscarriage that had caused the death was too early for the death to need to be registered. In the old days, the mother probably wouldn't have even had a chance to see this tiny protohuman, the hospital staff would have whipped the child away and incinerated him in the furnaces that lie within the bowels of all big hospitals.

But times have changed and it is understood that a mother who has lost her baby at any stage is entitled to grieve with the body, to take them home with them and, in this case, to entirely legally cremate them on a pyre.

The parents of this child were incredible. Loving and open hearted with some young children of their own already. We didn't put the idea in their head, we all talked our way gently to the same conclusion, the way we do with each funeral. The father was a vet and so had a deep sense of the practical, and it was he who worked out that it was legal to do so.

And so we prepared a time and a place. We would cremate the child in the ceremonial fire pit that we had hand dug ourselves when we set up a natural burial site for the Sharpham Trust.

His parents wanted to have some ashes, rather than allow the remains of his tiny body to mingle with the cinders of the fire pit, which already contained the cremated bone ash of at least eight other people. So we brought a fire bowl, the type which is used to sit around when camping, and the parents brought some dry wood to build a good fire.

We were mindful that the experience had to be handled sensitively and that keeping the body of the child hidden at all times during the process was essential – legally as well as emotionally – so I gathered some evergreens from some special trees that I knew. I took some bright green pine branches from the enormous cedar tree that stood outside our office. I visited the ancient yew tree that stood by the remains of the old church on the Dartington Hall estate, rumoured to be at least a thousand years old. I collected some branches from the mighty giant sequoias in the nearby forest and sprigs of holly, complete with red berries, all of which we lay over the soft shrouded baby as the fire roared.

The green wood and the pine needles crackled and spat, curls of sweetly smelling smoke rising up into the air as the child's parents spoke to their son, dead long before he had even started, about how they wouldn't forget him, the impact he had had on their lives during his short gestation, the happy future they had imagined for him and the sad reality of what his life would have been like, knowing what they knew of the difficulties he would have faced, had he lived.

After a bit, Claire and I quietly left them, dusk falling on that hilltop, as they placed branches on the fire and quietly held each other tight.

Cremation needs to be better. That's it. It needs to have the universal emotional punch that the huge pyre of Dr Price had. Crematoriums need to be redesigned so that they are more like temples than waiting rooms. The time slots need to be changed. They should be run like monasteries, always open, a place of contemplation for everyone, with the people who work there paid well, maybe even taking on the role of almost priests. We all need to become our own priests.

Technology is coming along in the form of alkaline hydrolysis or, to put it simply, water cremation, a high-tech version of dissolving the body using a strong alkaline solution to replace the outdated Victorian gas ovens, but we need to go further than simply replacing the actual way we do it.

A bold new secular vision of how we deal with our dead is needed. And that lies at the heart of what we have been trying to do for the past twenty-one years.

CHAPTER TEN

Bodies in extremis, grief in extremis

Our bodies are all we know and have for certain in this life. It is what carries us through it, even though we may believe it is simply a flesh puppet that houses some interior essence that stands outside of the physical.

I don't know about that. People often assumed that because Claire and I were undertakers, we had some sort of inside knowledge into an afterlife or, at the very least, a position.

I don't. I have hopes, but these are probably traceable to a Philip Larkin fear of oblivion. I have definitely had some experiences around death that make me feel that time is not as linear as we assume. Perhaps any hope (and terror) I have about an afterlife is based on a feeling that everything that has happened is happening simultaneously, that there is no death because there is no time.

But it quickly became obvious to me that any idea either of us might have about an afterlife was completely irrelevant, indeed detrimental, to helping a family. The grieving grasp at straws of comfort, it's why mediums are so irresistible to the violently bereaved. But all we could do was be there for them in the rawness of the physical truth of the matter.

Regardless of faith or the absence of it, when someone dies, they are indisputably not here. That does not necessarily mean that they are somewhere else, but so much of our meaning of what it is to be human hinges on this contradiction. It is fascinating, and heartbreaking, but it is an important step in accepting that someone you love has gone from this world and that sooner rather than later their earthly vessel, the only thing we know for certain about ourselves, the thing that is 'me' in the world, needs to be taken care of.

And so the first step in handing back control to a family lies in helping them to raise the courage to see the body of the person they love, so profoundly and mysteriously changed.

More often than not, a person dies within a medical establishment framework: a hospital or a hospice or a nursing home. If it is the latter, they often ask that they are collected immediately.

Some nursing homes have a very strange attitude. They like to keep the news that a resident has died from the rest, have them spirited away. I get that in a specialist dementia home the lack of understanding around anything that is really happening is tenuous to say the least. But in some nursing homes where most of the residents are simply very frail, it must be a very weird sensation to suddenly find that chatty Mary from Room 28 has just left in the night, like they were doing a flit from a hotel to avoid the bill. Some nursing homes usher all of their residents into their rooms and lock them in while we stretcher out their companion. The poor sods rattle on the door handles wailing plaintively. In others, the staff ask us to come during mealtimes, when everyone is in the dining hall.

So weird. How must these other residents feel? I know nobody really wants to die, except the extremely infirm, but surely they must feel that death really is a thief in the night?

More obfuscation. More treating people like they can't handle the truth, which more often than not is really about avoiding our own feelings to their reaction.

So much of the etiquette around death, bereavement and funerals is about stopping the contagion of fear, stamping out the wildfires of panic and distress that we all feel, at any age, at the abyss we all drop off to who knows where.

The best of nursing homes treat the death of a resident with all of the appropriate ceremony and clarity that you would hope for. They tell everyone that sweet, dotty Mary has died, that the nice undertakers will be coming to take her body at a certain time, that they can visit her in her room before she goes.

And when we come to wheel her out on our stretcher, covered with one of the brightly coloured silk cloths we choose on a whim, based on what we think they might like, the other residents line the corridors and the communal spaces and applaud. This is so rare, but when it happens, it feels like a moment from a Robin Williams film. This calmness around death does not come naturally to anyone.

I believe all of us who work around the sharp edge, where life cuts into death, tries to put our fear aside. We all feel our hair stand on end at the incomprehensibleness of death, the inevitability of our own, the terror at how it might come, but we make a decision to overcome that, or at least to convincingly hide it, in order to help the really traumatised.

My encounters with the dead, mine and Claire's acclimatisation to the oxygen-thin atmosphere that surrounds death, was simultaneously gradual and immediate. I was and still remain preoccupied by death. I have thought about it every day since I was seven and my father's disappearance across that literal drawbridge from life to death. The sense that people you love can just suddenly and irrevocably disappear is eternal. That tensed-up existential anticipation is like tinnitus – you can sometimes forget about it, but it only has to be mentioned and it makes your head vibrate with a shrill alarm.

My first experiences around bodies were through the liminality of hospital mortuaries, and they remain largely so, apart from this past two years of the pandemic, when more and more people died at home, too frightened to go into a hospital, to be separated from the people they love. Good grieving decisions as it turned out.

And hospital mortuaries are good places to be initiated into the world of the corpse, they are simultaneously high tech and deeply medieval in atmosphere, cheery and everyday in their work place chatter, but solemn and sad with the reality of what they are for.

Generally, in my experience, the people who work in hospital mortuaries are a wonderful blend of the deeply competent and the quietly compassionate. There is no ghoulish banter, probably because they live locally and the people that come into their care are their friends and neighbours, relatives even.

The staff in my local big hospital mortuary were incredibly kind to me – and curious of me – particularly Tim, the now-retired head mortician, who was so generous in teaching me the ropes.

One day, a long time ago, I was buzzed in and walked into the mortuary complex. I had been in and out a few dozen times by then and was getting used to it, this windowless burrow in the depths of the hospital.

I was no longer awed and fascinated to be in what looked so like a television drama set, the long line of floor-to-ceiling doors with shelves of the dead behind them. I was getting used to the technician pulling one of the shelves out, unzipping the bag and seeing what my next dead client looked like. I was getting good at balancing that with the everyday chat, the ordinariness of it for them.

I was even getting used to the almost magical way they could transfer even the seemingly heaviest body from their fridge tray to my gurney with a simple one... two... three HUP! Still don't really understand how they do that, something to do with using their own body as a fulcrum. It might be a form of levitation for all I know.

But this day, as I was buzzed in, the place seemed empty, no one in the admin office, no one waiting to cheerily greet me. Not even any other undertakers looking like penguins in their pinstripe trousers wondering why I looked like I was in an indie guitar band. I wandered around saying 'hello?' loudly as I did so.

And then I pushed through some swing doors at the end of the main refrigerated room into a place I had not been before.

It was a large, brightly lit room, surgically lit. There were probably six stainless steel raised slabs in front of me and, lying on them, heads towards me were six bodies, mid post-mortem. The room was empty of the living. I had wandered in at a time when they were probably descrubbing for lunch.

The bodies were of mixed sex and age. They all had their chests cut and clamped wide open, spreadeagled, Viking style, with their viscera visible. Some of their organs were out of the body for examination. They all had the top of their skulls missing, neatly removed like a bowl. Their brains had been removed and the skin of their face was slightly rolled forward like a mask.

I don't know how long I stood there, probably not long. It was an off-limits area that I had stumbled on, but it was enough to deeply rattle any romantic fantasies about our higher identities.

What remains of us? They appeared to be meat puppets, animated by electricity and kept running by fuel until the wear and tear of their bodies meant the spark puttered out and they were done. It was a chilling blast of existential loneliness, the deep space of non-existence beyond the skin-thin atmosphere of the mortal.

It didn't change things for me. It didn't break any notion of the sacrality of the human body. It was just my first proper look at what lies under the skin, what lies backstage to our huge, sweeping psychological and emotional dramas – the unsung heroes of existence, the plumbing, winches and pumps that are what allows us to move through the world, experiencing it, enjoying it, being ambushed by all the little failures of system that can send a life spinning off down another track.

If you are at a stage in your life now when you are healthy, perhaps at that middle ground where you are old enough to feel some appreciation for your body, the kind of awareness that really is impossible to the young, in that space before the moving parts, the hips, the knees, godhelpus the heart, start stuttering, then just take a second to feel into it and thank it.

Maybe you will live long enough to miss the things you took for granted, the ability to run over uneven ground at a steady pace, the stamina to make love long into the night, to dance until dawn at a party. These are the great moments when our minds and our bodies work together in our lives and, if you are lucky enough to have a broadly working model, then just occasionally allow that to be enough, to let a brief wave of pleasure and satisfaction wash over you. All of these things will be missed as they go. All of these things make us as human as composing a symphony, or making big emotional mistakes.

◆ ◆ ◆

When we started, the body was what we started with, and it remains the centre of what we do. It is the solid earth of this frighteningly ungrounded experience.

A funeral usually starts with the phone ringing and the sound of their voice tells me what side of the event horizon they are.

The first and sometimes the only question I might ask is, 'What happened?'

Within that phrase can lie a whole life and everything that is within in it, from the medical details of what has led the person to their death to a broader question about how they lived their life and who is in it and who is not.

So we begin by slowing everything down or rather by joining the family in the same time-space, that slightly buoyant unreal time, freed from the dull tyranny of routine and propelled into the world where things that happened forty years ago are more important than the whole unthinking world that carries on around a bereavement, as blind to the loss as a commuter hurrying past the ranks of damp sleeping bags of the homeless.

It is a process of careful descent for us, acclimatisation to the pressure, making sure our own systems of survival are working properly.

There is no rush after someone dies, despite the implied urgency that you are sometimes placed under by funeral directors and family and friends who, bereft of knowing what is the right thing to say, adopt an air of practical urgency.

When is the funeral? What is the date? Cousin Mark is coming from Düsseldorf and he can only get four days off.

Stop.

Stop.

They are dead, it has happened. Allow that incomprehensible phrase to rattle around your head a little, it won't be denied.

Stop and gawp at the still-revolving world, the indifference of the everyday, the astonishing idea that this thing that has happened happens to everything that lives, yet feels like an original one-off event each time, a smashing of a mould.

Let's talk. What happened? Yes, how did they die, but how did they live? This is going to take time, but we have it, because time has stopped.

I go to the hospital, do that balancing act of being casual and friendly with my colleagues in death, alive, still with the quick, but beginning to bring my awareness to the person who has died, to start the process of taking temporary ownership of the body of the person who has died.

I bring them back and we look at them. Sit and look at what life looks like when it is removed, that extraordinary trick, the tablecloth of existence pulled sharply away like a whip leaving the cutlery of our bodies in place, a little moved and rattled, but still recognisable as a place of feasting, of civilised discourse, the set where all the drama happened.

I always talk to a body, certainly when I first meet them. This feels instinctive, not an affected thing, not the deliberate overcourteousness which some very traditional funeral directors do. Some of them knock on the door of their mortuary each time before they come in. I feel a little uneasy at the Victorian children's story that this kind of behaviour implies, the naughty dead talking to each other like puppets in the dark.

I don't believe they can hear me or see me, but I think at the very least pretending they can is a good way to approach the dead with some physical respect.

Once, in the very early days of this work, Claire and I had a short marital row while dressing an old man. Nothing too bad, an irritable domestic spat as we were dressing him, doing practical things like putting our hands down the sleeve of his jacket in order to grasp his hand and pull it through, just like you put a coat on a toddler, snapping at each other as we unfurled his socks onto his cold waxy old man's feet.

We both went quietly back in afterwards without telling the other one to apologise.

He had long been married and, had he been aware of this little exchange, it would have amused him. It would have amused me. And it did feel a little strange to be apologising to someone who I was sure was not really there. But I was starting to understand that we form a strange metaphysical bridge between the living and the dead, and to build and maintain the structural integrity of this relationship it is necessary to perform a little hidden magic, to pretend a little.

We do stand in between the living and the dead, and hold hands with both. We bring the living into the presence of what the person they love has become, and we hold them through the shock of it. And we do that again and again, endlessly introducing this deeply familiar stranger, this heartbreaking contradiction that is the newly dead.

For the families, we are often heroic liberators.

We have returned their beloved's body from the theatre of war, the hospital or the mortuary, where the tumultuous events of the end of their lives happened. The illness, the accident, the slow painful descent into death, the place they changed sides, became part of the past tense, moved into the realm of the ancestor.

We start by bringing them back to a place that is as normal as we can make it. Now we can begin. That medical bit – the drama and urgency, the interventions and dashed hope, with its cast of characters who loom so large and so briefly, whose kind faces or sudden solemnity accompany a family through the agony of loss – is gone. Let's bring them back to a quiet place where we can sit in that ear-ringing vacuum left by the departing life, sit around the matter of them to adjust, all of us.

In some ways it is so simple. Since the beginning, I have been returning the dead to be with their living, making sure that they are clean and dignified, but unadorned, freed from the oddness of embalming and makeup.

We lay them out in a room and fill it with candles and flowers. We have bamboo blinds on the windows to allow as much of the outside in, while protecting the family from passers-by.

Sometimes we just quietly let them in, having explained in detail what they look like, and sometimes they want us to come in with them.

These moments come close to a metaphorical version of the Catholic idea of transubstantiation, what is to us a logistically physical thing to be prepared for being seen becomes, in the presence of the family, the essence of the person they loved.

A presence returns, like a breath of wind on the still surface of water, but it is always that baffling presence of an absence, and that first heartbreaking moment can be too much, and the living need to leave the room.

But they nearly always return within a few minutes, and each time they re-immerse themselves, things start to settle. Their cultural fear of the body disappears and the purity of loss kicks in. And then the beginnings of stability can reestablish itself.

The ever-present, entirely subconscious hope that there has been a mistake leaves us and with that departed hope comes a steadiness that is always surprising to people. It is like watching someone take their first wobbly bike ride or push themselves through the water without immediately sinking. There is a real sense of achievement that can go with being in the presence of your dead.

At this point, often the living are still looking to us to show them the etiquette. We gently show them again and again that the etiquette is to reassume whatever was the tone of their relationships. People die, but relationships don't. They change, but they are still relationships and remain so until we ourselves die.

'Do not speak ill of the dead' is another old mechanism of control, a way of dampening down the flood of raw emotions, that contagious fear again of hobbling the messy, complicated way we relate to each other.

So much is missing from the modern traditional funeral, but one of the most obvious absences is anger. We buried a woman who died from complications from drug use. A complicated and messy life that had broken the hearts of all of her family, one by one, until some of them had hardened enough to think that they didn't care. And then she died and her siblings and parents soon stood around her grave, looking at her coffin resting at the bottom and talking about her – and to her. Suddenly one of her sisters spontaneously and uncontrollably shouted at her, cursed her lack of self-care that had led them all to the lip of her grave. It was unplanned and electrifying, filled with savage love, and one of those moments that taught us an enormous lesson.

Anger is valid, should be welcomed and could be held and facilitated by us, but it hadn't occurred to us until it happened that it was both missing and welcome. That we should be alert to it and try to bring it out to the surface as much as we were trying to bring out the love and the gratitude.

It is okay to speak ill of the dead. It is okay to rage and curse at the dead, if they deserve it. But these are complex moments which need to be uncovered with the delicacy of an archaeologist brushing away the soil from a long-buried artefact and built up to with the steady hand of a model maker.

One of the first emotions to present itself to someone in the first blast of grief is guilt, warranted or not. Guilt is an incredibly opportunistic and adaptive parasite that senses the psyche's vulnerability, that can move into the vacuum created by the protective airlock of shock.

It happens to the most loving and functional of relationships. It can bring enormous shame and, if not gently challenged, can begin to police your entire experience of bereavement, start to whisper persuasive nonsense about what you could have done differently in your relationship, even that you didn't really love them. The shock and the guilt work together like a pair of scammers.

Shock in itself is a wonderful thing, nature's anaesthetic. People always think of shock as being a state you find yourself in after a car crash that needs strong sweet tea, when in truth the shock of bereavement is a much deeper, longer-lasting state, an existential one, which needs all sorts of soothing and accommodating.

Shock is our friend, there to remove us a degree or two from the loop of loss that spools between our head and our heart. But if that conman guilt manages to get his toe in the door, then shock curdles into self-recrimination, turns inward like a hair and can send your bereavement off down a horrible tunnel, a ghost ride where all you can think about are the messier moments of your relationship, the times you let them down, or vice versa, or the last few excruciating months of their illness.

It's normal, it's almost inevitable, but it needs to be nipped in the bud because an exaggerated sense of grief does not help you get to a state of acceptance, does not help you remember them as they were by dealing with how they are.

Sometimes families help us to dress their dead although, as we warn people, it is a deeply practical and sometimes undignified process. But again, we just keep opening doors that people ask if they can come through, checking every time that they know what is going to be on the other side.

I have been showing the living their dead for over twenty-one years now. Leading them into the room like I am introducing them for the first time at a party. The effect it has on people is extraordinary.

We don't force people (how could we?) and each time there is a delicate assessment as to whether it is appropriate or not, and this equation we figure out involves the state of the body and the state of the relationship, and whether the person died unexpectedly or was gently nursed at home.

All of these give us the factors that allow us to make an emotional risk assessment. Our bottom line is that if someone is in two minds about it then they should probably see them. If adamant not, then we respect this.

Some people won't be denied under any circumstances: mothers. There is no power on earth that can stop a mother from cradling the body of her beloved child after a violent death.

Being around the grief of a mother is among the most testing of experiences. Nothing sets off the flight or fight response quicker than somebody embodying your own worst nightmare. Their pain is often unbearable. Paradoxically, some of these mothers we have helped over the years have become our deepest friends. Incredible that they still want to see us, let alone be friends with us, and the relationships can at first be complicated.

We represent that bridge of connection, we become what Freud would see as the transitional object between their child's life and their child's death and sometimes, as their grief advances, we become too painful a reminder of that time and they drop away. But some do stay and we have formed deep and loving relationships, filled with all the normal warm banter of a friendship, but solidified by this extraordinary experience we went through.

One such mother is called Ali and her daughter that we buried was called Anna. Ali is a small, beautiful, funny and earthy woman, with three other children and a lovely husband called Mo. Ali and her family are an incredible unit. Mo and Ali were tight together, and still are. Her courage is a prime example of the extraordinary strength and bravery and love of a mother bereaved, both at the same time the strongest thing in the universe and the most vulnerable.

Anna died in every parent's nightmare, a car crash on the way back from a bacchanalian party.

Anna was twenty-one, strong and beautiful like her mother, the eldest child of her four, growing into that wonderful bit of parenting where they move from being a much-loved child to a genuinely liked adult.

Doesn't always happen, as my mother once pointed out to me, in that short time we had together as adults. You always love your child, she explained, with an unbreakable, visceral violence. Even if they become a grisly serial killer, you can't stop loving them. But sometimes, as they grow into the person they are meant to be, you realise that you like them too, that if you were to meet these fledgling adults as someone else's child, you would like them.

Anna and Ali were in this golden stage. Anna was not perfect, but she was magnificent and a little bit fierce, like most young women today, women that have been parented by strong women and good men, fierce and uncompromising. They have reached the end of the limit of what women have had to take since the dawn of time and it is so heartwarming to see. The revolution will be feminised, not televised.

Anna had gone to a party about thirty miles away from her home town with her boyfriend. Anna had danced until the small hours and then got bored. She was sober, but tired and wanted her own bed, so she got a lift back with a young man who was ready to leave. The driver was probably drunk, over the limit, but perhaps not visibly so – Anna was fiercely against drink driving. They started the relatively short distance home down the motorway.

There is strong evidence to suggest that Anna was asleep when they had their catastrophic crash (they drove into the back of a motorway maintenance lorry), but no way to confirm that. What is certain is that Anna was killed instantly and any awareness and suffering was as short as is possible. These details are deeply important to a family when you have no clear answers.

Anna had suffered catastrophic head injuries. In this country, we don't do as a matter of course the sort of extraordinary, reconstructive post-mortem techniques used by American embalmers, such as the fictional Rico in *Six Feet Under*, the incredibly gifted Puerto Rican 'restorative artist'. Here it is almost unheard of, but we did consider it for Anna, to allow her mother to see her face.

But Ali is a realist and a warrior of the heart. We knew that whatever reconstruction might be able to be done would still be an artificial and uncanny simulation and not what this woman of truth needed. So we had to work around this, and it was Claire who came up with the solution.

Anna's body was largely unmarked. Her primary head injury was what had killed her but, apart from some small cuts and scratches, there was nothing too bad on her torso. Claire prepared a space for Ali where, together, they gently washed Anna's body while her head was covered with a soft cloth. Ali had asked Claire if she could wash Anna's hair, and Claire had kindly but firmly said no, but covering Anna's head, allowed Ali to touch and kiss the body of her beloved daughter, to physically feel her, mother to daughter, to examine each little cut, to weep with her head resting on her daughter's body. There is no grief therapy that can replace that experience. A mother knows her child's body as her own, it is her own. They needed to connect to separate.

When someone dies at twenty-one, they know a lot of other kids, hundreds of them. And the death of someone in this age group is a big social event, so there were close to three hundred young adults for Anna's funeral at a rain-soaked natural burial ground near her house.

I held the ceremony and I talked, as I often do, about how she died. It is the most central and the most unpalatable part of the story, but it nearly always needs to be told, and I am usually the best person to tell it. It spares the family.

People's imaginations fill in the narrative gaps and somebody's death, even one as violent as Anna's, is less brutal than the imagination paints. They needed to know that she was most likely asleep when it happened. They needed to know that it was instantaneous, that she suffered as little as is humanly possible in that situation.

After others had spoken, her mother stood up to speak, the most important, the last word. She told those kids to go home and kiss their mothers and tell them they loved them, that life was short and unpredictable and risky, and there might not be the time they thought they had to say these things that were assumed.

She told them not to get into cars with drink- or drug-impaired drivers. She didn't tell them not to drink or do drugs – she is too savvy a mum to go that far. Her words were unjudgmental and wise, full of a love that visibly burned like a roaring pyre.

Ali later took this message into schools as part of a programme of interventional warnings that she did in conjunction with the emergency services. Ali was the family speaker at these events and her clear testimony without a doubt saved lives, caused young teenagers to reassess whether to get into that car.

I saw Ali recently. She and her husband had moved out of the town they lived in and up on to a village on the moor. She told me that they had a lovely garden, that the moor was all around them and that, on a walk, she had decided she would bring back a large stone in memory of Anna that would form the central part of the fire pit.

Ali is small but, as you have gathered by now, tough, incredibly so. The stone she chose was heavier than she realised and the distance home longer than she realised, but nowhere near as heavy and far as the burden of grief that she had carried and would always carry.

She refused all offers of help from her husband. Ali carried the granite of her pain by herself, the billion years old rock of her eternal love all the way back home.

◆ ◆ ◆

Sometimes the closed coffin is all we have, as time and circumstance have changed a body so much that any real contact with them would be far too distressing. People who have died at home and lain undiscovered for weeks. The man who died sleeping on a beach and was taken out to sea by the incoming tide before being returned to the very same beach a month later. There is no comfort to be had from sitting beside these bodies, they have become something other than recognisably human.

Yet even amid these bodies far gone in decay, there is a beauty and a strange dignity.

I once had to do a funeral for an old man whose body had for some reason been held until a couple of days before by another undertaker. We collected him forty-eight hours before the funeral and, when doing so, it was clear that the elderly undertaker was not coping, seemed close to a breakdown and this was probably, or should be, his last funeral. His fridge didn't appear to be working properly and the old man we were collecting had begun to smell.

It happens. You can never quite tell how quickly a body will begin to decay. A young healthy person killed in some kind of accident will often remain looking like they are just sleeping, whereas someone who has been through cancer and undergone a lot of aggressive radio and chemotherapy, well, their body is ready to go as soon as they die and the decay begins almost immediately.

This man was neither of those, but he was old, the same age as my father would have been had he lived, and they shared some history, both having fought in Burma during World War Two. We brought him back and put him in our mortuary fridge.

His family was small and had been with him at the nursing home when he died, the best place to experience the tipping fulcrum of life seesawing down to death – the slow changes that happen, the relaxing of the features, the disappearance of the minute, etched frown lines of anxiety and pain that almost everyone wears on their face as they die. The simple act of post-mortem physical relaxation is enormously comforting to someone who has had to watch someone they love die.

They weren't coming to see him again before his cremation and, with the slight smell, I was glad. He was being cremated quietly in a day or so in a simple, sealed wooden coffin and he would be in a body bag which would keep the family from the smell. It is very difficult once this process has begun to disguise it. A decayed body is well past embalming, even if we didn't disapprove of it on so many levels, and many undertakers simply try to mask the smell with chemical deodorisers that to my mind simply add another layer of olfactory hell to the proceedings.

It was high summer, hot and beautiful, and at the time we were still living in the mill. We had friends camping in the field and the children were all playing in the river. We had had lunch and with it a glass of wine. I was relaxed, sun-buzzed and content and, after lunch, I went to check on the body of the old man.

I was aware that something was wrong from the moment I opened the fridge.

The correct low temperature of our fridge, as opposed to the insufficient broken one of the ageing undertaker, had definitely lessened the smell, but when I opened the body bag, I saw what had happened.

At some point between the man's death and us collecting him, flies had entered his nose and mouth and had lain eggs in the soft tissue there. They must have hatched into maggots before we picked him up, but were invisible when we collected him.

Even though the coldness of our fridge had made them sluggish, the sight of them was the most shocking thing I had seen so far. They were pouring out of his eye sockets, his nose and his mouth in an almost cartoonish way, like the cover of a lurid horror comic book. I was stunned and appalled.

It was not my fault, but that was irrelevant, as was the fact that his family were not going to see him and the funeral was the next day. I could have resealed the bag, turned the fridge colder to slow them down to torpid inertia and sealed him tight in his wooden coffin; no one would have been the wiser.

I don't know how you think you would react on seeing a sight like this; certainly before it happened to me I knew how I thought I would react – with revulsion and fear – but in fact those were not the feelings that came over me.

I was filled almost immediately with a mixture of compassion and awe, gratitude even. I felt the reassurance one gets when the thing you have been dreading finally happens – and it is nothing like what you expected at all. I felt weirdly but deeply privileged to see this entirely natural process happening, the reality of a decaying body being consumed by maggots. I felt honoured to witness it close up, to see this moment of extraordinary, natural, symbiotic intimacy. But I knew I had to do something about it, to intervene as best I could.

I was completely out of my depth, well beyond anything I had experienced so far and, despite my tenderness towards his body, I still had passing shudders of horror at what was happening.

I decided to try to expel the maggots as best I could, even though they were deep inside his head. The only thing I could think of was to pour small amounts of bleach into his eyes and mouth and, as the maggots reacted violently and tried to escape, scoop them out with a teaspoon.

I knelt beside him on the mortuary floor on that summer afternoon for four hours, murmuring to him the whole time, talking to this man, seemingly far gone in his humanity, but as full of what it was to be human at that moment as I ever would be. I talked to him constantly, apologising for the indignity, speaking to him as if he was a wounded soldier, as in many ways he was. It helped that he had fought in Burma. I knew the sort of horrors he would have seen and this vision would not have been unfamiliar to him. He would also have understood my impulse to try to help as much as I could, the urge to give the dead as much respect as it was possible to, even though it was of no meaning to them.

I thought of all the bodies he had seen like this, that he had been unable to perform this service for, the dead sprawled in ditches and impaled upon bits of splintered wood that would have just been passed by in the shock of battle. I thought of all the horrors my father and grandfather had seen, and for them as well as for him, I attended his body as best I could.

I have never taken a body into my care since without checking the nose and mouth for flies' eggs. An almost vertical learning curve was climbed that day.

CHAPTER ELEVEN

All that is wrong and how to right it

So we went from funeral to funeral, family to family, taking a little bit of knowledge from each of them and passing it on, learning how to do this work through their openness and courage.

At first our funerals, and those of other secular movements, were a bit… busy. There was a feeling that all of the things that the Christian liturgy provided – shared singing, readings from the Bible, call and responses – all of these had to be replicated in a non-religious funeral.

And so there were a lot of things going on: local choirs singing, poem after poem, perhaps even some kind of a ritual that we did together with a vaguely New Age-y feel. All sorts of different things to fill up the space between gathering together and burying or burning the body.

The humanists are a fine organisation and have done so much to keep church and state separated. Their work at protesting against things like faith schools or a visit by the Pope being paid for out of the public purse is exemplary, and they were one of the first organisations to start doing non-religious funerals to any big degree, but their funerals and their celebrants used to be a little preachy about their atheism.

A lot of the families who would say to us they wanted a humanist funeral weren't actually humanist, they were just non-believers. They often used to contradict themselves by asking if they could sing hymns, which was clearly quite irritating to any humanist celebrant who, at that time, used to start their service with a slightly inappropriate, little bit passive-aggressive sermon about humanism and how they strongly believed there was no God.

This was fine if the deceased was a fully paid-up member of the Humanist Association, but often these families just didn't want a fusty vicar and had inadvertently found themselves with the secular equivalent, who would follow up their swipe at organised religion with some rather dull and unimaginative homilies about the seasons changing and leaves falling off trees.

This post-mortem crowing over the absence of God felt at times as grabby as a Catholic funeral mass could be when someone who was brought up a Catholic but lapsed comes back at the last minute for a deathbed welcome back into the bosom of the church. Both felt a bit point scoring. One for God, one for science.

Then there was a sort of gold-rush time for secular celebrants, with several organisations starting up to cater for people's desire to have a meaningful job by training them into this new non-religious priesthood. These new clergy were usually middle-aged retirees, often middle class, with a professional job behind them and an experience around the death of a friend with an inadequate funeral that suddenly meant they wanted to change life direction and become a non-religious celebrant.

No shame in that. It was a moment of vocational vision that had propelled me into this work, and indeed anyone who is working around the dead and the dying who doesn't feel driven to do this work is quickly tossed around and out, but the trouble was there just wasn't the space for the number of secular celebrants who were being trained.

At one point it felt like that for every person who died, three new people had just 'graduated' from some training organisation and were naively presenting themselves to funeral directors, expecting to be doing three funerals a week. The funeral directors were less interested in the content of a ceremony than they were in the cost of the coffin and the number of attending limousines, and indeed the cost of the person taking the ceremony is still generally less than the main floral coffin spray costs. And most of them, frankly, were no good. Not all, but a lot.

It takes a lot of different strengths to be able to successfully hold a ceremony. You need to be part actor, part therapist as well as a good writer, and you need to be finely tuned to the currents of a funeral, able to respond to a shift in mood, think on your feet, let things go which clearly aren't going to work. You need to bring a whiff of a priest about you or, at very least, the air that a powerful lay preacher brings. You need to have big clanging brass balls, an outrageous amount of front.

One of the problems with the religious funerals was not just that people didn't believe any more, it was that the format had become stale, that the congregation weren't listening really – they were quietly murmuring in the back row, while a dusty dull vicar, and now a dusty dull celebrant, started the ceremony with some rather flat preceremonial 'housekeeping' about who the collection was for, where the reception afterwards was going to be, that sort of banal but somewhat necessary information with which a bad funeral starts with.

After forming such a deep connection with a family, having them open up to us about deeply painful family secrets, having worked out for ourselves and clearly seen the structural dynamics of their relationships, it felt a betrayal to hand them over to the ceremonial equivalent of a primary school teacher, who was either going to patronise them about the superstitious beliefs of religion or lose them in the opening salvo by giving it over to administrative details. So we stopped getting in other celebrants all together; unless a family arrived with a specific one in mind, I would take them all.

This was to prove an incredibly powerful thing to do and meant that once Claire and I had met a family and started to form a relationship, we didn't have to bring anyone else into the bubble of intimacy we had started to grow around us.

The downside is that it meant that on top of all the practical things around organising a funeral, not to mention the hours and hours of talking to a family, I had to craft a meaningful and powerful ceremony that was not cut-and-paste predictable, but original and genuine and, above all, honest.

Every time.

I believe you have one good shot at the beginning of a funeral at catching everyone's attention, by setting a tone that shows the celebrant has grasped the essence of someone, flaws and all, and that we might well be talking about these flaws, these blemishes and twisted shapes we all throw. This startles people and grabs them into the moment.

There is a boldness if, as a stranger, you start talking honestly about the dead. A current snaps open and runs around the room. People both tense up a little about what you might say next and relax a bit because it is becoming obvious I have understood who they really were. This initial burst of disarming honesty about them, about us, about life and death, is where it begins and suddenly you are deep in ritual space.

You don't need to blow a conch or ring a singing bowl, though both of these things are fine if appropriate. You just speak clear words of truth and that immediately forms the container within which the thing can be done.

This carries risk. The way that a trained secular celebrant works is that they try and act as the voice of the family. They say what the family want them to say and this involves a lot of checking with the family that the script is correct, that biographical details are all in order, that there is nothing in it which is going to upset anyone. The trouble with this method is that with the endless reading and amending of the script, it can become stale and familiar to the family, and come the actual ceremony, they are barely listening.

Of course it is fresh for anyone at the funeral who is not part of the family, but then the whole thing becomes a performance for them, rather than a ritual that helps the family. Everyone becomes an audience at it, rather than immersed participants in a communal rite.

My ultimate aim when I take a ceremony, when I eulogise the life of someone I have never met, is to show to the family that they have revealed something about their relationship with the deceased that they haven't voiced out loud, that there is something so strong in their connection that it is obvious to me, a stranger.

If I can do this, it feels like the greatest gift I can give them; a vindication of the complexities of their love, an acknowledgment of the entwined nature of our relationships and the hugeness of the human character which can still reveal itself when they are not there. This is a form of afterlife as well as almost an act of a spirit conjuring – to be able to raise a recognisable figure of the person we are there to release, to actually see them. Isn't this all we really want? To be seen in our totality?

And so I took over the ceremonial role, speaking with an earnest urgency and a reckless intensity about people I had generally never met. My way of assessing whether this was working was whether anyone was chatting quietly in the back row. My aim was all in, everyone present to the moment, or I had failed. And that meant carrying along with me the people who did have religious beliefs, who were slightly defensive about what might be about to happen, bracing themselves for a brusque denunciation of the old beliefs or being cajoled into an awkward sharing of a ritual borrowed from another culture, the passing around of a talking stick, that sort of thing. They had to be embedded in it with the rest of us – and this meant not saying anything they could disagree with.

The definition of something we all can agree on is called the truth. It just meant I had to make a leap of faith and judgement that what I was saying actually was the truth. I can hear Pontius Pilate snorting derisively in the background at that.

It still scares the shit out of me over twenty years later, but to date no one has ever said to me that I've got them wrong. But I live in fear of it and it means each eulogy is preceded with a surge of self-doubting adrenaline.

Meaning comes from doing. Our philosophy revealed itself to us as we did it. It began to appear around us naturally. We started to discard all the overbusy ritual substitutions, to strip the experience back and back.

We worked out that you can have too many poems and bits of music, you do make people feel uncomfortable by shoehorning them into cultural behaviour that is outside of their world view, but you cannot have too many people who loved that person talking about them in their entirety.

Talking gently but firmly about a person's faults over their dead body feels like absolution, not condemnation, and in doing so, it releases us all from the guilty secrets of our faults. We are human, and that is an incredible gift and burden, a struggle and a triumph.

But words, powerful though they are, are not enough and, for some people, the possibility of talking at their dead mother's funeral is just too much. I didn't. Too shocked into an awkward silence, an inarticulate numbness of the heart. But there are other ways of participating and these ways started to reveal themselves as we started to instinctively do them.

In a conventional funeral with a traditional funeral director, you have bearers. I have maligned these nearly always gentlemen before and I am going to do so again, though it is not their fault. They are nearly always retired men of roughly the same height. They have usually come from a background which means they are unfazed by death, but they aren't drawn to the job with the sort of emotional zeal that a wannabe celebrant is. They are often retired policeman and they enjoy the blokey bonhomie, the cash in hand and are often just getting out from under their wives' feet for a few hours.

Their job is to carry the coffin shoulder high into the venue, the crem or the church, place it down in a military-style fashion, bow deeply and then skedaddle. If it is a cremation, then their job is done as soon as the coffin touched the catafalque. If it is a burial, they carry the coffin to the grave and lower it down. All important, practical parts of the job.

Straightaway we knew we didn't want them. They were anathema to the participatory feel we were trying to achieve and part of that very male display of the control of tradition. We decided that we would get each family to be the bearers. Now, the ubiquitousness of bearers at the modern traditional funeral is because those chipboard veneered coffins with their gaudy plastic handles have to be carried on the shoulder; if you tried to lift them by those handles, they would simply tear out. So you need men of the same height who are familiar with the raising and carrying of a coffin on the shoulders, a heavy and intimidating thing for someone who has never done it to do.

We don't use those coffins. They are aesthetically ghastly, overpriced and filled with terrible chemicals. We have a small range of environmentally friendly coffins, mainly willow, bamboo or cardboard. And all of them have load-bearing handles. Which means anyone of either sex and height can carry them.

The downside is having to explain to a new bunch of people at every funeral how to do it at a time when they are least able to retain instructions. That's okay. We don't aim for military precision, we aim to offer families the chance to do the last practical thing they can do for a person in this life: carry their earthly remains and lower them into the ground or put them at the edge of the fire.

The day of the funeral of someone you love is a deeply hallucinatory experience, utterly unreal. There is a sea of faces of people you often haven't seen for decades, some since you were a child.

You have been in that strange emotional waiting room, the place between the death and the funeral, for some time now. Hopefully you have had some profoundly moving experience with their body or were lucky enough to have been with them when they died or immediately after their death, but however good these experiences are, the funeral is another level of trippy.

Most people don't want to speak at a funeral and the anticipatory anxiety of doing so often ruins the whole day for them. That doesn't mean you shouldn't do that, and a lot of people think quite wrongly that if they try to speak and become choked with emotion they have failed, but for some people it is their worst fear. The two top recorded most feared things are public speaking and funerals, so when you combine the two, well, boom! Cortisol explosion.

But, if you do the simple non-verbal practicalities – if you assemble with your siblings, joking with each other about the unexpected weight (everyone is constantly surprised by how much the dead weigh, as if it isn't called a dead weight for a reason), feel the physical reality of it all, the rope handles biting into your palms, the lowering straps slipping through your fingers together, as a family, until the coffin rests on the floor of the grave – then you have done more for yourself and the dead than the recitation of a thousand poems can do.

Like everything, grief has a muscle memory, but you have to activate it. Doing these things – carrying the coffin, picking up a shovel to fill in the grave – these things take you out of your head and into your heart through the use of your body. You are imprinting the moment into your collective psyches and you are laying down the framework for good grieving.

I know because I did not do these things as a child or as an adult. Had I done them, I am not sure whether I would have spent twenty-one years urging people to do it themselves.

This 'we're all in it together' approach is particularly useful around children. A friend of mine, who is the youngest of four, like me had her father die when she was young. When she was well into her twenties, she was talking about her dad's death with her siblings and sighed sadly about how much she would like to have actually been there at the funeral. Her brothers and sisters were incredulous. 'But of course you were there, we all were, don't you remember?' She had no idea.

Kids are remarkably blasé around death because up until a certain age, and it is generally agreed to be around seven, the age I was when my father died, you don't have a proper grasp of the finality of it all. Also, you don't yet have the cultural baggage that we all drag around with death as adults, the fears and the beliefs, so if you are a child at the funeral of someone who is central to your life, it can just be another day, albeit a slightly exciting one.

So we bear this in mind when there are children present. We look at their grief, and this day, as a thing that will grow in significance for them as they get older. We try to create a map so they can find their way back into the past.

The image that always comes to my mind is a series of brightly coloured flags, each a hundred yards or so apart, on a snowy landscape. Grief to me always feels like a blizzard, featureless, disorientating and numbingly cold. The idea is that there are actual mementoes of their presence at the day, physical things for them to do, like drawing on the lid of a cardboard coffin or tying labels with messages of love on to the handles, and photographs of them doing these things.

All of our coffins have six handles. The most important ones are at each end, the middle ones are less important, so if a child wants to be part of this experience they can. We have had some very small children actually hanging off the handles going 'wheeeeee!' as they swing from their father's coffin. The idea is that when they return to the whiteout landscape of their long-past grief, as they surely will, then they have a map to guide them back into it, an embodied memory with physical proof, a series of visible flags that takes them back to that moment and their part in it.

We have come a long way from the day when I was absent from my father's funeral and we have brought a lot of people along with us.

To some of the funeral industry, we were not only upstarts, we were traitors to the theatre of it all, Penn-and-Teller-esque, revealing how these incomprehensible tricks were done, all of the ways in which funeral directors proved their worth and made their money. We were turning up in a Volvo, with the dead in a cardboard coffin in the back, getting the family to help us to lift them out and carry them in, and then standing up and talking about their failings. To a working model based on a slightly camp spectacle, with some trite homilies said over the body by an authority figure who would ruffle no one's feathers but conjure no essence either, it was outrageous.

They were right. We were determined to pull down the edifice of low expectations. We were against the theatre of it all – because so much of it is bad theatre.

CHAPTER TWELVE

Extraordinary ordinary people

We had wild plans, some of them outrageously ambitious. We dreamed of opening a combined maternity unit and hospice, a sort of hatchings and dispatchings, with the two units situated around a ritualised central space.

The idea was to try to reintegrate these two ends of life in a way that was different from the drama of a hospital death or birth, to transfer some of the deep peace of the hospice experience to a maternity unit and to bring some of the joy of birth to those who were dying. We imagined this all centred around an inner atrium, a secular temple-like meeting place, where both life events could be celebrated and held in equal regard.

I had visions of the nursing staff being able to switch from one to the other, and what this freedom to move around these most important parts of our lives would do to their emotional morale – how nourishing it might be to be able to move professionally between the end of life and the beginning.

Pipe dreams, perhaps. I think it would be easier to persuade the dying to go there than the pregnant. It takes a certain type of person to get this integrated cross between a monastery and a hospital. Perhaps someone who has had a relative die in a hospice and knew what extraordinary atmospheres they have.

We dreamed, and still do, of redesigning the modern crematorium. Other countries have made much bolder, architectural statements with these utilitarian buildings, creating places of great beauty and contemplation. Here in the UK where our modern architecture bumps along the aesthetic bottom, we are used to things being grim. The Aztecs used to hang gold in the branches of trees they felt the different worlds intersected in. We just make sure that there is sufficient parking and a water cooler in the waiting room.

We dreamed of setting up a natural burial site, which really was a dimensional crossroads, a place of great beauty where the living could be with the dead, and create and perform rituals that were both new and extremely atavistic in their feel. Somewhere where all of our instincts around what and how to be with the dead could arise naturally without any of the embarrassing and self-conscious ways the secular funeral could go, all cosmetic fluff and no heart.

Everything about the way we do death can and must be done better. We were hungry to shake it all up. I still am. That revolutionary fervour has grown not subsided.

The main thorn in the side of the various patriarchal players, the church and the industry, was the charity that had inspired me in the first place. The Natural Death Centre, a tiny volunteer-run organisation set up by that public-school dropout and social engineer, Nicholas Albery, the quiet genius behind so many great ideas such as The Institute of Social Ideas.

The commitment that this generation held to their youthful ideals was so impressive and showed me the oft-confused difference between growing up and selling out. I have tried to do one without doing the other. When they asked me to become a trustee, I jumped at the chance, even though I would be jumping in way out of my depth.

The charity had found itself in a precarious position after the untimely death of Nicholas in a car accident at the age of just 52. It was a bitter irony as Nicholas hated cars and had been on his way to one of his simplest and enduring of ideas, the regular Saturday Walkers Club.

He had broken his neck and been killed instantly, and his death had thrown the charity into disarray. It was Nicholas's enthusiasm and love of self-publishing that had driven the charity along and produced four editions of his *Natural Death Handbook*, a densely packed series of self-published books, filled with information and experiences from people who had stepped outside the mainstream, all of it with a strong countercultural vibe, talking about transcendental things like the death of Aldous Huxley who was injected with LSD by his wife as he lay dying, as well as the deeply practical, such as how to lay out a dead body and how to carry a coffin.

In some ways I was an obvious candidate to become a trustee. A fellow public-school dropout like Nicholas, I had become extremely good at being around the swirling currents of grief and I was not frightened by the horror of death or disgusted by the physicality of some of the situations I found myself in. I was also probably the only trustee of the charity to be directly influenced by the charity in what I did for a living.

I had been an undertaker for ten years when I joined the charity and had one mission – to take the handbook and change its publishing model. Since Nicholas had started the handbook, written by himself, edited by himself and self-published to great acclaim, the internet had become a thing and most of the information that was contained within these densely packed books could now be found online, yet the charity relied upon these book sales to keep it afloat.

It was clear to me that the publishing model had to change. We had to raise this up to what it clearly was: culture. We had to produce something that both inspired people on a practical level to free themselves from the grindingly dull funeral machine and give people the historic and social context for what they were doing. In other words, it needed to move from being a practical yet inspiring directory into art.

This was a slow-burning revelation to me. But I knew one thing. I knew I could rewrite the handbook to make it a combination of a rousingly seditious pamphlet and a practical guide, with an accompanying book of essays covering all of the fringe subjects around death and dying that the Natural Death Centre had been inspired by and alluded to: the inclusive and imaginative rituals that the hippies and their forbearers had inspired, the anarchic and creative nature of the counterculture, the positive experiences of the drug culture that were starting to permeate mainstream society – and what might happen if we started to apply these lessons to how we die and how we cope with dying.

I wanted people to feel the warmth of their spiritual ancestors at their back, to feel their excited encouragement, just as I did. To know that the progressive path was not a new one, that it was as old as our ideas of a struggle between light and dark, and that its central idea, that people have the power, was all we needed when facing any kind of solid authoritarian block.

So we changed the model, we upped the production values and we created a slipcase which contained three volumes. The first was co-written by each of the trustees, each one expert in a specific area. One had run a very successful natural burial ground, another was a palliative care nurse who had helped people die at home for nearly twenty years, another was a fellow alternative funeral director, a solid former academic from Sheffield, on my side but not from my tribe.

There are chapters about grief, ritual and home funerals – all of the practical things that make up the movement.

In my chapter, I covered the timeline, as I saw it, of the birth of the movement; always attempting to link it to the various progressive movements and youth cultures that I saw in its lineage, always trying to honour the ancestors both living and dead, always trying to show that, paradoxically, we walk in the still-warm footprints of those we are overtaking, that progress is really following, not leading.

There was a slim directory of services in the third volume such as good funeral directors, burial grounds and organisations that could help with alternative rituals, but we knew this was all available online.

I had no experience of editing. Still don't really and everybody who contributed to the fifth edition of *The Natural Death Handbook* was unpaid, so it probably still retains an enthusiastically amateur vibe, but one thing I did have was good taste as a curator. I knew exactly the sort of people I wanted to write essays and the sort of diverse subjects I wanted to stitch together.

I wanted the second volume, a book of essays called *Writing on Dying* to range freely across the subject taking in all sorts of ideas, from the very concept of what it meant to be alive, through the beliefs of Animism, to what it felt like to be actually dying. We had essays on the art of funeral death masks and the history of the modern death from the perspective of the history of medicine. I persuaded Dr Sheila Cassidy, a pioneer in the hospice movement, to imagine her perfect hospice in a perfect world, and to talk about that most taboo of subjects, euthanasia.

I brought in artists such as Bill Drummond, the most original man in Britain, whose unfiltered thoughts are always a bracing bucket of ice water to our complacency. Former Blondie guitarist turned esoteric author Gary Lachman wrote about Jung's belief around death. David Jay Brown, a Californian, wrote about the bourgeoning use of psychedelics around the terminally ill, particularly the use of psilocybin and MDMA to treat the anxiety around dying.

I managed to persuade the artist Maggi Hambling to contribute. She had nursed her lover, the muse Henrietta Moraes, to her death and had drawn her dead body over and over again before the undertaker arrived to take her away.

I wrote about my desire to be burnt on a funeral pyre and how the showy, elemental pyre of Dr Price had morphed into such an apologetic non-event that was the modern cremation. A Geordie practitioner of Haitian Vodou wrote a psychically dismembering account of ancestral practice, but the most moving essay came from an American woman called Carla Zilbersmith, a former actor and theatre director who taught at the prestigious Marin College in California.

Carla was filthy, hilarious and dying rapidly from the dreadful Lou Gehrig's disease, or motor neurone disease as it is called in the UK. Her essay was delivered to me under a month before she died. There is an incredible documentary about her called *Leave Them Laughing*, but I would strongly recommend you watch the video on YouTube that she surprised everyone with at her funeral. It is utterly heart-breakingly funny, dirty and deeply moving.

I am so proud of this volume of essays and I tried to spread the remit of the book to include the wide cultural ripples that bounced through the experience of death.

◆ ◆ ◆

The funerals kept on coming, anxiety-inducingly slowly at first, but the strength of our position, the sheer barefaced cheek of our mouthiness struck a chord with people, people like me who had been let down by the industrial religious complex.

We were helped by the quiet support of professionals along the way who could see the power of what we were doing. Recommending a funeral director is an ethical minefield and many old-school funeral directors grease the wheels a little by dropping off crates of wine at local nursing homes and hospices. Some of the large chains resort to some incredibly crass marketing opportunities.

One bunch was looking around for couples in nursing homes who had been married an impressively long time, celebrating, say, a golden wedding anniversary. They would appear with a bunch of flowers, pose for a photo with them for the local press and then disappear, presumably after slipping a card somewhere saying 'Don't be a stranger!'

Our recommendations came from people at the very sharp end of the work who were in a position to gently help people choose. Long-retired coroner's officers, those people who have to deal with the family of people who have died in an accident or an unclear manner of death, would nod approvingly if a family mentioned us. Hospice chaplains, always mavericks, got what we were doing too, could see that it was the opposite approach to the flowers and the wine bribe and would steer people towards us.

And doctors. Doctors who work alongside undertakers in a weird re-enactment of the different levels of our class system and who know more about who is a good undertaker and who isn't than most, doctors would help us.

In the past we have had rival competitors take a body from a hospital mortuary that had been assigned to us, blustering with the mortuary staff that the little old widow had meant them all along. Their mistake at that time was misunderstanding the nature of this little old woman and assuming that because she was relatively poor and living in a caravan park in a static home, she had no power.

Wrong. She was a retired head teacher of a primary school and had been very clear about which undertakers she had instructed. Our rivals, who up to that point we had simply thought of as local competitors, colleagues even, had to sheepishly bring round the body of her husband to us, incredulous as ever as to why anyone would want to use people so defiantly un-funeral director-like, never able to grasp that this was the very reason we had been chosen.

So I make a point of telling people to speak to other undertakers, not just us, to understand that they have time. Even if the body had been collected by a funeral director and they had started to feel uncomfortable with them, they were fully within their rights to change undertakers in midstream.

When we are engaged by a family, we are in each other's life in an intense way and it needs to feel right for everyone. It's rare that we have ever turned a family away because they haven't felt the right fit, but we are not for everyone and this might take a few days for everyone to realise. We don't charge for these brief, failed relationships.

If someone dies in a hospital, the family receive a bereavement booklet outlining some of the practical things that need to be done. Hardly anyone takes this stuff in, being in the first nanoseconds of one of the biggest emotional events of their life, but amid the legal requirements such as how to register a death, there is good advice about shopping around for funeral directors, for not allowing yourself to go with the path of least resistance or, in other words, the first funeral directors you speak to who isn't actually rude. Hardly anyone does this – to look around and contact different undertakers to find the right fit.

Sometimes in this work, quite often, actually, you fall in love with a family. It is one of the best things about this job. So it was with these guys. They were a father and his two children, a son around thirteen years old and a daughter of around fifteen, whose wife and mum, Julie, had died.

They were an ordinary working-class family who had been through an extraordinarily difficult few years and this had knotted them even tighter together than they had been before. Steve, the husband, was exactly the same age as Claire, an old punk music obsessive, and I imagine this was just one of the reasons they chose us.

Unlike nearly every other family who had undergone a family hospital death, they had actually read the bereavement booklet and were interviewing funeral directors in the security of their own home. I think we were probably the fourth or fifth undertakers who had passed through their front room, the rest having been politely dismissed.

It really was like an interview panel. The son, Tommy, the youngest of the family and one of the most extraordinarily emotionally empowered kids I have ever met, sat in the middle of the family group with a notepad, giving off a strong senior vibe.

I don't remember which bit of our conversation swung it for them, where it became obvious that we were a fit, but I can remember the three of them exchanging a glance when we had clearly passed a major test.

Perhaps it was Claire and the husband enthusing over Iggy Pop. Maybe it was our gleeful approval of the way the dad took his son along to wild punk gigs. They would always get tickets which were age appropriate, and this would usually mean that they had to sit in the balcony. They had an agreement where the son would usually allow his dad to go down into the mosh pit for one song. It wasn't a given and the dad would look pleadingly at the son each time. The boy would grant permission with a sigh of 'go on, then'. It was an adorable image, the son looking down with a benign patience at his dad thrashing around in a melee of surging bodies.

They were a great threesome, doing the painful work of becoming one from a foursome. Their mother, Steve's wife, had been through an unfortunate arc of illness which had brought out the best in all of them. What looks like a deep tragedy, a horror show of awful luck can, in the right family, be another chapter of an unfolding love story.

Julie had been a strong, bright woman, gently fierce in just the right way, living the life of a working mother until she was diagnosed with multiple sclerosis. This ruthless and relentlessly progressive illness had put her into a wheelchair, but her family had adapted, skilfully and naturally swapping the roles around from cared for to carers.

It is a hard thing for children to have to suddenly grow up in the face of implacably bad circumstance – to have to let go of their carefreeness, their innocence – but with a tight and loving family, it is second nature. You do all these previously undreamed of things because you love that person – of course you do these things. And life grows around the rocks of misfortune, and things are done and lived with because you have no choice.

And so this family carried on and things were good or as good as an illness like MS allows you to be, but then in a devastating twist she fell gravely ill with sepsis. She never fully recovered and it was a testament to her strength of character that she survived the initial crisis at all as this form of blood poisoning is a vicious merciless illness. But Julie survived, although she remained in hospital for the rest of her life, in a state of semi-permanent coma.

Her family kept her enfolded in their daily life in a way that was incredible. Every day after school, her children would go to the hospital and Tommy would talk to her about his day, keeping a steady stream of loving inconsequential chat, which must have been like the balm of Gilead to her.

It is a much-repeated trope that the last sense to go is our hearing, and new technology, which allows accurate brain mapping to take place, can now stimulate a simple conversation of yes and no between the living and those deep in a coma. I dearly hope this is true because the number of people I have buried whose last days have been soundtracked by the loving murmurs of their family is too numerous to count. The idea that these dying people can hear the litany of love being poured over their bodies is such a comfort.

Julie's condition became worse and her family had to make the heartbreaking decision to turn off her life support. I can't imagine what this feels like. We can empathise and feel into it, but I don't think we can really get close to the depth of sadness that such a moment in life actually feels like.

Tommy had been reading a book to her in the last weeks of her life, picking it up when he had exhausted himself with the idle chatter of his day. It was his idea that he would continue to read to her as she died, and so he did.

I have never come across a more simple act of loving bravery than the one this boy performed for his mother. It was saturated with love and so clearly the thing she would have done for her son, had the situation been reversed. So she drifted out of this life, with the sound of her son reading her a bedtime story.

They constructed the funeral with us, none of it clear in their minds beforehand, just the solid certainty of what they didn't want and who they didn't want looking after them and their mother and wife.

Steve and Julie's punk roots revealed themselves to be the thirsty, strong, nourishing support system that we all knew it was. That freedom from conventional pressure allows a huge uprising of creative energy to rise up, that enthusiasm for creating a ritual which is authentic to your own culture is such a powerful thing that you cannot help but do the right thing; it is the natural flowering of such personal integrity.

So, between us, we created a ceremony that reflected Julie's life and one in which each of them played a part. Julie and Steve's daughter, Rosie, now a talented writer, spoke lovingly about Julie. Steve spoke, and of course we played music that was part of the family anthems.

Julie was buried in a wood at a local natural burial ground and the sincerity of everything that was done that day was deeply moving for everyone, standing in that sun-dappled glade amid the young birch trees and the bindweed.

A traditional Christian funeral ends with a committal, a blessing to send the deceased off into the afterlife, but it is hardly ever appropriate for anyone but a serious believer, filled as it is with certainty of 'the sure and certain hope of resurrection to come'. This is one of the things which happens at a funeral that we have felt the need to replace with a secular alternative. This moment, this consignment of what was a life to the fire or the earth is, after all, always a ritual ending which needs to be properly marked.

It's usually up to me to do it and it can be all sorts of things – poetry mainly, the warm earthy rumblings of Walt Whitman or the speculative mysticism of Kahlil Gibran work particularly well. Or something more obvious but timeless in its sincerity: a word of farewell from each person, the throwing into the grave of a flower or a letter – but it is always up to the family as to how they bring this to a close.

Julie's son decided what we would do. After he, his dad, his sister and a family friend had lowered Julie down into her grave, Tommy pulled up a chair beside her grave and sat down. He had been reading to her as she died, but she had died before the end of the book. There were still four pages left. That boy took out the book and lovingly read it out loud to his mother. We all stood around him, eyes wide with tears, shaking with emotion. When he had finished the book, he put the book down, stood up, took off his jacket and picked up a spade. He and his father started to fill her grave.

We have moved through our working life from goosebump moment to goosebump moment, stood as if in a waking dream while family after family have welcomed us into these incredibly intimate life events.

We have carried coffins onto windswept beaches to the bewilderment of dog walkers to hold ceremonies down by the spume-flecked shoreline.

We have carried an old man in a midsummer twilight into a mature wood he planted himself forty years previously, toasted him with dandelion wine he had brewed weeks earlier and set off a rocket into the deep blue night.

We have helped children fire flaming arrows at an enormous pile of wood, their father's ashes encased in a wooden boat made by the eldest, while the mourners gawped at the audacious spectacle.

We have carried people on circuitous winding journeys that they used to walk around their land, backtracking on ourselves to enter a favourite clearing, stand by a stream, to listen to the birdsong, as they did. Turning the practicalities of such an undertaking, the fording of a stream or the crossing of a fence into a shared task, a practical embodiment of help that is familiar to the farmers who were the mourners that day. This, they understood – the lifting, the doing, the shared struggle to move an object around the land connecting them to the moment – much better than any fancy words or sentimental songs.

We have sat in pubs, the coffin sitting on a table surrounded by quietly attentive dogs, hopeful of a thrown bar snack, while the mourners chatted to each other and the dead, lapsing into silence broken by the sound of pint glasses being put down.

We have followed where people have led us, astonished at the creative bravery of people who take to the challenge as if they have been devising new ceremonies their whole lives, following through doors that we have simply opened to them by pulling down all of the flimsy gaudy falseness we have all put up with for so long.

From the outside, what we were doing looked pioneering, but I was always aware of our roots, the spiritual ancestors who had paved the path before us. We were not just following the families' leads, we were following a well-trodden path.

◆ ◆ ◆

The war on drugs is over fifty years old now and has caused devastation around the world, particularly for the poor and dispossessed. Our hypocritical attitude to the crutches we use to ease our own way through life and the way we view other people's props has long been pointed out. We rush to condemn the use of disassociating and painkilling drugs like heroin for the socially dispossessed, yet cling on furiously to our own painkilling drugs like wine.

The drugs that have benefited me the most have been infrequent treats. I would go so far as to say that the uplifting surge of ecstasy probably taught me to properly love after the trauma of my childhood. And the bewildering visions of psychedelics have placed me humbly within the cosmic tapestry, made me feel no more or no less than everything else that exists.

I have publicly stated my position on this in interviews and articles. I felt it important to jolt my generation out of the amnesia that was setting in, the hangover after the euphoria. I could remember the utopian excitement and optimism, and didn't want that swallowed up and compromised by the pragmatism of old age, put down solely to youthful hedonism. I believed those feelings of solidarity and transcendence were not just drug induced, but glimpses of a different way of being with each other in this world, and I still do.

Upsetting apple carts is a risky business. People always get upset, particularly those selling apples.

One night, early on in the winter, November, a short but bitter hailstorm blew through the town where I lived. It killed a homeless man who was sleeping under the shelter of the Methodist church right on the High Street on which I live.

I knew him a little. He hadn't been there that long and this was 2012, before the current epidemic of homelessness. He was young, just gone forty, and I was shocked by his death. He wasn't a drug user, and only a moderate drinker, it was the sudden soaking and drop in temperature that had given him hypothermia.

I was more shocked to discover that he was actually the third homeless person to die in our small town within the year. I thought if I don't know and I am the local undertaker, then nobody must know.

It seemed obscene to let the council quietly cremate him, so I stepped in and offered for us to do his funeral. I made it clear that we would be doing a public funeral, that Michael deserved to have his life and death publicly discussed, the same as any of us, and that anyone was welcome.

It gathered some traction in the media. The plan was to carry Michael's cardboard coffin up the long High Street that had been his home for eighteen months, carry him up the steep hill that ran from the tidal river at the bottom to the Norman castle at the top. The idea was anybody who wanted could carry his coffin and that we would stop every so often before arriving in the market square near the top, where I would deliver a eulogy, before carrying him to the town cemetery on the outskirts.

When Claire and I arrived with Michael in his coffin at the bottom of the hill and we got him out and placed him on the trestles, my heart sank a little. There was plenty of media – reporters and film crews – but no mourners that I could see, just ordinary shoppers going about their business.

I had heard rumours that some people felt this very public funeral was inappropriate for someone who was homeless. Michael was complex, of course, who isn't, and could be a little hostile and wary of people. I heard that some of the more conservative townsfolk felt that giving a street drinker, possibly a drug addict, such a showy send-off was unbecoming.

Michael did drink a little, perhaps two cans of cider a day, what I would consider the minimal numbing for someone forced to live a harsh life on the streets. Michael's real addiction was gambling – slot machines in particular. Around ten years before he had died, Michael had had a small pay out on a slot machine, just under a hundred pounds, and that was that, he was hooked.

What a brutal pointless addiction that is, the empty promise of another tiny pay out constantly dangling in the imagination. Out of all of the ways we allow ourselves to be distracted from the hardships in life, I honestly believe that gambling is the worst. A miserable form of slavery, capitalism at its worst.

I did a few pieces to camera about why we were doing this, talked to some reporters and then, at the appointed time, turned around to discover over 150 people had silently gathered around Michael's coffin.

Every vulnerable person in town was there, every homeless person and every nearly homeless person. There were off-duty policemen and -women, parents of teenagers who were dangling over the precipice of problematic drug use and toying with the slippery slope of sofa surfing. There was a local woman who suffered from schizophrenia and regularly accused passers-by of being paedophiles. She looked as calm and as present as I have ever seen her, as if her reality and all of ours had finally aligned.

We carried him slowly up the hill, blocking the traffic as we went. We stopped every thirty yards or so to allow other people to carry him by the rope handles of his cardboard coffin. Around eighty people in all carried Michael's coffin.

Fellow homeless men read poems when we paused, but mostly we simply processed in silence. When we reached the market square, I stood up on a bench and said my piece.

I was angry, angry at this preventable death. Angry at a society that actively encouraged this money-stripping parasitic 'game' that took cash off our most vulnerable, and I was angry at the hypocrisy of judging this man and his life. I pointed out that most people I knew with a comfortable job, a loving family and a nice house still anaesthetised themselves each night with half a bottle of red wine, and yet, as Dr Johnson said, we cannot help but delight in stripping the pill barer for the poor.

It was wrong to let these people slip quietly from our conscience, wrong to judge them for their coping strategies, wrong to let them die unnoticed. It was preachy, without a doubt, and, as you've no doubt noticed by now, I am a little preachy, but a good funeral should be anyway. This is where the power of the church worked so well hundreds of years ago. It took an individual death and turned it into a universal lesson because humans are quite selfish and distracted and, unless something is about us, we tend not to pay attention.

Someone described this as funerals as activism and I was certainly seizing the opportunity to say something important because at a funeral everyone is briefly jolted out of their everyday apathy and there is an opportunity to teach everyone an important lesson. I took these opportunities, liberties some might say, to spread our wider agenda about how the way we approach death can ripple through all areas of our lives, particularly around the people we love and interact with.

I laid out these beliefs in my part of *The Natural Death Handbook*, conjured up the spirits of my ancestors, living and dead, calling out not just the funeral industry and the church, but all of us, for our failures, for allowing death to become trivialised, almost privatised, parcelled off from our collective experience, separated from the consequences of our lives and the inevitable indifferent response of a society we tolerated and enabled.

And we acted out our opposition to this state of affairs through the funerals we did, striving for honesty and context, participation and understanding, forgiveness and redemption. All old ideas, but ones which were not owned by religion, but were part of a deep, shared morality that everyone recognised.

Co-writing the handbook with my fellow trustees felt like setting out a manifesto. All of our ideas about how death and dying could be different were refreshed and restated. In it, we began to turn information into culture, advice into philosophy, grief into art.

CHAPTER THIRTEEN

Tending the bone orchard

It felt as if things were really coming together for us after the publication of the handbook – and so they were, as we finally were offered the chance to start up a burial ground.

To set up and run my own natural burial ground had been one of my ambitions from the moment I became an alternative undertaker. When we started out, there were hardly any natural burial grounds in the UK. The first one was started in Carlisle by a visionary man called Ken West, who ran a large municipal cemetery.

The idea was simple. Cremation was an environmental nightmare, belching out chemicals, heat, gas and actual tiny particulates of people in the form of sooty ash. Churchyards were full and, besides, people were less religious, so an idea formed of burying people simply, unembalmed and with the minimum of chemical makeup, in their coffins on land, which would then be managed for the benefit of the local ecosystem.

Some of them were set up as woodlands, with a tree planted on each grave (sometimes a bit problematic in a practical sense as trees are often fickle creatures that die or have to be thinned and nobody wants the tree that marks their mum's grave to be the one that dies) and some are managed as wildflower meadows.

They are unconsecrated ground, in other words, not blessed as a designated burial ground by the church, mainly because in doing so they became subject to an enormous and ancient rule book about what could and couldn't be done.

They have a number of obvious social benefits. They protect land by establishing a serious community interest that any developer would find extremely hard to challenge – digging up dead people to allow an out-of-town retail park to be built is a tough sell. They provide a haven for flowers, insects and wildlife in general and they allow people to have a little bit of a natural wilderness that they can visit, a place of quiet contemplation that is much needed in our busy urbanised lives.

You would think that this idea would be universally accepted as a good thing, but you would be forgetting the powerful fear that is unconsciously raised around death and anything to do with the commercial nature of how we deal with it. At the time, I had not realised how society's discomfort around death would coagulate around something so obviously needed as natural burial sites.

People really don't like to be reminded that we die. I get it. Not a day goes by when I don't think of it and this bothers me. It is always there, gaining ground on us all, like a posse sleeplessly riding through the night. And this discomfort around death manifests in all sorts of ways.

These feelings of disgust and horror manifest themselves in all sorts of ways. When a funeral director might try to set up a new premises on a high street or when someone tries to establish something as obviously good and benign as a natural burial site. I have seen these things happen, and I have had them happen to me.

I tried to establish a natural burial site, while in the first flush of my messianic enthusiasm, on a field I owned behind my house. I naively sent everyone in the parish a letter explaining what I was aiming for before I applied for planning permission. When that planning permission was turned down, I had the chance to see what the local objections were.

It was interesting to say the least. My neighbours – those who had lived there the longest, some of them for fifty years – were filled with enthusiasm and wanted to book their plots there. The newest arrivals, people who would generally sell up within the next few years, objected the strongest.

Traffic was the peg they hung it on, even though I proved it would be so negligible in its use that they would barely notice it. One neighbour complained that it would spoil their view of my house as they drove past because there might be cars parked outside.

Another strong and repeated objection was that it was a 'get rich quick' scheme. They had done some rudimentary sums based on the size of the land (about two acres) the size of a grave (roughly seven foot by three foot) and had come up with some ludicrous figure.

To anyone with an ounce of common sense it was clear that these figures were nonsensical, that people were buried one grave at a time, not en masse. That it would take decades to reach the sums they were talking about and it would, in fact, be a modest and steady income for what was extremely hard work.

But this kind of thinking bypassed their logical side and went straight to their reptilian brains, which told them that here lay death, and this person wanted to profit from that death, that this person was a cheerleader and enabler for death. Deeply buried in their head was a commingling of fear and disgust, appalled that anyone could do this work and would repeatedly put themselves into the furnace of sadness, and loss over and over again. I have to say it sometimes baffles me.

I saw this when a friend bought an old carpenter's yard in Kentish Town in order to move her high street funeral parlour off the main road and into a leafy back street. It was completely unobtrusive, but an enormous grassroots campaign sprung up among the largely middle-class professionals who lived in the area to prevent it. Her car was vandalised, graffiti appeared as did posters everywhere. It was utterly bizarre. This was a small, local, progressive undertaker serving the area she lived in, who was being used by these same professionals when their mothers and fathers died, but somehow its discrete assimilation into their street tainted it. And in a part of London plagued by street crack use, prostitutes and often murder. But the silent corpse of a local grandmother? Fetch the flaming pitchforks.

Such is the power of revulsion that death brings. Such is the strength of the social othering that people who work with death attract. So when my application for a natural burial ground on my own land got turned down and I went to a public meeting for another proposed one that had such a strong negative turn out you genuinely would have thought they were suggesting setting up a halfway house for sex offenders, I realised that this was not going to be an easy sell and that if we genuinely wanted to set one up, we would have to find a large private landowner to do it with, somewhere where any nearby houses wouldn't be able to object.

We tried a couple. Port Eliot, the former monastery that lay on one of the arms of the Tamar Delta between Devon and Cornwall, was a possibility but, when you deal with the aristocracy, they often have a financial attack dog between you and the final goal. We failed because our bank accounts were empty and we were thought of as part of a long line of chancers wanting to milk the estate with an idea. Deeply annoying and a little humiliating to be sent packing by a Thomas Cranmer-style figure – but that's how aristocrats keep rich and fools like me shed it all in the name of conscience.

We crossed the Tamar border into England and the slightly more forward-thinking county Devon, particularly the town in which I now live, Totnes.

The forward-thinking and alternative reputation of Totnes comes from the patronage of one of the richest women at the time and certainly one of the most visionary, Dorothy Elmhirst. With her husband Leonard in 1925, Elmhirst bought a stunning, ancient and crumbling medieval estate and poured money and ideas into it, particularly those of the artistic and intellectual polymath Rabindranath Tagore, whose revolutionary ideas about education and the emancipatory ability of arts and crafts to regenerate a stagnant rural economy were to create one of the richest idea generators of the twentieth century, the Dartington Hall educational and rural regeneration project.

The Elmhirsts implemented Tagore's idea of a democratic school with no set hierarchy or division between the sexes, but with a broad liberal agenda and, while the school was eventually to end in an inevitable welter of sex and drug scandals, finally closing in 1987, the college and the Elmhirsts' artistic influence would go on to have an incredible influence on post-war liberal culture, good and bad.

The bad took the form of questions raised in 1938 in the Houses of Parliament by MP Captain Arthur Smith who said the school was raising children to hate their parents. His heady take was that it was a protohippy commune with satanic communist undertones and was satirised in a novel by the right-wing horror writer Dennis Wheatley in *The Haunting of Toby Jugg*, a frothy concoction of sex and socialism, giant spiders and black masses. I know that kids had a good time at Dartington but I doubt it was that good.

The upside was the fertile European cultural mix, particularly around the staff of both the school and trust, and this mix of art and intelligence, of culture and progressiveness was to ultimately flower into the policies that became the Welfare State, probably one of the most important political ideas the world has ever seen.

Dartington was the Mecca for the liberal intelligentsia of the twentieth century and was frequented by people like the Huxley brothers, Stravinsky, Virginia Woolf, even Paul Robeson, the Black American actor, athlete and baritone, and radiated art and culture far beyond the environs of the immediate town. But, by the time we became tenants on the estate, decades later, setting up our premises in one of the old school stables (coincidentally where an extremely unhappy Lucian Freud spent much of his time at the school, sleeping on hay among the steaming horse flanks), the Trust was in some disarray. The art college, which was the final legacy of the school, was shut down to public outrage, and the Trust became an organisation in a messy retreat from possible bankruptcy.

Such is the curse of being bankrolled by such a genius philanthropist with seemingly bottomless pockets. As soon as Dorothy died in 1968, her family swooped in to reclaim what they saw as an incredibly costly vanity project and, over the next few decades, the entire project slowly collapsed; first the school, then the art college.

It is now in a state of rebirth and a smaller version of the art college has been reinstated. I wish it all the luck in the world – its legacy extends throughout the arts, educational and the environmental world in ways which people just couldn't conceive of – but they were not at their most visionary when it came to giving us some beautiful land in which to try to implement our own vision for the best natural burial ground in the UK, despite having invited us to work on the estate with the intention of us establishing one, due to being in an advanced stage of crisis management.

So we were headhunted by Dartington's sister estate, the Sharpham Trust, a stunning house on one of the serpentine twists of the river Dart that flows from Dartmoor to the sea through some of the most beautiful countryside in Britain – the Dartington Hall estate and the town of Totnes, where it becomes tidal.

Sharpham was set on one of these bends of the river and the hilltop they suggested as a burial site is one of the most beautiful places I have ever seen. We accepted their offer to set it up and run it immediately. This was to prove one of the best and most challenging things we have done in our twenty years so far.

Stephen Grasso, a working-class Geordie practitioner of African diaspora religions like Haitian Vodou, describes setting up a burial ground as 'planting a bone orchard'. He is right. It is a serious business which requires attention on many different levels, practical and metaphysical. In fact, Stephen Grasso's practice of diaspora religion, which he sees running strongly through the cultural currents of immigrant Britain, particularly South London, as both a haunting of and a reckoning of our colonial past, was to strike a particular chord with me, immersed as I was in the world of the dead and draped in the bloody bodies of my own colonial ancestors.

By now we had used dozens of natural burial grounds and I had seen almost all of the rest of them in the country through my work as a trustee of The Natural Death Centre.

They varied so widely, from token unmown areas of municipal council-run cemeteries to small, one-acre sites adjoining the cottage of an eccentric old lady, who in past years would have been undoubtedly condemned as a witch because of her knowledge and understanding of the natural world, to giant corporate beasts with a tranche of shareholders pushing for more and more bodies in the ground, more sales, more money.

Some of these green burial sites were just corporate bandwagons jumping on greenwashed versions of the real thing and it showed. They ignored core ideas about natural burial such as burying bodies in shallow graves to ensure as rapid a decomposition as possible. The whole six-foot deep thing means that there is almost no bacterial action to break a body down, it is just too deep and, in traditional graveyards which bury spouses on top of each other, the graves can be even deeper. Of course, burying two people in one grave up to eight foot deep means more money for the operator, so it was a very good way of separating which sites were purely about the bucks and which sites had a philosophy that prioritised the natural world as much as it did the human.

Some of the sites were beautiful and genuinely managed with the ecosystem in mind. Others were serried ranks of neglected graves, allowed to overgrow without any intervention at all. Graves in these sites would be quickly lost and relatives would hunt forlornly for their relative among the undergrowth. A betrayal of the whole idea of natural burial and its benefits for grieving – the inevitable moving in on a good idea by venture capitalists.

The Sharpham Trust couldn't have been further removed from this type of organisation. A charitable trust established by one of Dorothy Elmhirst's children, it had begun as an informal Buddhist community and grown into an organisation that offered young people, often with severe physical or social difficulties, an immersive rural experience.

The hilltop they gave us to use was incredible. It looked straight out over the serpentine mud-flanked curves of the River Dart as it made its way to the sea in the distance, and it had a 360-degree view of the surrounding undulating hills, including a dramatic panorama of Dartmoor on the horizon to the left. With sharp eyes you could, on some summer days, see in the distance the crop circles with which I was slowly encircling the town.

The land had been farmed organically and had never been ploughed, just grazed by sheep and cattle. It was and remains one of the few fields in the area that maintains a traditional wild natural grassland, untreated by chemicals and intensive farming and home to an astonishing variety of insects and animal life.

Hares, those most haunting and otherworldly creatures, lollop through the high grass. Skylarks rise into the sky with great theatrical timing and, as we started to lay people down into shallow graves and leave the turf on top to become what Walt Whitman described as 'the uncut hair of the graves', there was an explosion of field voles, mice and insects, who found the grave mounds irresistible.

This, in turn, attracted more birds of prey; raptors like kestrels and buzzards and also the stealth fighter, silent, ear-popping flights of barn owls. At the last funeral we did there, there were at least 150 people present, but this was not enough to stop the steady hunting of a kestrel, hovering over the mourners as she calmly tried to fill the beaks of her nearby brood. It seems that the more we fill the field with humans, dead and alive, the more the animal world returns to thrive on the deliberate and thoughtful physical management of it.

But this was many years away from when we first stood on that hill, breathless at the beauty and possibility of it all. For me, everything starts with a circle and so we made our first move in demarcating this land from agricultural to ritual by making a fire circle.

Even the best burial grounds were missing what we felt was a ceremonial heart, a fire to gather around after the grave had been filled. A shared point of remembrance, the ritual centre of it all.

We chose a point in the exact middle of the field, drew a circle with paint about ten feet in diameter, and dug the turf off it.

This would become what is known as The Ancestor's Fire and, if you were to wander up to Sharpham Meadow today, it is not unusual to feel the warmth of the embers from a recently lit fire. Give people the tools for ritual and they will use them. The first fire that was lit in the pit was on the summer solstice of 2014, when the burial ground officially opened. Since then, it has burned well over a thousand times and at least eight people have had their cremated bones scattered in it. The idea is that each time it is lit, the fragments of bone deep within it emit a glow of remembrance, even if those stood around it don't know this.

We remember each other in ways known and unknown. The fire radiates out its physical warmth and its emotional heat to the graves, which would soon begin to creep nearer it. The fire became a focal point for rituals around release and transformation. Unread letters to the deceased would be burnt on it, families would sit there on short summer nights until the dawn came up and the tiny fragments of bone would glow, unbeknownst to the mourners, a fiery fragment of remembrance that turns the fire pit into half human-half carbon, mingling with the others into an anonymous permanent remembrance, marking the ground, which will be physically measurable to archaeologists in an unimaginably distant future.

The rituals grew quickly as people 'got' the fire. The eternally familiar crack and hiss of a fire would immediately transport people to a place of semi trance; it would activate deep things inside them, prehistoric feelings of the importance and symbolism of a fire, intentionally, on our part, echoing our ancient history of pyres that stretched back to Stonehenge and its ritual burnings of high-status people.

We are the fire people, not just the Vikings, and the transformative nature of fire, the energetic chemical exchange is about so much more than the release of solid into gas and heat; it is about beautiful but permanent change, security and warmth, and the visions we see in its shifting heart.

Now the fire has a surround of eight small weathered wooden plinths, just short enough to comfortably sit on, and all with representations of the setting sun and rising moons in their different stages facing the right directions. The physical limit of the fire is bound by a beautiful iron uroboros, the symbol of a snake eating its tail and representing time and rebirth, death and the underworld that came from ancient Egypt and is found in all cultures from Norse and Christian to Amazonian Indian tribes.

The sculpture was created by the artist Robin Lacey and it is inscribed with brass lettering that says 'In my end is my beginning', the brave final words of Mary Queen of Scots and used by T.S. Eliot in his circular poem of existence *Little Gidding*. He and a few women who have spouses buried there quietly maintain it, like priestesses guarding an inner chamber, so when we come to use it, it is fresh and bright.

The fire has become a focal point of group ritual and we all, both guardians and bereaved, meet up there once a year on the second of November, All Souls Day, to perform a fire ritual of remembrance with the families and friends of people buried there.

It is our misty and damp take on the Mexican Day of the Dead, which I feel is too often imported over to the UK inappropriately culturally intact, with its warm and spicy Catholic, Amerindian roots jarring with our dour Northern nature, our dark and wet November, the autumnal rot and decay of our wild hedgerow fruits, the cut and blackening stubble in the fields – all of these, to us, are a long way from the heat and the sugar skulls and primary colours of the Día de los Muertos.

But these pagan-ish gatherings were far in the future when we dug out the turf circle and I raked out the stones that lay just under the sod and threw them on the edge of the field. It would take a while to encourage families to incorporate fire into their burial rituals and use it to mark dates on the calendar. First we had to start to bury people on the land – and what an extraordinary process this was, planting people one at a time into this hillside, far above the glinting estuary.

A cob shelter was slowly constructed, made using the traditional method of mixing clay and straw and stone that is called wattle and daub, all sourced from the estate and slowly sun baked into a version of a solid wall, a technique used since pre medieval times. The roof was turf and this beautiful ellipse-shaped shelter, with its open side perfectly framing the hillside and the view of the estuary and far-off sea, is now the start and often the focal point of the ceremonies.

Word was spreading that this beautiful field was to become a burial site and we intended to open it officially on the summer solstice in 2014, but our first funeral came unexpectedly early and was for someone who so clearly should be buried there that we had to do it.

Andrew Peterson was a gloriously eccentric individual who lived in a caravan on the Sharpham Estate, actually in the farmyard that was the nearest dwelling to the burial ground, just a bit down the side of the hill. He was an odd job man, a wild bearded eccentric who performed the twentieth-century role of the eighteenth-century hermit for the estate to perfection. His wild ways were tolerated, his practical skills much needed and he was greatly loved for his hedonistic freedom and love of homemade wine and weed.

Too unkempt and ornery, he was one of those people that the modern world has little time for. Nowadays social services would have swept in and placed him in some sort of sheltered accommodation, where he would quickly have died of ennui but, as it was, he managed to maintain a wild and free life right up until his end, his caravan always a source of much merry befuddlement for his frequent visitors.

At the same time as we were busy setting the ground up, Andrew was diagnosed with diabetes in the most horrible way possible. A neighbour in the farmhouse heard him screaming in pain and called an ambulance, and it soon became clear that his diabetes was advanced and his leg needed to be amputated. He returned from this surgery quite quickly and put an extremely brave face on it, managing to adapt his Land Rover to drive with a homemade hand-held clutch. Undoubtedly illegal, but Andrew wasn't much bothered by the law.

He soldiered on in his modified vehicle for a while, but it soon became obvious that his life mission of being the person you called when you need a wall rebuilding or a tractor restarting were over, and so he quietly and undramatically drew up plans for his own death.

Andrew left a note on his caravan door telling whoever got there first not to open it but to call the police. He shot himself through the roof of the mouth and the calibre of bullet was just enough to pierce his skull on entry and kill him, but not to leave an exit wound. Neat and as untraumatic as possible for those, including us, who had to deal with his body.

There is no one form of suicide, no one common theme. There are the spontaneous suicides of teenagers, swept away in a storm. There are those overwhelmed by the black fog of depression that has haunted and goaded a person their whole life. These are the most frightening, the most unable to reason with. They carry the gravity of a black hole.

There are the terrible self-obliterations that come when a person has done, deliberately or accidentally, an awful thing that haunts their every waking moment. And then there are the rare suicides like Andrew's, a deeply pragmatic and understandable thing, not entirely free, I'm sure, from a last-minute surge of fear, but different from the others. A grown-up decision that life isn't going to get any better and that what they actually live for has gone.

Claire and I hastily dug our first grave, months before we had planned, and dressed Andrew and placed him in his willow coffin. His funeral was large and took place at the burial ground, all within sight of the caravan he had taken his own life in. The mourners were a mixed bunch of people who had enjoyed his outlaw company and local farmers who had valued his gung-ho approach to a farming crisis.

The farmers, themselves a profession much given to suicide and notorious for not expressing themselves verbally, did exactly what they should, grabbing shovels and taking it in turns to fill his grave, silent tears running unremarked down their sun-browned cheeks. This is how you sculpt grief. Physically, wordlessly, or at least after the truth has been spoken by someone.

Andrew's burial marked the opening of Sharpham Meadow with what felt like an ancient and deliberate dark blessing and that feeling of maintaining a temple, performing an ever-unfolding ritual never left me for the four years we ran it. Even now, as we return to bury folk, I feel the same sort of connection and obligation that those who created those ancient stone circles of Avebury or Callanish must have felt. Our interaction with these places is as significant and important as the places themselves. We are our own sacred sites.

Of course, for some of the more mainstream funeral directors who use Sharpham, they see a lovely view but no more. They rarely offer families the use of the fire pit and perhaps consider the beauty of the place and the reluctance of mourners to leave it as an inconvenience, used as they are to multiple visits to a crematorium in one day, in and out, rather than hours and hours lying on a hillside watching the clouds of our mortality scud away.

One funeral we did quite recently involved a small number of family mourners, led by the daughter of the woman who had died in midsummer. They were an adventurous gang, filled with the roaming spirit of the naturally curious. The funeral was small, just six members of the family, and they arrived the night before, a glorious July evening. We brought up the body of the mother in her coffin, opened it and placed her in the cob shelter. Her family lit the Ancestor's Fire and sat around it, even pulling out sleeping bags and a picnic.

Claire and I went home, and they sent us a photo of them lying in their mum's grave. It was eerily beautiful. We returned at around 4 a.m. and they were gathered around her, laying flowers inside her grave and her open coffin.

As dawn came up, we carried her to her grave and lowered her in. Very little was said, it didn't need to be. What could beat dawn rising up over an open grave? This is the essence of the funerals we tried to facilitate at Sharpham Meadow.

Setting up and managing a natural burial ground was both the best thing we did and the most stressful. It was an incredible privilege to have some input into how to fold ritual and intention into this hillside, to facilitate the growing of a commingled community of the living and the dead, not bound by religion but forged in the fire of mutual loss, to bring us side by side with our ancestors, and to offer a space where ritual could naturally evolve.

The funerals were all very different but even if I wasn't doing the undertaking, I felt that each person being laid down there was entering my care. The place was open to other undertakers, so I would greet them and make sure that the grave was dressed for them, that they had everything they needed.

I began to formulate a series of rituals around the running of the place. As each funeral left, I would pull the still-smouldering logs apart, so the embers from that fire could be used to light the next, an eternal flame sleeping within the blackened charcoal. I would rake the fire pit before the next funeral came, whether they were using it or not, clear it of any nails or extraneous pieces other than the charred remains of the wood from the previous fire, which would be used to light the next.

It was extremely important to me that the fire pit stayed ritually clean, especially once it held cremated remains in its bed. It could not be used to burn rubbish, paper cups and the like. Fag butts or beer bottle tops were a desecration. It is The

Ancestor's Fire. And I would rake the soft grey sand that lay in the middle of the ceremonial shelter into zen-like circles, swirls of shapes that would welcome the mourners, whose first footsteps onto this swept ground would mark the start of ritual space, the beginning of the funeral.

The way we ran the graveyard was the same way we ran our funerals generally: communally. There have only ever been two people working in The Green Funeral Company. Even when we tried to bring in other people we could barely afford to pay, it would be to help with the admin, we would still operate in a two-person team.

This, of course, meant that the carrying and lowering of the coffin had to be done between us all. It is such a simple and powerful thing, to remove those professionals who do the lifting and the lowering. Each time, as a funeral comes to its ceremonial conclusion, I gently approach the family members who have agreed to do this thing. Each time they look startled and out of their depth. We go through the same simple reassurances, repeat the simple instructions as if we were instructing them to step slowly out of the wreckage of their car: 'Not that hand, the other hand, yes, facing towards their feet. Yes, we always carry a coffin feet first, otherwise it feels like you are carrying them backwards. Ready? All lift together. Yes, they are heavy. It's not called a dead weight for nothing.'

They follow me across the meadow, threading our way between the grave mounds until we reach the open mouth of the grave. Everyone leans out awkwardly as we shuffle along the planks, placing the coffin on two hazel staves, beside the thick webbing of our lowering straps. Hands grip the material as they take the weight, Claire removes the staves, the straps slip through their hands, soaking up more sweat and dirt, more emotion.

The weight is what stays of the day, the muscle memory of loss. The heft, the solidity of it all.

It is only a couple of feet down until the coffin is resting on the bottom. The straps are pulled up, the portal begins to close. By this stage, even the most detached people are fully involved, are completely in the moment.

The grave suddenly seems less daunting than when we first talked about it.

The surrounding planks are pulled away, jackets are taken off, ties loosened, and folk start to pick up the four shovels lying on the pile of grave earth. The filling in of the grave doesn't take long and is a hypnotic spectacle. Men and women passing shovels over and backfilling, doing the last thing they can do for anybody on this earth, covering the coffin until it is gone and the cut turf is heaped upon it.

Long after each family had gone, I tended each grave after it had been backfilled, met the stone mason there to lay the hand-carved head slate flat into the ground. I cleared the flowers a week or two after they had wilted. I marked the ground out for the gravedigger for the next one, even thinking about who would appreciate being buried next to whom, or more often, which family of mourners would benefit from bumping into each other.

I got the men who cut the grass to make paths through the heads of the long grasses connecting the fire pit to the graves, corridors that led from the roundhouse to the mounds of the graves, so that a visitor would be led naturally around the nervous system of the place, find themselves at the ritual beating heart of the fire and then be led back down to the graves or back up to the head of the field and the ceremonial shelter.

I would walk out of the town and up onto the hill in the evening, accompanied by my old dog and my teenage stepdaughter. She would try to hula hoop her troubles away in the dusk as I patrolled the growing aisles of the grassy dead, my fellow townsfolk, their fathers and wives, their sons and their daughters. The hill started to fill up with the long lived and the cut too short.

We had been undertakers for thirteen years before we started running Sharpham Meadow and we had got used to the level of stress that went with the promise, the undertaking, to look after the living by dealing with the dead. I had got used to the idea of being told that we 'held' things very well.

Holding things. Such a delicate, nebulous term, and one that is very hard to understand until you 'drop' the space you are meant to be holding. Once you have accidentally dropped the holding of the space, then you have some appreciation of what it is you are doing when you successfully take a group of people through the process of mourning a life and laying that body down in the ground. The margin for error around a funeral is minute and things do go wrong, especially in the intense and stripped back way we do things, and what might make one family roar with laughter and say 'that is so like her' can make another family's pent-up disfunction explode with anger.

In running a burial ground, you lay yourselves upon the longer-term, more complicated parts of bereavement, what psychologists call 'distorted grief' and you can become a lightning rod for the currents of rage, reasonable and unreasonable, that swirl around death. Trivial but actually environmentally important things like what can and cannot be planted on a grave, exotic plants, solar-powered fairy lights or the permitted lettering on the headstone can suddenly assume the importance of the Paris Climate Accords.

You become a human manifestation of the rage people feel at mortality and that is a hard burden to carry, seeing as death is already a permanent floater on the greasy surface of my mind's eye.

Running Sharpham Meadow was where we first felt something from families other than the utter relief and gratitude for helping them through a death. We felt their anger, and it shook us and lit the process of burnout that we both had to pass through.

We ran the burial ground for about four years, before handing it back to the Sharpham Trust to administer. The paperwork was becoming a full-time job and the unresolved grief that accompanied it was an added stress. Managing something like a burial ground wasn't really what we did. We were a tight two-person team who parachuted into the most traumatic moments of people's lives to attend the wounded and get them through the immediacy of what had happened, we were not administrators. But we had shaped the burial ground to the pattern we thought would work and we had enabled so many people to have a funeral experience they couldn't have dreamed they might be able to have.

The people of the town had taken it to their hearts and the framework of rituals that we had established around the fire pit continue to this day. It is a place where the people of Totnes meet in sorrow and in love. On summer evenings, it is dotted with families sitting beside the graves of their families, sharing a beer or eating a picnic. The fire pit is often warm from recent use when I walk up there. Perhaps in our own way, we have managed to create something closer to the communal rituals of Mexico than we ever thought we would.

CHAPTER FOURTEEN

Don't be afraid, you're already dead

As a way of trying to cope with the stresses of both managing a burial ground and dealing with the pressure of all of the grief I carried, I turned more and more to ritual.

And through this strange mixture of land management and the entwining emotional architecture of grief that grows through it like bindweed, I began to examine with my own beliefs further, practising what I used to think was a form of magic, but what now I realise is probably closer to art. Perhaps I just discovered that art and magic are either ends of the same bootstrap.

Some of my magical acts, such as the more extravagantly ritualised making of crop circles, were about the desperate need to release the growing load of grief I carried. But these were small, brief events, land punctures, mirages almost, a part of my increasing practice of dabbling with forms of magic and art to try to drop the emotional weight of what we did in order to keep from having a breakdown.

We had begun by burying strangers, then friends' parents and now we had begun to bury friends. It hurt. The weight of tragedy that we encountered on an almost daily basis needed to be lifted somehow and playing around with ideas of magic and the occult really began to help. It gave me a point to focus on while everything around me was spinning.

Some of my ideas around magic were about trying to act with intention in the world and pay attention to the remarkable everyday. The difference between stage magic and the sort of magic that could be described as modern occult is obvious.

One, magical entertainment, relies on distracting the attention, getting you to focus on something trivial while the swap or exchange, which is the magical punchline, is sneakily performed. The other, the occult, requires you to do the opposite – to see the miraculously mundane all around you, to focus on the dazzling obvious that we overlook all the time, the transpersonal coincidences that bestrew our paths that we can read meaning into as we like. Modern occult practice, particularly that of chaos magic, involves trying to align those coincidences to act as stepping stones for your own advantage.

Nearly all of the things that I classed as magical, or shall we say accidentally occult, I have interpreted retrospectively. I am a great believer in doing something, then realising what it was about later.

I started to play around with these ideas, looking for something to bring me some relief from the ever-present feeling of omnipresent death. I realised there was an itch to be scratched through the repeated practice of ritual.

In our house, I had a Perspex square of shelving that Claire found in the dump. It probably came from a school lab or somewhere similar.

It's about three-foot square and the shelves are random sizes, some only an inch or two wide, all about six-inches deep. I hung it on the wall in an alcove and behind it I stuck a collage of all of our dead relatives as well as heroes of mine, photos of ourselves and our families, spiritual ancestors like Malcolm X, even photos of some of the people we had buried. I filled the shelves with all sorts of weird things: dried sprigs of gorse handed out as buttonholes at a moorland funeral, images of skulls and saints, odd objects that had to be explained to the casual viewer: foxes, teeth, my mother's perfume bottle, old clay pipes, small silver cups my grandfather had won in 1919.

It became an ever-evolving thing, which could be looked at a thousand times from many different angles, casting many different shadows and revealing different lines of connection and transmission – every time a candle illuminated it from a different angle, new lightning bolts of generational pain or inspirational influence would light up like a computer graphic. It bears more than a passing resemblance to the author Iain Banks's divination machine in *The Wasp Factory*.

On the flat shelf that lay underneath this ever-shifting bank of images and objects, I put a life-sized plastic skull I had bought on eBay. In one of his eye sockets, I put an old acid-house Smiley badge that wedged in perfectly. I placed a cigar in between his teeth and poured a glass of rum to stand beside him with a tin enamel mug half filled with clean water. Next to this I put a clear white candle that I would light in the evening. This is basic etiquette if you are going to try and interact with your ancestors in this tradition.

This plastic skull I chose was meant to represent Papa Gede, one of the Haitian pantheon of spirits that the slaves took with them from Africa and syncretised with the Christian beliefs they were exposed to. He is the embodiment of the corpse of the first man to die. He has spectacles with one lens missing in order to look into both worlds, hence the Smiley monocle and, like most of the Haitian spirit world, he is an interesting mix of lusty and mischievous. He is the guardian of the graveyard.

My colonial past haunts me. I could think of nothing more appropriate than for me, a Scotsman, whose family history was probably soaked in blood and sugar, the theft and rape and genocide of empire, to adopt as a household deity an African spirit whose role was as the gatekeeper to the graveyard.

I get that I can be accused, with some validity, of cultural appropriation. Partly I feel that a culture that does not appropriate from another culture stagnates, but I also feel that I approach this idea of Papa Gede with a sense of generational atonement– and I feel my work holding the hands of the living and the dead gives me an inroad with him. Pape Gede, and my offerings and interactions with him and all my complicated family mosaic, became the everyday ritual that I choose to begin to try to filter my ancestral awareness through.

The longer I worked with the living and the dead, the more the mounds of the earth of the buried dead grew around me, the more I felt into my relationship with my own dead family through a playful interaction with a plastic representation of an African spirit, the more I came to develop a slightly disorienting view of the way the pyramid of generational influence was placed.

I started to feel that we, the people living through our time now, are the wise ones, that we have grown better and further from the deeds of our ancestors simply because history progresses and we are always wiser than our ancestors; in fact we are probably the ancestors, setting an example to those who went before us.

These ideas, of our true moral placement within the network of the living and the dead, felt important to try and share with people. It was both liberating and challenging to think of yourself as being the apex of progress within your bloodline. It frees you from the guilt of feeling that the modern world had in some ways become wrong, that humanity had become so far adrift from itself that you are missing crucial ways of being human that were effortless to your ancestors.

It calls you to the seriousness of recognising the responsibilities that come with existence, that only we are still able to make an impact, only we are in complete possession of the full facts, there is no wiser person looking down on us from an afterlife. We are the wise ones gazing down into the grave of the past, offering forgiveness and understanding for the failings of our forefathers, and able to formulate a plan to do the right thing. It is up to us. We are the ancestors.

◆ ◆ ◆

I started to write some of these ideas down, to script a dialogue that Claire and I would deliver together, one that would ultimately become a spoken word performance ritual, which we would perform at festivals and cultural events – an unexpectedly hallucinatory blast of images, an upending of it all, a reversing of positions; the dead alive and the alive dead.

I wrote it deliberately unfiltered and it plunges you without warning into images of your own death. It muddles with ideas of time, disorientates you into a nightmarish state in which the very idea of your present existence is called into question. It probably should come with a trigger warning.

I didn't really know what I was writing it for when I started. I knew I wanted to try and shatter this false respect we automatically gave to all who went before. I wanted people to feel dragged underneath the surface of existence by swirling currents, to bring them face to face with their own skull, then show them that their flesh still glowed on it, that the blood of life still pumped around their heart with purpose, that they were, in fact, everything that they were projecting onto the dead.

The first time we performed it was as a support act to the book tour of a music journalist in our local record shop. The author, the lugubriously dark and funny genius that is John Doran, was doing a slightly manic one-month dash around the UK, a nightly reading from his autobiographical account of his recovery from long-term drug and alcohol issues, accompanied by an impossibly cool Norwegian heavy metal guitarist from the band Årabrot.

Kjetil, for that was his name, looked like he was straight out of an Alejandro Jodorowsky film, with a pencil-thin moustache and a livid scar from a recent operation. He had an enormous hat like an ancient preacher and a silver necktie. He looked like a killer.

The tour itself was a crazy idea, physically punishing and emotionally exhausting, retelling the story of John's troubled twenties and thirties every night in an assortment of art centres and music venues. Each night he and Kjetil would arrive in another town, after another night in a cheap roadside motel and meet the support act.

John said afterwards that he had no idea that the people suggested to him by our mutual friend as a suitable support act when he played Totnes were actual undertakers. He assumed The Undertakers was the name of a local synth-based two-piece playing something moody and complex. Had he known we were actual undertakers, he would have dismissed the idea as ludicrous and refused.

We were nervous as to how this strange thing I had written would be received. Claire had rewritten bits for herself in her voice, but the main narrative came from me and it had the breathless immediacy of a psychedelic experience, dropping you without warning right into high weirdness. I wasn't exactly sure what it meant or how it would be received.

As a record shop, there was a turntable handy, so we put it on the counter and placed Papa Gede on it, with his smiley badge monocle and his plastic teeth clamped around a cheroot, and turned it on. We surrounded him with candles and photographs of various ancestors we thought it would be appropriate to honour at the launch of a music autobiography. Amy Winehouse, recently dead, was one of them. The idea was to introduce people to the concept of their cultural ancestors, living and dead and light a candle to honour them.

The plastic skull slowly revolved in a frankly unsettling manner as we begun. We had a haunting soundtrack to accompany it put together by my brother-in-law Daveid Phillips. We pressed play and begun.

'Don't ever be afraid, of anything, ever, because you are already dead.

This moment, here, now, this is the moment between the click and the bang.

You are already dead.

The truth is the glass of life. It is not half full or half empty; it's smashed on the floor and every drop of experience that passes your lips is sucked from the lip of non existence.

We are all absent friends in waiting, ancestors already, peering out through the fabric of our burial shroud, the soil of our graves filling our mouths, the flames from our funeral pyres scorching the inside of our greasy, cracked skulls.'

There was a stunned silence. Someone whispered, 'Fucking hell.'

We knew it was a heavy opening, so we lifted it a bit. Claire said, 'By the way we're available for children's parties, christenings, summer barbecues, out-of-town superstore blessings, whatever. Usual rates apply, plus forty pence per mile if it's any further than Exeter.'

A nervous giggle ran around the room. She carried on.

'We are undertakers, and we run a burial ground. That's how we know we're all already dead. We buried you, shortly before we buried each other.'

By now it really did feel like all the oxygen had been sucked out of the room. Papa Gede slowly revolved in front of us all at 45 revolutions per minute.

'When you talk about ancestors, people automatically think you are talking about genetics, and it's true, your forebearers are extremely important. You literally have life because they lived, and from time to time, they should be acknowledged and thanked because knowing where you came from helps you to be clearer about where you are going and gives you some personal perspective.

And sometimes, actually always, their actions need to be atoned for too because our ancestors gift us their blood guilt as well as their hard won wisdom.'

We were into our stride now. The audience were listening, even if they looked like they felt trapped.

It was time to explain the spinning skull.

'This real, plastic skull sits on our family altar.

He is a representation of, and a vessel for, Papa Gede, a folk deity who comes from Africa via Haiti, LA, Miami, Rio, Louisiana, New York, Cardiff, Brixton and now here.

He is the guardian of the graveyard, the corpse of the first man to die, a psychopomp who waits at the crossroads to take your soul into the afterlife.

Like many memes of belief, he picks up and integrates elements from the different cultures and realms of existence he passes through; Catholicism, slavery, jazz, pop art, hip hop, the occult, films, even cartoons. He moves through them all.

Tradition says he is short, with a top hat, he carries an apple in his hand and wears spectacles with one lens missing, so as to see into both worlds, but since arriving in Devon, he has developed a taste for old skool acid house, so he wears a smiley monocle instead. Same vision, different tune.'

We tried to lighten it every so often. Holding your audience's sympathy and attention while making them think of the moment of their own death is a fine art for sure. We were treading a razor-sharp line between a vaudeville act and a genuine summoning. The least we could do is insert the odd laugh.

'Remember, this is all imaginary, just play. Magic can just be psychology dramatised. Ritual is the raising and focusing of energy that moves us towards a goal.

This skull is plastic, but hey, one day soon all our skulls will be plastic, our microbead evolutionary leap is well under way, but by treating this as if it had consciousness, and offering him rum and smoke, then we spread our awareness outwards towards endless possibilities, other models of thinking and being, the idea that we don't own the patent on consciousness, that life moves through more things than we will ever know. We start to drift into the mystic.

And we smeared a lot of acid on the door handle earlier, so if you came in, you're coming up. Helps move things along a bit. An old witches' trick, henbane on the bicycle saddle. Hoffman was not an incompetent chemist but the victim of a fairy gangland hit. Probably.'

The acid spiking gag was risky, but it did make people exhale with a hiss the breath they had been holding since we started. And the atmosphere did feel solid, thick with the presence of something; spirits, ideas, visions of worlds all around us and in us. Psychedelia can be induced in many ways.

After we had finished our disorientating, psychedelically menacing ritual, John Doran slowly walked out of the door of the shop and we saw him walk across the road before resting his head against a wall. John had recently had a close friend die unexpectedly and this unforeseen immersion into the world of the dead had profoundly shaken him.

John later wrote about it in his book, *Lucky Lad*, saying 'I don't want to state the obvious, but I've taken a lot of drugs and had more "visionary" experiences than I'll ever remember, but most of them pale next to what real life has thrown at me. The birth of my son is probably the most genuinely psychedelic thing that has ever happened to me, in the sense that it altered my perception of the world irrevocably, and by the same token, undergoing this ritual, presided over by a couple of youthfully middle-aged countercultural funeral directors in a record shop in Devon, surrounded by people I don't know, ends up being one of the most mind-altering experiences I will ever have.'

We had successfully jumped into the world of performance art. We had something more to offer now than the talks we would give to the Women's Institute or The Sunday Assembly, something more to say than my eulogies. Weirder too, and this strange and slightly disturbing performance would lead us into some interesting places. Once again, Death introduced us to a scene.

It would be adapted to whatever situation we were performing it in, but it's essential essence, that of an upending and reversing of the idea of who was alive and who was dead, would be at the heart of it. It does sound a bit mad, a bit self-consciously affected now that I have put it down on paper, but people are as hungry for a meaningful but playful encounter with death as we were to give it to them.

Bereavement comes to all of us, over and over again, and it is always surprising in its intensity and simultaneously deeply familiar in its pain. By holding these rituals, exploring the concepts of existence outside of the actual reality of day-to-day grieving, I found a bit of relief, playing around with these ideas of ancestral influence, flickering back in between existence and non existence.

I would take Papa Gede up with me to the burial ground as I tended the fire pit. He would accompany me into the fields at night as I pressed my portals into the wheat, trying to fling the accumulated grief down into the underworld.

It was, of course, all a form of bastardised prayer. My magic was really art, my spells offerings of thanks or acts of propitiation, attempts to ward off the dark tides of sadness that swept so many people away, so many men. Suicide was the dark secret I carried with me, the despair I needed to keep at arm's length. I could understand it only too well and I grew wearily familiar with the terrible eternal gouges it took out of the survivors' lives, the way it trickled down through generation after generation.

Our own intergenerational trauma can take a long, long time to reach us. The bullet that rattles down the barrel of life after life can take decades to strike home. Often we are not even aware of the reality of our ancestor's pain physically encoded in our DNA, the way it leaches into our own psyches, the sins of the fathers complicating our own life-given wounds.

But with a suicide, the trauma is instantly inescapable. It soaks not just into the lives of all of the families, but all undertakers, all police officers, everyone who comes into contact with it, and the socially acceptable way to deal with it was by drowning those feelings with alcohol and antidepressants, drugging yourself to sleep with benzodiazepines.

I was far too at risk from all of those addictions, being hard-wired with trauma already, so these private theatrics became the thing that I tried to grow around me, a protective weave of ritualised performance to try and keep me safe and alive.

The lesson I had learned so early on in my career as an undertaker, the shattering of the notion that it was only the old who died, was buried on the hillside in the bodies of the children and the young people who dotted the ground, the graves of those who had taken their own lives or been caught up in accidents of physics and bad luck, the men and women who had been swept away by a surge of bleakness.

This was what I needed to keep myself safe from. This was why I took a plastic skull into the fields at night and onto stages around the country. This is why I threw spells into the darkness.

CHAPTER FIFTEEN

The North shall ritualise again

One of the places that our performance ritual took us to was Liverpool. I come from the north and am familiar with most northern cities, but, until we were asked to be part of a weekend of performances to accompany a play written by Daisy Campbell about the works of Robert Anton Wilson, I had never set foot in this extraordinary city.

There is an energy that flows through the city, which comes from being the civic outsider, on the back foot. It has an almost overwhelmingly welcoming cheeriness that comes with an edge. Liverpool is the last stronghold of socialism in the UK and was targeted by Margaret Thatcher for that very reason. It has, and still does, suffer from enormous social deprivation, and has at least a million less people than the infrastructure could deal with, but it throbs with grassroots culture.

Art is not a middle-class preserve there, it is shared by everyone, particularly music – the incredible musical heritage of which that began with the Beatles, but certainly didn't end with them, instead kickstarting a homegrown boom of incredible bands in the late 70s and 80s including Big in Japan, Echo & The Bunnymen, The Teardrop Explodes, The Mighty Wah!, Frankie Goes to Hollywood – a whole scene of genuinely original creativity.

It is also, of course, one of the most slave-heavy historical cities in Britain; the logistical epicentre of the UK transatlantic slave trade, and that legacy of racism and violence is also stained into every quayside cobblestone, every grand Victorian building that escaped the pummelling that the German bombers gave it night after night.

Most of the jobs came from the huge docks, which was one of the main transatlantic hubs for everything that came into the UK. The docks employed thousands of men and women as well as a large number of manufacturing factories that grew alongside this hub of commerce, but these all withered away during the twentieth century. In an apt metaphor for the atomisation of our society, it was the increased use of storage containers that saw the decline in dockland jobs.

By the 1980s, it was one of the most deprived cities in England, a country which has always been much more deprived than it likes to admit to the rest of the world. Places like Toxteth had become ghettos, no employment and policed by a racist police force. When it erupted into riots in 1981, no one was surprised, and the stark racial and social divisions in Britain were brutally laid out.

The smearing of the good people of Liverpool after the awful disaster at Hillsborough Stadium by a collusion of police, politicians and the tabloid media reinforced this idea that it was Liverpool against the world and that anything that was going to happen there had to happen from the ground up, from the good of its ongoing cultural revival to the bad – the establishment of the worst drug gangs in Britain. Outside help was not going to come. Outside of Liverpool lay Babylon.

Being invited to perform our ritual, which we called 'Don't be afraid, you're already dead' after a line in it that was taken from a song by the American band Akron/Family called 'Love is Simple', in a converted warehouse down by the docks as part of a celebration of the weird hybrid countercultural joke religion Discordianism, a situationist spoof religion created by a couple of American High School students that worshipped the Roman and Greek goddess of chaos, known as Eris in Greece and Discordia by the Romans, was the beginning of a love affair with the city which was to develop in ways I couldn't possibly have imagined.

To stand on a stage with a representation of an ancient African spirit god, smuggled into the west as spiritual contraband in the hearts of those poor miserable shackled men and women, felt an appropriately dissonant thing to do for an ex-posh white man making his living from a traditional working-class trade.

It went with the upending nature of the whole ritual – the dead brought to life and the living consigned to the past – and when we performed it in Liverpool as part of what was basically a chaos magic cabaret to celebrate the rites of Discordianism with an audience who were used to such far-out things, it had a big impact.

In fact, the creator of the festival and the writer of the play it was arranged around was so moved by the urgency that it brought to the everyday that she and her partner decided there and then to get married. Such is the power of speaking the right words at the right time, even if you are not entirely sure what they really mean yourself. It was an extraordinary way to enter the life of the city, even if I didn't know that this was what I was doing.

◆ ◆ ◆

Bill Drummond and Jimmy Cauty, two of my favourite musicians and artists, had a strong association with Liverpool. Jimmy had been born in the Wirral, which lies a couple of hundred yards across the Mersey.

Jimmy left Merseyside when he was young and moved to bucolic Devon. He found early success as an artist at the age of seventeen by drawing a poster of Gandalf from *The Lord of the Rings* for a national retailer of poster art called Athena, which became a huge bestseller, before becoming a guitarist and joining various bands.

Bill Drummond, the Scottish son of a Presbyterian minister is a genius of late twentieth-century culture. He arrived in Liverpool to work as a set designer at the Everyman Theatre in 1975 and soon became involved in the local music scene, being in and managing several bands, such as Big in Japan and Echo & The Bunnymen.

To describe Bill and Jimmy simply as musicians would be like describing Charlie Chaplin as a slapstick clown. Yes, they have had an incredibly successful and varied music career, both on their own and with each other and – as one of their most famous incarnations as the KLF, they have created the soundtrack to my generation, the anthems to my early Dionysian raves – but they are shapeshifters, refusing to settle on one form or another and have been accused, with some justification, of being art terrorists due to the controversial way they played with the commodification of art, particularly through the destruction of money.

They formed a band called The Justified Ancients of Mu Mu, a reference to Robert Anton Wilson's and Robert Shea's The Illuminatus Trilogy, a sprawling satirical dismantling of conspiracy thinking that unwittingly spurred such thinking on to greater heights. As The Justifieds, they sampled from other people's records so provocatively that ABBA tried to sue them and, because of this, many people think that the name KLF, their next incarnation, stands for Kopyright Liberation Front. Perhaps, but Bill and Jimmy know that an unexplained acronym is a much more powerful imaginative device than anything that can be definitively explained.

Oh, and they are mad. Delightfully but completely, unpredictably, mad. In 1992, despite never having played one live gig, apart from DJing at a couple of raves, they won an award for the best band of that year at the Brit Awards (shared with Simply Red) and were nominated for the most awards of any band that year – which apparently disgusted them, or at least bewildered them.

It wasn't the quality of their music they struggled with, which remains to this day some of the most diverse and innovative stuff of the late eighties and early nighties, music that shaped and defined rave culture (they describe themselves now as being in a 'rave heritage' band), but their extraordinary meteoric success and what they saw as their collusion with a capitalistic music industry.

Becoming a money-making machine had not been part of their plan. The disruptive betterment of society was the plan, and the disconnect between their anarchic natures and the cosy embrace that the music business was tightly holding them in clearly grated.

Their acceptance of their award, which involved one of their only live performances, was a typically discordant clash with the self-congratulatory smugness of the music world. Live on television and surrounded by the industry heavyweights, they performed a version of the hit they were nominated for, '3 A.M. Eternal', but a thrash metal version with the band Extreme Noise Terror, whose name said it all.

Drummond swayed onto the stage, limping and kilted, in a leather trench coat. He snarled the lyrics, leaning on a crutch while the band roared and pummelled the audience, before he pulled out a semi-automatic weapon and shot the audience with blanks. I hasten to point out that this was before the days when mass shootings in the States were a phenomenon, but it was still a shocking thing to behold.

As soon as the performance was finished, a voice announced over the tannoy that the KLF had left the music business and they promptly shapeshifted into an art institute, the K Foundation. Incredible. Literally at the height of their career, they renounced it all and within a month had deleted their back catalogue completely, an act which would cost them millions in future earnings.

But this act of artistic contrition wasn't enough for Bill and Jimmy and they did something for that they will evermore be associated with: they took out from the bank the remaining money that they had earned as the KLF, which amounted to a million pounds, and they chartered a small plane and flew to the Scottish island of Jura, where in the company of their roadie, Gimpo, and one journalist, they unceremoniously burnt the lot in the fireplace of a deserted croft.

This simple act provoked outrage and continues to divide people to this day, with many people still refusing to accept they even did it. Believe me, they did, and, if you look closely enough into their haunted eyes, you can see the reflection of the flickering flames as bundle after bundle of twenty-pound notes rages in the hearth.

I was intoxicated by the idea of what they had done. I never doubted for a second that they had actually done it and I thought from the moment I heard of it that it was an act of staggering brilliance. It caused my first proper argument about art with my then girlfriend, who thought like many people that the money could have been donated to a hospital or a homeless charity. The world is divided up into those who think it is an act of artistic genius or an act of wanton vandalism.

Any attempts to explain why they had done it were hamstrung by their ability to fully understand it themselves, so they drove a hire car to the most northerly tip of Britain, the cliffs of Cape Wrath in Scotland, and painted a contract on that car in white emulsion paint, in which they both pledged not to speak to the press or anyone about it for 23 years. They then tipped the car over the edge so it smashed on the rocks one hundred feet below.

At the time, I was as gripped as anyone with this saga of what I could see was genuine outsider art. This was an act which had managed to outrage half of the world and delight the other half – proper art. I couldn't have foreseen in my wildest dreams the part I would play in the ending of that contract of 23 years' silence.

I met Bill when I commissioned him to write an essay for the book I was editing, which I had called *Writing on Death*. It was a brilliantly Drummond-esque piece of writing and I edited it with a very light touch because I was so in awe of him. In fact I didn't change a word, even though he said some pretty challenging things. You can read it in the fifth edition of *The Natural Death Handbook* to see what I mean.

As for Jimmy, well, his artistic output continued to be provocative and diverse and he had started to build incredibly intricate miniature models of an unexplained but very dystopian near future, including a sprawling diorama of an urban landscape in which clearly something awful had happened, as it was completely empty of people apart from hundreds of seemingly rampaging policemen, engaged in disturbingly joyous destructive rioting.

It was haunting and brilliant, the attention to detail was mind blowing, and you could walk around it looking at it for hours and hours and never see every darkly funny detail. Jimmy put this shrunken square mile of looted town into a shipping container with hundreds of viewing holes drilled into the side like bullet holes, squeezed it on a flatbed lorry and started touring the country with it.

I hosted it when it came to Totnes and that was where I first met Jimmy. Totnes was Jimmy's home town, and he has lots of family and friends who still live here, so the visit of The Aftermath Dislocation Project, as it is called, was a homecoming of sorts.

My relationship with Jimmy was to deepen when a few months later his younger brother and longtime collaborator, Simon, took his own life.

Simon Cauty had been an integral part of the KLF and had built many of their sets. Simon and Jimmy shared a hive mind. Simon was responsible for one of the most iconic outfits that Bill and Jimmy wore as The Justified Ancients of Mu Mu – the long cowled robes that hid the face but from which a huge rhino horn jutted out, making them look like mysterious shamanic priests from some sort of deeply pagan rite.

By now, the presence of suicide in my story should have stopped being such a shocking surprise. The death of Jimmy's lovely, talented but ultimately troubled brother was an event like all of these deaths; it shot around his family like an electric shock, a shock that burns and scorches permanent wounds. Simon has four sons, all in their early twenties, beautiful boys, and it fell to them to organise his funeral.

Simon's kids are brilliant and we inhabited that strange place with them where humour is never far away, albeit streaked with darkness, and we helped them, their big family and Jimmy decide on what was to be the right thing to do.

Simon had played such a big part in the whole grandiose aesthetics of the KLF that, at first, we seriously considered burning him on an enormous pyre, but such a publicly theatrical funeral felt too exposing to his sons, understandably so. We compromised.

One of Simon's sons made his coffin, a rectangular even box that looked like the sort of thing you would expect to be filled with a consignment of guns. It was covered in stencils of the KLF's logo, surrounded by artefacts of Simon's, like his chainsaw, which was as much an artistic tool to him as a paint brush.

On top of the coffin, Jimmy put the horn that Simon had made for him for an appearance on *Top of the Pops* and that had become their trademark. It was strange to see such an iconic thing just resting there, its inner workings of welded metal and skateboarder helmet holding the battered and chipped plaster-of-Paris horn.

We held the ceremony in the Great Hall at Dartington. I am used, by now, to the atmosphere of these funerals of men who have killed themselves, but there is always that feeling of disbelief, the feeling I had from that first suicide funeral, of being stuck to the walls while the floor drops away. I held the service and various people spoke, including one of Simon's close friends, Paul Conroy, the war photographer who had been blown up in Homs in Syria with the legendary journalist Marie Colvin.

Paul is a Scouser and has seen enough death in various war zones to be the right person to talk at Simon's funeral. The eulogy he gave was so powerful. He told the boys that this unbearable pain they were feeling, this unreal horror, would one day become one of their most precious possessions because it would hold them tightly to the memory of their father and would be one they would not swap, or let go of ever, even if they could.

It was the sort of truth which sounds absurd, but comes with the experience of having lost friends and colleagues in violent ways. He was right. There is a precious intimacy to the depth of this pain, which does indeed grow into something that the heart refuses to let go of. It fuses into a smelted ball of memory that is all you have left of that person and you guard it as fiercely as an inmate in a prison with a hidden piece of contraband from home.

It was decided to do the funeral ceremony somewhere other than the actual crematorium, as we do a lot of our cremations. After that, Claire and I accompanied Simon's sons to the crematorium, where a very simple farewell was held, just the boys carrying the coffin up to the catafalque and having a moment's silence, before leaving to go home and light an enormous bonfire and send screaming fireworks up into the sky, another of Simon and Jimmy's loves.

The horn of Mu, Jimmy's horn that Simon had made, sat on top of his coffin but, as we suspected, the crematorium refused to burn it with him. We had talked about this possibility and Jimmy had said to me that if it happened, I was to bring it back home and keep it with me. He said he would be down to collect it from me 'when the wind changed'.

I brought it home like the Holy Grail and I put it on my altar, underneath my Perspex shelves filled with family ghosts, where it sat next to the plastic skull of Papa Gede. I spent a lot of time staring at it with disbelief.

I was at this time spending a lot of time standing in front of my altar, trying out my own rudimentary form of magical wish fulfilment, scrying for meaning within the traditions of Haitian Vodou and my own psychedelic visions of my complicated family matrix. Returning again and again to see new lines of trauma, new visions of intergenerational connection was absorbing and enlightening. It swayed and shimmered in front of me like a TV set, struggling to find a steady signal before suddenly revealing a series of connections that weren't really there, but would bring up strong feelings of sadness or understanding about my life path.

Much of my magical practice was based around spells to try and hold my faltering marriage together. Claire and I were struggling under the pressures of running a business that had such enormous depths of emotional pain within its everyday structure, as well as raising my stepdaughters and trying to hold them through their teenage struggles. For at least seventeen years, Claire and I were never apart, night or day, and this pressure began to show, especially as our intense work isolation (it was always just the two of us) magnified any friction between us.

I had taken to casting spells in the style of the sigil magic created by the painter Austin Osman Spare, a method in which you write down a short statement of intent, then remove the vowels and then the repeating consonants until you are left with about four or five letters. You then form these into a symbol which you mediate on for quite a while. You then destroy the symbol through a highly charged manner, the traditional way being to visualise it at the point of orgasm. The idea is that this is a symbol of your desire and will pass through into your subconscious and manifest in real life.

Like a lot of practical magic, it is one of the last acts of the powerless and, at that stage of my life, I was desperate to hold on to our union, my early feelings of abandonment making me cling to the familiar, however painful it had become.

We had intertwined our lives together so deeply that it was impossible to see where we stopped, and what we did began. Falling in love while being in an intensely niche job together was always a high-risk strategy and for years it had bound us together on an incredible adventure, but after seventeen years together, it was starting to fall apart and we were making each other unhappy.

And the grief of this and the death all around me was beginning to calcify on me. My rituals, cobbled together as they were from a strange range of sources such as English hoodoo, crop circle art and spell making were another attempt to keep me from being dragged under into the dark underworld.

I could see all around me examples of people who had been overwhelmed by the tragedy they worked with, deathcare professionals who were committing a sort of passive suicide through self-destructive behaviour, of which I was prone to myself. It had been years since I had used the transformative power of regular raving to heal me, and it was unsustainable, yet the things I needed to shake off still clung to me.

And now, on my strange magical portal, with its photographs of my family dead, my keepsakes from funerals, my coils of lowering straps and my cheap plastic skull, sat something that had been an icon of my cultural youth, a fragment of the true cross of acid house – one of the two horns of Mu as worn by Bill and Jimmy.

One night, I was standing swaying in front of my altar, a little bit altered. I had lit candles and turned off the lights, so the usual shifting wisps of meanings were showing themselves through flickering shadow play, unseen connections appearing and then disappearing again.

It is quite a painful way to explore my family past and examine my own psyche. The revelations that came clearly showed the struggles my parents and grandparents had gone through, the sadness that they had experienced in their own lives, the lines of transmission of ancestral woundings which then fed down into my life. But suddenly my altar had this powerful artefact on it, filled with all the jokey seriousness which marked out my own lightly held ritual behaviour.

It was just a carved piece of plaster of Paris yet, for my generation, it was the symbol of two shamanic pop stars intent on dismantling the established culture framework around them. I couldn't quite believe the circle of events which had led to it sitting on my altar.

I very gingerly picked up this cultural artefact, this weird rhino horn that I had seen in their provocative videos, and placed the horny crown on my head.

Instantly, my phone buzzed with a text. It was Jimmy, and it was so unexpected that for one moment I thought that somehow he had me under surveillance.

It said: We need to talk, we have a plan.

CHAPTER SIXTEEN

Building The People's Pyramid brick by bony brick

Jimmy Cauty and Bill Drummond are not people to let an obsession go. For decades, they had harboured an obsession with pyramids, Jimmy in particular. A pyramid featured in the band logo of the KLF: a pyramid with a ghetto blaster superimposed on it.

At one time, a time of shared manic grandiose delusionality, they had intended to build a pyramid with a brick for everyone born in the twentieth century, but sheer logistics got in the way – where to put such a huge edifice and how to fund this thing, which would dwarf the efforts of the Pharaohs, being the main stumbling blocks.

But Simon's death had reignited this pyramidal obsession for Jimmy and provided a neat creative way to focus his grief, and so they arranged to come down to our house to put a proposal to us.

They were reaching the end of their self-imposed moratorium on talking publicly about the burning of the million quid and, while they still hadn't really figured out why they did it, they decided to use this ending to relaunch themselves as a duo again, but with a new artistic project that had nothing to do with music.

Their proposal was that Bill, Jimmy, Claire and I would form an artistic and business partnership called Callender, Callender, Cauty & Drummond: Undertakers to the Underworld. They would, in effect, join us as honorary undertakers and we, with our twenty-odd years of actual undertaking experience, would provide them with some deathly credibility. The purpose of this partnership was to at last build Jimmy's pyramid – but the twist was that each brick would have a small portion of cremated human remains fired into it.

The pyramid was to be exactly 23 feet high and this would need precisely 34,592 bricks to create. The process of turning a brick into a bony memorial was to be called MuMufication and would take place gradually, going at the speed of the idea catching on which, given the KLF's oblique marketing strategy of doing things, like announcing ideas by defacing billboards, might take a while.

The bricks would be fired once a year at a traditional brickworks in the south east of England, a place where Bill and Jimmy had history. When they burnt the million quid, they brought the ashes back in an attaché case. They took the attaché case to this brickworks and asked them to turn the burnt banknotes into a brick.

It is an extraordinarily ordinary thing to look at, a rather beautifully rich-coloured, Victorian-style London house brick, made from the sieved remains of one million pounds worth of sterling cash. When Jimmy first held it in his hands, he knew that one day he wanted to become a bony brick.

Once a year, we would take the bricks that had been fired containing 23 grams of ground human bones and ceremonially lay them in the Toxteth district in Liverpool, at a site not yet secured. Around this practical thing, we would drape a loose nebulous ritual framework and call it the Toxteth Day of the Dead.

We in Britain have long been envious of the way other parts of the world celebrate their dead, refusing to see that the grand and ambitious ritual statements made by the Victorians were in themselves magnificent. In particular, as I mentioned before, we appear to have been smitten by the rituals of the Mexican Day of the Dead, in which families come and decorate their graveyards with coloured lanterns, feast upon sugar skulls, dance with people in beautiful skeleton costumes and generally have a grand old carnival time. But our attempts to culturally appropriate this always seem to me to strike a bit of a bum note.

The Toxteth Day of the Dead is designed to be a loose template on which the people of Toxteth can impose their own rituals, their own meanings on the day – and already they have begun to do so, parading around the boundaries of Toxteth, commemorating local people of note, both real and fictional, conjuring up a vibe which is pure Liverpool, and has their dead at the heart of it.

We are trying to do this thinning of the veils, this slow, close dance with our ancestors in a way and a place that reflects Britain; the real Britain of mixed racial communities and defiant strength, unstoppable artistic creativity in the face of crushing poverty and political indifference.

So. A 23-feet high pyramid built from bricks filled with burned and crushed human bones, assembled over a period of probably no less than a hundred years, within the framework of a day dedicated to the ritual celebration of the dead but without any specific religious origin in one of the most deprived yet vibrant areas of the country.

To announce this new incarnation, Bill and Jimmy fly posted a poster in their trademark font at a place they were known to make announcements. It proclaimed there would be a three-day event in Liverpool:

'Welcome to the Dark Ages
a three day situation by
The Justified Ancients of Mu Mu
23rd–25th August 2017

day one:
Why did the K Foundation burn a million quid? – a hearing

day two:
2023, what the fuuk is going on? – a reading

day three:
The Rites of MuMufication – a ritual

All ticket holders are volunteers. All volunteers will be called on to perform duties. Duties directed by agents of The Justified Ancients of Mu Mu. Only 400 tickets will be on sale. There is no guest list or red carpet.

£100.
Tickets will be on sale at 11.23am on 23rd July 2017.'

It sold out within minutes.

Bill and Jimmy had written a book together called *2023*, a sort of rewriting of Robert Anton Wilson's *The Illuminatus! Trilogy*, and the start of the situation (for they are, at heart, situationists, a philosophy which feels human beings are trapped by surrounding circumstance and so seek to break that spell through unexpected and bizarre happenings) was the book launch in Bold Street in Liverpool at 23 minutes past midnight.

(By now you should have noticed the proliferation of the number 23. You'll have to do your own research if you want to know what that is all about, but I will say that its origins lie with that old occultist Bill Burroughs and it runs like a Golden Thread through his work.)

They asked for an advance of £23,000 for this book, which they promptly spent on an ice cream van, another of their old classic signature props, and they arrived at the launch in that classic ice cream van to a crowd of hundreds, much to Bill and Jimmy's utter astonishment.

This moment was deeply moving. Jimmy had adapted the song machine of the van to play the four-note hook of their hit, '3 A.M. Eternal' as well as the classic 'O sole Mio' and, as both these tunes rang out, the crowd roared in appreciation. This was the bit that the press covered as it made for a great photo and a simple story, which is a shame because really the big reveal – the adapted Rites of Mu (the first rites having been performed on the isle of Jura to a series of endlessly bemused journalists) in which we announced they were now undertakers and building a pyramid of the dead – was lost to the media. If I sound bitter, it's because I am but, if you hitch your wagon to people who insist on doing what you least expect, what do you expect?

The grand finale to this announcement was a carnival-like procession in which everyone had had their faces made up like skulls and wore robes emblazoned with the KLF logo on it, like some weird scene from an Indiana Jones film in which a dark cult is discovered in a subterranean cavern practising some ghastly rite.

Half of the participants had been hurriedly trained as a scratch choir to perform a vaguely church-like choral version of one of their big hits, 'Justified and Ancient', and everyone was packed into a large hall in Toxteth affectionately known as the Florrie. It looked incredible, and while everyone knew their part, only a tiny core knew the whole point and substance of the ritual.

The only two people who weren't dressed in strange robes were Claire and me, who were dressed in our funeral suits, faces unmade up, looking disconcertingly out of place.

After some strange slow motion interpretive dance, it was our turn. Claire's brother, Daveid Phillips, known as DP and a music curator responsible for some of the best festivals of the eighties and nineties, stepped up with us onto the stage, went to his laptop and pressed play. The uncanny soundtrack to our ritual began and we stepped up to the microphones.

'Don't be afraid of anything, ever, because you are already dead. This moment, now, this is the moment between the click and the bang.'

I have no idea what the four hundred people dressed like refugees from a haunted ghost train version of Jonestown were expecting, but they weren't expecting us.

We performed our destabilising rite, spinning the living dead and the dead alive, rubbing out the clarity of death's line to bring everyone in that room into a state where they could imagine themselves dead, picture themselves already dead, already ancestralised, while strange and unsettling music accompanied us.

We have performed this odd ritual in a variety of settings and amended it each time, but nowhere has it been as powerfully received as it was to those four hundred people, stretched as they were by three days of disorientating ritual play. People started to cry, the black makeup of their skull sockets running down the bony white of their chalked cheeks.

It climaxed with us announcing that Bill and Jimmy would be joining us as undertakers now and that, together, we would be building the People's Pyramid, brick by bony brick.

The audience looked at each other to make sure they had heard that right.

At this point in my memory, it starts to become like a film. Jarvis Cocker, the Sheffield lead singer of the band Pulp, suddenly revealed himself from under a hooded cowl and led the choir in a hymnal version of 'Justified and Ancient' as bearers carried forward two coffins made by Bill and Jimmy, which symbolised the death of their old personas. Probably. They never said, as they never do.

As Jarvis crooned like a comically sexy Scott Walker at evensong, the coffins were borne aloft on the shoulders of the robed masses outside the hall, placed inside the ice cream van, which was hooked up to two long ropes, partly because the petrol tank was contaminated.

I have had some experiences in my life, been part of things which are distinctly odd in the best sense, but nothing will come close to the exhilarating feeling of being part of a procession that literally dragged that ice cream van for three miles through central Liverpool, dressed as skeletons, all singing, 'We're all bound for MuMu Land.'

Bill and Jimmy sat in the ice cream van, their coffins, sorry Koffins, behind them as we pulled onto the dual carriageway. I was marching alongside, carrying Pape Gede with me, his smouldering cigar clamped between his plastic teeth. I quickly realised by the hurried arrival of police cars that of course none of this was being done with any official permission. A senior policeman strode anxiously alongside the ice cream van, rapping on the passenger window. Bill stubbornly ignored him, like the art terrorist he is. At one point he vaguely gesticulated that the window didn't work. To their immense credit, the Liverpool police bowed to the inevitable and started to direct the rush-hour traffic into the fast lane, pleading to know how far we were going.

We were heading to the city waterfront and what was known as The Great Pull North. There, by the Mersey, was the outline of a pyramid formed by steep-sided bits of four-by-two wood, with a pyre at its base.

The ice cream van came to a halt and the Koffins were taken out. The four hundred formed a wide encircling of the pyramid frame and, as the sun set over the Mersey, Bill and Jimmy ceremonially donned their horns. The Koffins were placed on the pyre and they lit it.

And so begun the consecration of the idea of the People's Pyramid.

As the pyre raged, Claire and I began signing up people for MuMufication, selling them bricks and certificates to take home with them – to try to explain to their families that these three days had culminated in them buying this brick, which was going to sit on their mantelpiece until they died and then they were going to be cremated with whatever ceremony the bereaved seemed appropriate, but a small portion of their ground bones were going to go into this brick, which would be laid into a slow-growing pyramid.

We immediately uncovered a fractally complex world of technical complications around every practical aspect, particularly the firing of the bricks. At first we thought they could only be fired once, and this meant that pre MuMufication, they were incredibly vulnerable, just held barely together and prone to crumbling, breaking and, if exposed to the damp, dissolving into a damp mush. But after some trial and serious error, we worked out that they could indeed be fired twice, which gave them some much needed longevity, and by the time the first Toxteth Day of the Dead rolled around, one year after we announced the KLF's inauguration into the world of undertaking, we had the first brick of the People's Pyramid to lay, the MuMufied remains of Jimmy's brother, Simon Cauty.

Right up until the moment we revealed that this first brick was Simon, until we laid the first brick and read out his name, people still thought Bill and Jimmy might be joking. They have long suffered under the accusation that they are pranksters. This is incredibly unfair. Jeremy Beadle was a prankster; Loki was a trickster. Pranksters fool people for a cheap laugh; tricksters change culture through acts of creative deception. Bill and Jimmy are tricksters and suddenly everybody grasped the seriousness of the intention.

Once one brick had been laid on the foundation stone, the building of the pyramid was underway and, when it was joined the next year by the kiln-fired bones of eight strangers, the last shred of doubt fell away.

As it should. Anyone who has followed the unpredictable career of these two men have known that while it is sometimes ludicrous and seemingly frivolous, it has a deadly serious heart to it. They mean everything they do.

And so Claire and I are committed to turning up to build this pyramid every year, even though we have released each other from our own mutual emotional commitment, even though Claire no longer works at The Green Funeral Company. She and I, and Bill and Jimmy will build this ziggurat, brick by bony brick, until we ourselves are absorbed one by one into its sandy embrace.

The People's Pyramid will be built.

CHAPTER SEVENTEEN

This is the moment between the click and the bang

I have slowly but steadily become this town's undertaker. I am firmly stitched into the fabric of this community as surely as a corpse is sewn into its shroud.

I live on my own now, in a first-floor flat above an ice cream parlour in an ancient house on its ancient high street, just above the former town gates and within the palisade of the original Norman fortification. Within the pale, not beyond it.

The ground behind my house is higher at the back than it is at the front; a good twenty feet higher. My front windows look down on the tourists struggling up the picturesque hill of the high street and my bedroom windows look out onto the graveyard of the town's fifteenth-century church.

I am poised, like all undertakers, between the bone orchard and the shopfront, decay and commerce, the showroom and the furnace, trade and dissolution, but in my case, with a sort of comic literalness, like some kind of an overdrawn archetype; the Undertaker as a tarot card.

The ground level comes halfway up the back of the house, so my bed lies a few feet underneath the sod of the graveyard outside, facing the same direction as the graves. I sometimes lie in bed and knock on the wall as if to rouse my long-dead neighbours to my presence; still here, my friends, still breathing, still above ground, brothers and sisters.

The whole back of the house is shored up, or rather, persistently leaned on by the ancient churchyard, and a deep plague pit rests against its basement, a pit that once memorably intruded in an avalanche of crumbled bones and powdery jawbones. The odd fragment still works its way up through the soil, like shrapnel to the surface of skin, to lie among the long grasses and the yarrow; the chunky knuckle of a femur, a broad, flat piece of stained rib. Once the pointing tip of an index finger – a phalange, accusatory and insistent in the direction I must go, as if I or anyone else has any choice in the matter.

Just under two hundred years ago, the occupant of the house was one John Shute and his wife, Elizabeth. He was a Radical Dissenter, a lay preacher, part of the English tradition that the Diggers and the Ranters and the Quakers come from, splitting from the authority of the established church to follow what they believed was the true message of Christ: liberation through social justice, dignity, morality and fairness over doctrine and corruption.

He was an outspoken moral voice in this town, much to the irritation of the incumbent vicar of the church at the time, the bilious and unpopular Reverend Burroughs, who kept pace with John Shute for fifty years, finally outliving him to preside over his funeral, proving sadly that often-smouldering spite is better fuel for the body than open-hearted compassion.

I am not sure what John Shute would make of my psychedelically tinged, occult surroundings that was his former drawing room, now filled with trinkets from funerals I have done; paper origami cranes, dried boutonnières of gorse worn by mourners, dead bees, figurines of Hindu gods and goddesses, a brass Pan playing his pipe with his lusty cock standing upright against his shaggy stomach.

There are photos of my long-dead ancestors, and my strange altar with its plastic skull and its corn dollies, napped flint knives, thimbles full of grave dirt, my father's medals, my mother's hospice brooch, glass vials of the ground bones of my dead dog – brightly coloured fragments that look more like coral or rare minerals than the bones of an old hound. Everywhere in my flat, weird objects throbbing with meaning.

A porcupine quill impales a crocheted devil to the wall and keeping him in place is a silver Tibetan knot of eternity. The door frames are lined with photos of my parents and my grandparents, and of strangers bought in market stalls in Marrakesh or table top sales in village halls: a man smoking a cigarette in a Moroccan house in the fifties, cross legged and beautiful but long dead, as is the young Irish lad in a tweed suit, proudly cradling the nose of his horse like a rural teddy boy with his best girl. They both look into the camera into the future eyes of someone they could never have conceived of.

One of my father, taken when I was probably five, shows him and a friend laughing at some agricultural show on the Isle of Skye. I remember that holiday. I remember the fog horn in the night and the loom of the lighthouse across my bedroom wall, the white rush of the waterfall onto the pebbles of the beach. The photo is old and yellowed, curved with age. The bottom left-hand corner never stays stuck down and so each time I pass it, I press it back with my thumb, where it stays for a while, a form of meditational remembrance, like absentmindedly spinning a prayer wheel as you pass by.

I Ching coins jostle for space with foxes' teeth. Shark egg cases, nicknamed mermaid's purses, hang from the mantelpiece, strange artificial-looking things made from collagen and keratin, the stuff of toenails and hair. They look like plastic purses made by H.R. Giger. It is like living in an occult museum of curiosities.

Would John Shute find the slate hearth of the grand fireplace, now engraved with the mandala tattooed on my chest and ringed with candles, amusing or appalling?

Would he find it blasphemous that I regularly light a cigar that is clamped in the plastic teeth of the skull, fill up a tin mug with water, refresh its glass with rum until it evaporates? Would he mind that I cast these spells to connect myself with my dead and the dead I bury, to shake off the foist of death that I have pledged to carry for others?

Hopefully he would find it more Dr Dee than of the Devil, but I think he would approve of my lightbox in the window with its ever-changing messages, proclaiming that this is still a house of Radical Dissent, that Black Lives Matter, No Pasarán – No Surrender, the passionate defiant cry taken up by the International Brigade in the Spanish Civil War. Sentiments, that though they exist two hundred years after John, he would surely agree with.

John Shute is an ancestor of mine, and I remember him in my orisons.

The walls of the church just sixty feet from my bed are scoured with gouges in the sandstone that I and most other people believe were from archers sharpening their arrowheads, part of a law made by Henry VIII that all English men must practise archery on a Sunday and that still technically stands.

An urban myth. The truth is far more interesting. They are from people scratching for Holy Dust to put into folk remedies, magic medicine. John Shute would have seen his fellow townsfolk engaged in these desperate acts of the powerless and hopeless out of his window and, I hope, be filled with compassion for them.

The rituals that I perform to try to make sense of this maelstrom of grief I work and live in have been practised here in other similar forms for hundreds of years; townsfolk desperate to save their child, desperate to tip the odds in their favour.

Jane, my girlfriend, who is an artist and academic, pointed out that I surround myself with these objects to protect myself, to keep away the deep-water pressure of my past, to prevent the emotional bends that go with such immersion. She showed me that my magic is art and my art is magic, and bought me a book on Joseph Beuys, the German artist and former Luftwaffe pilot who made art from mythologising his trauma. Once again I see that my ancestors are everywhere: alive, dead, and not just of my genetic lineage.

◆ ◆ ◆

I walk the streets of my town every day with my dog and stop every ten feet or so to embrace and talk with people whose husbands and wives, whose children and parents, I have buried or burnt, and their dead stand between us, invisible and mute.

I bridge the gap, and some people hold on to me for the passage to the past I embody; some turn sharply away for the same reason. Some of the living, many, have become dear friends of mine. People ask us how we met and I genuinely am surprised when I remember it was when I cremated their grandmother two decades ago.

One of these friends is Rosie, whose fierce warrior daughter Lydia died at just 21, when she was climbing the back wall of the Victorian terraced house she shared with some friends.

It was after a Christmas party at the skateboard shop she worked at and she had forgotten her key. She always hopped over the old brick wall when that happened, all her flatmates did, but this time, it gave way.

It was nearly twenty years ago, but Rosie and I and her partner, Joe, still talk about her as we stand in the market and gossip and snigger about our fellow townsfolk. Rosie describes how she used to lie in bed in the years after, awake in the dark, saying out loud to herself, 'I have a broken heart. My heart is broken,' over, and over again.

Rosie says that they, she and her other daughter Ione, were always a bit scared of Lydia and Lydia's Boudicca-like fierce directness. How she rushed through life like a wildfire. Rosie says how grateful she is that she didn't listen to her friends, who thought Rosie should curb Lydia's wildness a bit, that she shouldn't send her to the alternative school that was like an anarchists' commune, but instead make her focus on her future prospects and send her somewhere which would prepare her academically for a career.

She had no future, only a short, blazing vibrant now, a brief summer or two of adulthood, boyfriends and parties, before she vanished into the past.

Some of the dead are so sharp in my memory, their stories, their characteristics and likes so deeply ingrained, that I forget sometimes that I never met them alive. How can I know these people? How come I am still a bit scared of Lydia and her brusque magnificence? She was dead by the time we met, yet I flinch from her unasked-for opinion, delivered without a shred of doubt with the blunt confidence of youth.

How come I know how Rich, the crazy author with his tendency towards practical jokes, would be bored by some pompous dinner party – and how he would mischievously shake it up?

How do I know what a woman I never met would feel about a novel, or a person? Are they still living within me?

Am I accidentally holding them back in this material world, stopping them from rising to disperse into the cosmos? Or am I blowing the flames of their memory afire for those who still mourn them?

I remember these people in a way which is not really possible. I have absorbed enough of them to feel that part of me is in an in-between place with them, a place where remembrance and imagination keep them alive.

At times it makes me feel insubstantial myself, part ghost, someone who knows things they can't, they shouldn't. I worry that I am, in some way, becoming transparent, that my atoms have exchanged places with theirs as I dress them and hold them, that the dead are mingling with me until I become part of them. It makes me desperately try to understand linear time's illusion – that everything that happens is happening today.

That is what I hope, the nearest I can get to a belief in an afterlife. That some moments do last forever.

◆ ◆ ◆

Death rings in my ears all the time. And the only thing to stop the wailing fire alarm, this shrill existential tinnitus, is love: both Eros and Agape, desire and selflessness.

We know this. We all know this is all we have to jam against the doorframe, to keep out the howling monstrous darkness. We know it is probably going to give and we hope that the darkness is not a suffocating fog of dread but at worst the sweet release of gaseous nothing.

In the past, as you lay on your deathbed, whatever your beliefs, you knew that the world would carry on turning, that the seasons would go and return. That perhaps generations from now, someone would discover the story of your life, that you would fit into the narrative of history but, as we face a possible global existence extinction, what bigger picture is there to comfort ourselves with? I am not writing this with an eye to posterity, to the future great grandchildren I will not have, I am writing this to you, right now, to this moment we are sharing.

Apocalypse means The Revealing. 'That which is uncovered' and the truth is that it is the apocalypse for the 150,000 people who die on this earth every day. What lies behind life is revealed to them one way or the other, even if it is just the fading of vision, the dimming of the light of consciousness to an unknowing benign absence of everything.

Perhaps we will summer blockbuster our way out of this sixth mass extinction event with a cinematic ending. Science is incredible and people are working on ways to try and refreeze the Arctic, to try to buy us enough time to stabilise what feels like our mother planet catching a fever in order to kill the human virus. I don't believe we are a virus. I believe we have as much right to our lives as a whale or an ant.

But what if we don't? Aren't we then just all fast-forwarded to the brink of our own personal yet simultaneous apocalypse?

Sometimes, if one is lucky, there is a state of grace that people enter when they are dying. It doesn't happen to everyone and I think it needs many factors coming together to manifest: good relationships with those we love, a life that's long enough and filled with enough work satisfaction, the right amount of sadness and joy to have helped us fashion over a lifetime what some people might think of as a soul. And, of course, it needs courage.

For these people – and I meet them often, shake their hands and look into their eyes as I am part of them bravely putting their affairs in order – they have suddenly had their clock reset to the correct time. They mean business.

What do the hands on your clock read? And if it is too late, what are you going to do? These choices are being made right now, everywhere, and are perhaps the same few choices humanity has always had to face: how to live knowing that this life is seriously limited, whether you give into selfishness or whether you step up towards the best part of yourself.

All undertakers are either hypochondriacs or apocalyptic or both. It comes from the endless parade of the worst-case scenarios; the sense that, with each death, with each body, one is both drawn closer to the moment of your own death and somehow getting further away from it. Our darkest fear is that we have immunity from death, doomed to be alone, always the corpse bridesmaid, never the corpse bride.

And what about me? Being an undertaker for over two decades has brought me friends and opportunities, taken me into experiences that transcend time, and it has both healed my heart and broken it into a million pieces. I have created a job that fills my soul, which means I can sleep at night knowing that I am doing the right thing, and which gives me a living, albeit a precarious one in a competitive world. But I have singularly failed to grow it like a conventional business. I don't have lots of branches in neighbouring towns, I have no real exit strategy, no grand retirement plan, no pension. I am my own product and I have set myself up to keep undertaking until I am taken under, until I drop in the field like an exhausted donkey.

My back hurts, my head hurts, my heart hurts. I have seen much of love – more than most – but I have seen too much of death.

Who will take me under when I die, dress me and place me in my coffin, light the pyre? Who will hold those who love me through this storm?

Who will take the liberties with my story that I take with those I eulogise?

It preoccupies me, this fear of being unable to do for myself what I do for others. I fear the funeral I have been saving others from will happen to me, that an incomplete picture will be painted of me, my complexities unaired and so unabsolved.

Perhaps, as it is for us all, it is simply the knowledge that within a few decades of my death I will be forgotten. It is hard to accept that unless we are significantly famous or infamous, no one will remember we ever existed. This might be my stab at immortality, this papery tombstone. Ironic that it may be more enduring than my digital footprint.

◆ ◆ ◆

I still fear death, particularly the manner of it, and think about it every day, but with this constant hum of mortality, comes the understanding that ordinary people are far from ordinary, each man and woman a star. It has taught me that nothing matters apart from love, not status nor achievement, beauty or intelligence.

And I know that there is little point in being afraid, really, of anything ever, because we are, in some very real sense, already dead, and that right now, here, this is the moment between the click and the bang.

Acknowledgements

Claire Phillips, for building this thing together.

Ruby and Tilda, for being brilliant.

Thank you to my fabulous editor, Muna Reyal.

Thanks to:

Penny Wainwright; Tim Coombe; Barry's family; The O'Donnell family: Steve, Rosie and Tommy; Tallulah's family: Rachael and Lia; Lydia's family: Rosie, Joe and Ione.

Ali and Mo and their kids. The Cauty boys. Kate and Steve.

Thanks for the inspiration and encouragement to Mike Jay and Louise Burton, Sarah Delfont, Mark Pilkington, John Higgs, Nicky Bell, Salena Godden, Jane Grant, John Doran, Thomas Lynch, Daveid Phillips, Andy Bloor, Dom Dare, David Southwell, Katie Tokus, Jon Rae, Charles Cowling, Susan Morris, Sonny, Bill Drummond and Jimmy Cauty, and to all my friends.

Thank you to all of the families who have been generous enough to invite us into the intimacy of their grief. Everything I have learned is from you.

About the author

Jane Grant

Rupert Callender was moved to become an undertaker through his experience of bereavement and its aftermath. He spent much of his childhood in the hospice where his mother worked, and the caring humanistic philosophy of the hospice movement is central to his work.

He opened The Green Funeral Company with Claire in 2000 and the company is now among the country's best-known eco-friendly funeral directors. In 2012, they won Joint Best Funeral Director at the first Good Funeral Awards and were described as 'The best undertakers of all time, by a country mile' by *Good Funeral Guide* author, Charles Cowling. Ru and Claire spoke at TEDx Totnes on Death, grief, ritual and radical funerals. In 2021, Claire left the company and Rupert continues with a new colleague.

Callender, Phillips, Cauty & Drummond: Undertakers to the Underworld was established as a partnership between The Green Funeral Company and The Justified Ancients of Mu Mu (KLF) in 2017.

www.thegreenfuneralcompany.co.uk
T: @wayswithweirds
www.mumufication.com/about/